Dilthey Today

Recent Titles in
Contributions in Philosophy

DILTHEY TODAY

A Critical Appraisal of the
Contemporary Relevance
of His Work

H. P. Rickman

CONTRIBUTIONS IN PHILOSOPHY, NUMBER 35

Greenwood Press
NEW YORK · WESTPORT, CONNECTICUT · LONDON

Copyright Acknowledgment

Excerpts from Karl Jaspers, *General Psychopathology*, translated by Jon Hoenig and N. W. Hamilton (Washington, D.C.: Regnery Books, 1963), are reprinted by courtesy of Regnery Books.

Library of Congress Cataloging-in-Publication Data

Rickman, H. P. (Hans Peter)
    Dilthey today : a critical appraisal of the contemporary relevance
of his work / H.P. Rickman.
        p. cm. — (Contributions in philosophy, ISSN 0084-926X ; no.
35)
    Bibliography: p.
    Includes index.
    ISBN 0-313-25933-X (lib. bdg. : alk. paper)
    1. Dilthey, Wilhelm, 1833-1911. I. Title. II. Series.
B3216.D82R53   1988
193-dc19   87-31779

British Library Cataloguing in Publication Data is available.

Library of Congress Catalog Card Number: 87-31779
ISBN: 0-313-25933-X
ISSN: 0084-926X

First published in 1988

Greenwood Press, Inc.
88 Post Road West, Westport, Connecticut 06881

Printed in the United States of America

The paper used in this book complies with the
Permanent Paper Standard issued by the National
Information Standards Organization (Z39.48-1984).

10 9 8 7 6 5 4 3 2 1

In Memory of Muriel

Contents

Preface

The title indicates the book's intentions. It focuses on the relevance of Dilthey's thoughts to contemporary concerns. Recognition of his importance is growing, and some of the evidence for it—the testimony of major thinkers, the continued work on unpublished manuscripts, the appearance of a new U.S. edition of selected writings—is discussed briefly in the introductory chapter. This evidence of renewed interest calls for a critical assessment and provides the material for it.

The sheer volume of publications on Dilthey bears eloquent witness to his importance as a living influence. By 1969 a bibliography of books and articles dealing exclusively or substantially with his work filled a book.[1] Updates[2] for the next fifteen years up to 1983 take up twenty-three closely printed pages. Among them are eight books and thirty-four articles in English. This surely is an index of his stature as a thinker, even if it does not quite match the thousands of books that have been written and continue to be written on such philosophers as Plato or Kant.

However, when I quoted these figures to a friend, she said "doesn't this suggest that enough has been written on him?" So a new book may need a little justifying, all the more so because some of the books and articles figuring in the bibliography are mine.[3]

I want to make three points in such a justification. The first is straightforward and easily made. Substantial and significant Dilthey manuscripts—hitherto only known to those with access to the Dilthey archives—have been published in the last few years.[4] The most recent and most important of these publications is Volume XIX of the collected works.

It provides new insights into Dilthey's philosophy and made me revise or sharpen some of my conclusions on his work. So any book on Dilthey appearing after the mid-1980s can avail itself of an advantage no earlier publication enjoyed.

My second point in justifying the present enterprise is that I have linked my discussions to specific issues of contemporary relevance, such as the methodology of historiography or the philosophic basis of psychiatry. In these cases I have placed Dilthey's thinking into a context of quotations from modern authors.

My third point concerns the way in which this book diverges sharply from my previous publications. To mark the difference to the present undertaking, I must restate the straightforward aims of my previous books and the limitations these imposed on my approach. I wanted to introduce a stimulating thinker to a wider English-speaking public. I believed then, as I do now, that at the hub of his work was his philosophy of the human studies—that is, his attempt to provide theoretical foundations for the methodology of the disciplines concerned with man—and that his work was directly relevant to the future of the social sciences. I had personally found that university colleagues from such disciplines as sociology or anthropology were keen on the philosophic clarification of the concepts and methods they used, and they found Dilthey's work more helpful than that of the philosophic schools predominant in the English-speaking world.

When I wrote my first book on Dilthey (it appeared in 1961), there were very few books on him in English, and only a minute proportion of his writings was available in translation.[5] Additional translations were needed, and they and the author needed to be introduced to English-speaking readers. For these introductions I adopted a number of guidelines. I concentrated on the outlines of his philosophy as a whole and treated differences between his various writings as clarifications, as changes of emphasis, or as a matter of taking up one after the other different aspects of a problem or homing in on one or the other pole of an unresolved conflict. I did not try to trace to any extent the influences that shaped Dilthey's thinking, or the step-by-step development of his ideas. In these respects my aims have remained the same.

However, I also tried throughout to provide—at the risk of some simplification—a clear and straightforward account of a complex and tentative thinker. Exercising self-control, I avoided almost all criticism. I thought that the kind of introduction I was aiming at required careful and sympathetic exposition. Where there seemed to be ambiguities or, even, contradictions, I gave Dilthey every possible benefit of the doubt and offered what I considered the most reasonable, consistent, and coherent account.

In this book I have abandoned these self-imposed restraints. It is no longer necessary to introduce Dilthey,[6] although Chapter 1 does contain some introductory material to make it self-contained. As this book is intended for all those interested in Dilthey's contribution not only to philosophy but also to history, psychology, sociology, anthropology, and literary criticisms (all fields in which he was profoundly involved), I could not presuppose readers of this book to have extensive knowledge of the previous literature on Dilthey, including my own books. So something needed saying, though as briskly as possible, about Dilthey's life, personality, publications, and philosophic approach, which I had discussed in previous books. (I have, however, avoided quoting myself or reproducing quotations previously used.) What is new is that exposition takes second place to critical evaluation. My previous publications did not dwell on the fact that I am not, and never was, an unqualified follower of Dilthey.

To mark the gulf that separates my past writings on Dilthey from the present attempt I must make an admission of guilt. The other day a student of mine, confronted by my extensive writings on Dilthey, whom she had not encountered before in her philosophic reading, accused me of having invented him. Admittedly, she was joking, but there is an element of truth in her accusation. By simplifying and streamlining Dilthey's thought and eliminating or explaining away what seemed obscure or contradictory, I had perpetuated a measure of falsification, created my own Dilthey.

I do not feel particularly burdened by guilt, as my "deception" was not deliberate. I just wanted to do my best for the thinker I was introducing to the reader. I was also anxious to avoid the arrogance of a commentator who sets up his subject as a straw man on whom to demonstrate his superior perspicacity. Anyhow, there are excellent precedents for what I did. Without pressing the analogy beyond the point at issue, I might remind readers of what Plato did with Socrates.

Indeed, I would like to claim credit for having improved Dilthey. It would be pleasant to think of myself not as a supine expositor of Dilthey but as a contributor of ideas that arose from confrontation with Dilthey's philosophy. However, this is not the point here. As I continued my work on Dilthey over the years, I became increasingly conscious of the limitations of and contradictions in Dilthey's approach. My sense of unresolved conflict in Dilthey's thinking was greatly reinforced by the appearance of Volume XIX. It contained his drafts for the continuation of his *Introduction to the Human Studies*, which he had published in 1883. For the rest of his life—some twenty-seven years—he had struggled to complete the work to his own satisfaction. I share the sense of a deep-seated tension in Dilthey's mind with Dilthey scholars such as Professor F. Rodi, one of the editors of this volume, although I differ from his and other scholars in my view on how the conflict should have been resolved. It then became clear to me that the nonappearance of the second volume could not just be blamed on his general, well-known inability to complete the vast schemes he was always contemplating. It was due to his inability to resolve the conflict between different lines of approach, toward which he was equally disposed. It did not diminish my admiration for a great thinker, but it made me think that attention to his failures might be almost as instructive as retracing his seminal ideas.

It can be argued that Dilthey's refusal to streamline and simplify his persistent awareness of complexity and conflicting viewpoints is part of his greatness. Professor O. F. Bollnow, a disciple of Misch, Dilthey's most distinguished pupil and expositor, has argued to this effect. Bollnow, now himself the doyen of Dilthey scholarship, writes:

One must guard against seeing this indeterminacy as due to lack of intellectual power which one must try to overcome by sharper conceptualisations. Every conceptualisation is also a simplification. Something of the original plenitude is always lost. When Dilthey hesitates to develop a definite terminology, when he vacillates in his linguistic usage, when he leaves in balance right to the end, important questions, such as the decision between a psychological and a hermeneutic foundation of the Human Studies, it is due to the profounder awareness that premature determinations would do violence to the subject matter. His is a penetrating deep-searching thinking which cannot come to rest at any definite result. Instead of perceiving it as a weakness one must understand it positively as necessary expression of Dilthey's philosophising. One must, therefore, be very careful if one wants to conceptualise more sharply what he left in suspense.[7]

In this preface I finally want to draw attention to an issue of which I have become increasingly conscious during my study, but one I am not competent to deal with adequately—namely, the striking parallels between Dilthey's thought and American Pragmatism. Because of my limited knowledge and, of course, the limitations of space, I shall not elaborate on these parallels and connections in my text. Let me, however, list here a few of Dilthey's central contentions, which will receive fuller treatment in the text. I think those acquainted with the writings of thinkers such as Peirce, James, and Dewey will recognize familiar themes. (Indeed, I have received encouragement to think so in correspondence with Professor J. E. Smith, the author of works on Pragmatism.[8])

1. All knowledge is derived from experience, but this means the full richness and complexity of our encounters in life, not the reception of sense data, which traditional empiricists and positivists—by a metaphysical abstraction—call experience.
2. Within experience, the emphasis should be placed on personal, "lived" experience, rather than on simple observations.
3. The mental equipment for cognition is partly an acquired structure.
4. The present has duration: in it past, the immediate present, and the future are interwoven in a way that makes us historical beings.

5. An epistemology that treats us merely as spectators is mistaken, because we are also actors.

6. Awareness of the interaction between individual and the world is crucial.

7. It is important to apply theory to practice. "It is useless going on sharpening the knife if the wood is there waiting to be carved" (*C.W.*, Vol. XVIII, p. 1).

There are, of course, important differences—for example, different areas of inquiry are emphasized and dealt with in detail by Dilthey and the pragmatists, respectively, just as there are significant differences between the pragmatists. So knowing pragmatism does not make reading Dilthey superfluous. On the contrary, I should like to think that these parallels may help to throw light on the respective philosophies.

How these parallels have come about is not easy to say. Peirce, James, and Dilthey were close contemporaries, and the young James met the young Dilthey briefly in Basle,[9] but there is no evidence that they ever read each other's work. In any case, the Americans could not have read some of Dilthey's more important philosophic writings as they appeared some time after the death of both Peirce and James. Undoubtedly they had read and were influenced by the same thinkers. For example, Dilthey was extensively influenced by Kant, and Peirce says that he "had come upon the threshing-floor of philosophy through the doorway of Kant."[10]

I cannot pursue this matter further. I have mentioned it for two reasons. First, I hope that someone may take up the questions that cluster around these parallels and connections. Second, I should like to think that American scholars may find Dilthey's ideas more accessible than they had expected, particularly once they have become familiar with Dilthey's terminology, which differs from that of the pragmatists.

Abbreviations

Volumes of Dilthey's *Collected Works* are referred to as *C.W.* plus volume numbers (i.e., "*C.W.*, Vol. VII").

The *Introduction to the Human Studies* is referred to as "*Introduction.*"

My book, *W. Dilthey: Selected Writings,* is referred to as "*Selections.*"

Acknowledgments

As I have worked on Dilthey, and on some of the topics raised in this book, for many years, I have received help, stimulation, and constructive criticism from many people. I shall pick out only two for special mention. Professor O. F. Bollnow generously assisted my first steps into Dilthey scholarship; he remained a friend whose writings and conversations have helped my understanding of Dilthey. To Professor F. Rodi I owe stimulating exchanges of opinion. Above all, he has kept me in touch with current Dilthey scholarship in Germany, to which he has significantly contributed. Other authors to whom I am indebted are quoted (though only briefly) in the text or mentioned in my footnotes.

I should also acknowledge that, though I have not quoted from them, I have used ideas previously discussed in articles listed in my bibliography.

Dilthey Today

1

Introduction:
The Man and His Work

In November 1983, at the castle of Biebrich, fronting the river Rhein, a ceremony attracted a large crowd of local citizens. It celebrated the birth, 150 years earlier, of W. Dilthey, whom the Lord Mayor of Wiesbaden—of which Biebrich is now a part—described as the town's most distinguished son. After the Lord Mayor's speech, another town representative and a distinguished Dilthey scholar, Professor Bollnow, addressed the audience. Music was provided by the string quintet of the local Dilthey school. Afterwards selected guests were taken to lunch at "House Dilthey." Dilthey had grown up in what was originally an old farmhouse. Now it had been renovated and converted into an inn, where guests drinking their beer could look at old pictures of Dilthey.

Germany takes its philosophers more seriously than we do. I know of no David Hume secondary school, no John Locke public house in Britain. Are there any William James schools, any John Dewey bars in America? For that matter, are we celebrating the birthdays of our great thinkers? However, even Germans do not celebrate just anyone. The celebration reflects the fact that Dilthey is increasingly coming into his own, is recognized as a major philosopher.

The sprinkling of Dilthey scholars present at the ceremony celebrated two other events in addition to the birthday. One was the publication in 1883 of Volume I of the *Introduction to the Human Studies*, which was reprinted in Volume I of the *Collected Works*. The other event was the publication that very year of Volume XIX, which happens to be the first appearance in print of Dilthey's plans and drafts for Volume II of the *Introduction*.

The celebration in the great hall of Biebrich castle calls for a three-fold explanation. First, we need to answer the question: what makes Dilthey so important that a school and an inn should be called after him, that his birthday should be publicly celebrated, and, last but not least, that his posthumous papers should continue to be published sixty-two years after his death? Second, a little needs to be said about the personality and the life of the man who grew up in this little town on the Rhein. Finally, the fact that the sequel to one of Dilthey's main works appeared a hundred years later itself requires to be explained.

PHILOSOPHIC ORIENTATION

The claim that Dilthey is an important philosopher is supported by the testimony of distinguished thinkers. Husserl wrote that an encounter with Dilthey changed his thinking.[1] Heidegger acknowledged the indebtedness of his whole generation,[2] Ortega y Gasset called him the most important thinker of the second half of the nineteenth century.[3] A reviewer called him the Newton of the social sciences.[4] Hugo von Hoffmansthal—the poet and librettist of "Der Rosenkavalier"—wrote an enthusiastic and moving obituary.

Various facts can also be listed in support of such a high assessment. I have already referred to the hundreds of books that have been written about him, some during the last few years. Conferences to discuss his work have been held in many countries. The original eleven volumes of his collected works, which had been long out of print, were republished in the 1950s, and work has been going on since then to augment them by bringing separately published material—such as the Schleiermacher biography, book reviews, journal articles, and lectures printed in the proceedings of learned societies—under the umbrella of a truly comprehensive edition. It will also include unpublished lectures, manuscripts, and letters. The complete edition, which has now reached Volume XIX, is intended to comprise thirty-two large volumes.[5] Recently the first volume appeared of a projected six-volume U.S. selection of his writings.[6]

The first impression given by the vast volume of Dilthey's writings is of the enthusiasm and single-mindedness with which he dedicated himself to the job of philosophy and thus inspired his students and readers. From his student days to the end of his life, he worked endless hours—we hear of a twelve- to sixteen-hour working day—on his vast projects. Into his old age he remained an openminded explorer of new ideas who kept on revising his arguments, although the major themes around which his thinking revolved remained largely the same throughout.

The cause to which Dilthey was so enthusiastically dedicated was—put in the broadest terms—the practical relevance of philosophy. For him it was not just an academic subject confined to the classroom or the ivory tower.

Like his near-contemporary Marx, he believed that philosphers were in the business of changing the world, but he was not so ignorant of, or indifferent to, the history of philosophy as to claim—as did Marx—that this was a novel project.

There were then, as there are now, teachers of philosophy who out of modesty or timidity are content to treat their subject as a specialty among others, with no direct bearing on personal or communal life. Not so Dilthey. He was profoundly interested in moral, social, and educational issues. He wanted to play his part in politics, but he believed that he could best make his contribution to these different spheres as a philosopher.

Dilthey remained well within the main tradition of philosophy in believing that in it man reflects on himself and on his doings and that this increased self-awareness and critical attention to his activities can give rise to guidelines for action. Looking into ourselves, the study of history or the examination of literature, if undertaken with philosophic intent—that is, used as material for philosophic analysis—highlights what we are, what we need, and what we genuinely value. They thereby provide norms for educational policy, social engineering, and political action.

If, however, the study of different spheres of human life is to provide a secure basis for philosophical conclusions, philosophy must also consider critically the reliability of the material provided. In other words, it must consider the conditions on which the successful acquisition of knowledge depends. Pursuing this line of thought, Dilthey embarked on enquiries into the epistemology and methodology of history and the social sciences. This, in the view of many Dilthey scholars, is his most original and important contribution to philosophy. It also has the most immediate relevance to urgent contemporary debates.

It has been argued—by P. Krausser,[7] for example—that Dilthey provided the outlines of a general philosophy of science. In this he reflects a growing concern with this subject on the part of many philosophers. As science advanced spectacularly and presented increasingly challenging problems, while metaphysics, and with it, to some extent, general epistemology, became suspect subjects, philosophers turned their attention to the philosophic examination of science. However, this issue was never central to Dilthey's thinking, and I will not pursue the subject further.

From the outset, Dilthey's attention was mainly focused on the philosophy of the social sciences. In this he was a pioneer for his philosophic contemporaries, such as the neo-Kantians, and, indeed, philosophers until fairly recently were predominatly concerned with the physical sciences. Specific philosophic concern with the human sciences is more recent and continues, with increasing vigor, today.

The reasons for this turn toward the human sciences are obvious enough. In a world of great social complexity, unsolved human problems call for solutions guided by knowledge. But unlike the physical sciences, the social sciences have not proved themselves extensively applicable to the solution of practical problems. Quite apart from this problem about increasing their practical effectiveness, there are also uncertainties and confusions about their concepts and methods, their presuppositions and theoretical framework. Schools or movements such as structuralism, behaviorism, or psychoanalysis—to give but a few examples—are all controversial. In this situation social scientists themselves welcome constructive debate with philosophers. This is what makes Dilthey relevant to us.

A number of intertwining themes form the core of Dilthey's philosophy of the human studies. Foremost among them are his theoretical examinations of meaning, "lived" experience, expressions, and understanding. His account of hermeneutics ("Die Entstehung der Hermeneutik," in C.W., Vol. V) and his fragmentary drafts of a "Critique of Historical Reason" (C.W., Vol. VII) are attempts at a systematic development of these themes. Unfortunately they amount to less than a coherent and consistent system. For this his plans were too vast, his philosophic temper too tentative and undogmatic, and the problems too vexing. However, as is the case with many great thinkers, the unresolved tensions in his work, due to his refusal to streamline intractable problems, are themselves proving fruitful.

His inability to complete his large schemes was, indeed, notorious. He never produced the second part of his Schleiermacher biography,[8] and he never put together into the comprehensive work on the German Spirit that he had planned his numerous writings on German philosophers, poets, musicians, and statesmen[9]. The reasons were those I have already hinted at. The scholar Max Dessoir,[10] who had attended his lectures, wrote in his *Buch der Erinnerungen* [Book of Memories] (1946),

The master's mode of thinking and writing remained unmistakeable. Both are characterised by a certain restlessness and unexpectedness. Dilthey could never find the definitive end, could never resist the temptation to spread himself. His account most broadly planned and based on a wealth of preliminary studies all too soon loses its dynamic. His capacity to depict was not matched by that to construct. On his seventieth birthday Dilthey himself spoke of being surrounded by building blocks which as yet had not been put together into an edifice. So it remained until his death. He valued arriving less than being on the way. . . . What value his work has is decided by its joy and fruitfulness. In this respect Dilthey was among the foremost.

But there was a more specific reason for his inability to complete the systematic part of his *Introduction to the Human Studies*: an unreconciled conflict in his epistemology. It now seems to me that less than justice is done to Dilthey and to the issues he was concerned with if we do not address these problems squarely.

The epistemological fix in which Dilthey found himself is, I think, the most deep-seated of his problems and the one which has received least systematic attention, probably for the most obvious of reasons, namely that his epistemological concerns are revealed more fully than before in that recent volume of drafts for continuing the *Introduction* (*C.W.*, Vol. XIX).

Basically his problem in laying epistemological foundations for the study of the human world was this. He believed that intellectual processes were embedded in the process of living—that is, were psychological events in the context of peoples' mental lives. They were also part of, and colored by, historical processes. But he was enough of a Kantian to realise the danger of any conception of truth and objectivity being thus submerged in a flood of psychologism and relativity. (I deal with this issue in the last part of this book).

The tension between Heracleitos and Parmenides, between recognition of an all-engulfing flux and the need for something outside the flux, is not peculiar to Dilthey. Indeed, it is the mark of a major thinker that his confusions and, even, contradictions are not simply reflections of his own personal defects, but highlight shared problems that defy easy solution. The history of philosophy is full of illustrations of this. In pinpointing Dilthey's difficulties, we are not just niggling. They need to be taken seriously, because they are our problems still.

The problem about the line to be drawn between the fluid and the fixed is not confined to the epistemological level. It confronts us in different guises, and Dilthey's work, in one way or another, is much concerned with it. One significant form the problem takes is the question of how far human nature is fixed and how far it is changing and malleable. The historical movement that Dilthey supported and wanted to provide with epistemological justifications was instrumental in changing our views on this matter.

This is still a live issue, and the contemporary forms debates on it take can be illustrated from different spheres. In psychology, for example, debate continues on the extent to which the ability labeled "intelligence" is determined by nature or by nurture, by heredity or by environmental influences.[11] In social anthropology, evidence has been produced that what we used to consider part of immutable human nature was a product of culture.[12] There are strong suggestions that at least some of the manliness of men and the feminity of women may not be the inevitable result of physiological differences but products of upbringing. History itself has made it increasingly clear that we cannot take it for granted that people of different ages thought, felt, and reacted as we do—that, let us say, ancient Greek farmers were much like today's Midwestern farmers in historical costume.

It is easy enough, but nevertheless important, to say that a line can be and must be drawn somewhere. Not all is malleable in human nature, nor is all fixed. Historical change affects our ideas, institutions, and ways of doing things, but not everything changes in history. We would be misrepresenting those ancient Greeks if we did not recognize how different from us they were, and yet when we read the Greek historians, say Thucidides' description of the families saying good-bye to the army setting off on the expedition to Sicily,[13] or when we watch the tragedies of Sophocles, we are moved by the recognition of how much like us they also were.

But how and where are we to draw the line? The answers we give will colour our historical insights and our psychological theories, they will also affect our educational practices and our political assessments. Dilthey was very conscious of this issue, and much of his work is an exploration of it. The tension in his thinking that comes to the surface in his theory of knowledge but permeates his approach to a large range of problems can be characterized as the problem of drawing the line.

To some extent, although I do not want to push pedantry to its limits, I have tried to represent the two sides of the issue, the two poles between which the particular tension is located in Chapters 2 and 4 of this book. Chapter 2 deals with Dilthey's historical approach. We must note, above all, his repeated insistence that what man is, we only know through history. It is not in the laboratory—let it be clear—let alone in the armchair, that we can discover human nature and understand his creations. It is only what man has shown himself to be in his thoughts and actions throughout the time of which we have records. This in turn raises the question of what is involved in the writing of history, and the special role that the history of ideas plays in it.

Chapter 4 provides the counterpart by exploring Dilthey's philosophic anthropology. The question is: how far can we—despite whatever has been conceded in terms of historical relativity—specify abiding features of humanity? He also wrote "As human nature is always the same the fundamental features of experience are common to all" (C.W., Vol. VIII, p. 79) because he was looking for solid foundations for understanding human beings, in spite of the variations played on the theme of human nature in history.

With the methodology he planned to develop on this basis I deal more specifically in Chapter 3. One needs hardly reemphasize that divergences on these methodologies issues remain unresolved. One of the key questions is how, and how far, methods that reach below the surface of overt human behavior can yet be objective and checkable. The tension in Dilthey's thought is represented in his dual commitment both to a hermeneutic approach that radically distinguishes the human studies from the physical sciences and to the conviction that its findings could be testably true. The hermeneutic approach developed by Heidegger and his disciples[14] rejects this position as a failure in consistency, a compromise with an outworn positivistic tradition. However, I think Dilthey was right in his insistence on criteria of truth, however difficult it may be to defend his position.

There is a second methodological issue, implicit in his approach but not incisively tackled in his writings. The hermeneutic approach, seen as essential in the human studies, corrects and limits the "scientific" behavioristic approach but cannot—indeed, was not intended to—replace it.

Questions then arise about combining the "inside view" of hermeneutic understanding with the "outside view" of scientific observation. Explaining most historical and social events involves such a combination of viewpoints. The thoughts and purposes of human agents are, clearly, relevant, and to unearth them is the job of hermeneutics. But what actually happens is also determined by external circumstances and by the way in which interaction leads to unintended consequences (for example, inflation is man-made, but no-one may have wanted to produce it). Other methods than those of hermeneutics are required to evaluate these factors.

My emphasis on these tensions and unresolved problems that force us to continue the debate does not mean that I want to carp. I continue to believe that the positive contribution made by Dilthey to the philosophy and methodology of the studies concerned with man is immense. Himself a pioneer of intellectual history, he had much of interest to say on how the historian can tell a meaningful story and what contribution he thereby makes to our intellectual and cultural life. He tirelessly stressed the importance, both for research and for practical policies, of asking what man is, and he produced seminal analyses of how man experienced time, made sense of his life, and gained understanding of others. I hope to convey an idea of these achievements.

THE MAN

A little needs to be said about Dilthey's life and personality. But even this modest requirement for a few details draws attention to a paradox. What could be more appropriate than a biographical introduction to a thinker who himself pioneered the art of intellectual biography, theorized on the significance of such biographical work, and generally believed that intellectual products need to be understood within their context in human life? Yet Dilthey, though extremely articulate in pouring out, quite literally, millions of words in his scholarly writings, was extremely reticent about his personal life. Indeed, his disciples called him the enigmatic old man. In connection with an episode in his life—the sudden termination of an engagement into which he had enthusiastically entered—he wrote, "No friend will ever be allowed to understand the motives of the most important and striking act of my life so that, in this respect, my character will have to remain un-understood for all time.[15] His family, friends, and disciples respected his wish for privacy, and no biography of Dilthey has appeared to this day. When I started my work on Dilthey, I even had some trouble in discovering how many children he had had (and got it wrong in my first publications). Similarly, Müller-Vollmer in his otherwise most knowledge-able book mistakenly states that Dilthey died in Berlin.[16]

Brief sketches of Dilthey as a teacher are available in print, and his elder daughter published a collection of his letters and excerpts from his diaries under the title "The Young Dilthey."[17] These works reflect the warm affection that Dilthey aroused. But there remains much untapped material, foremost among it a large collection of Dilthey's correspondence, which awaits evaluation and publication. So far only some collections of letters of obvious philosophic significance have been published. The unpublished letters cover university matters, social engagements, financial affairs, the unhappy episode of the terminated engagement, the courting of his wife, correspondence with her about the children, and so forth.[18] In due course some of these letters will be published as Volumes XXX–XXXII of the *Collected Works*, and one day a biography might be written with the help of this material.

Such a biography is not likely to be sensational, for there are no spectacular public actions or horrific private vices to be recounted. The only thing striking about Dilthey is the breadth of his interests and his amazing industry. Apart from this, he lived the life of a typical scholar, and the main interest of his biography for a wider public could be a picture of what it was like to be a German professor in the Victorian age. These letters might provide Dilthey scholars with sidelights on Dilthey's scholarly activities, but they are more likely to assuage personal curiosity than to illuminate Dilthey's philosophy. Why did he expend so much time and energy on the large number of articles and book reviews, published anonymously, that were relatively recently traced back to him? (They are now collected in *C.W.*, Vols. XVI and XVII.) What were the moral scruples that made him break his first engagement? Was it really just the fact that his fiancée had had a baby some years before? What was his health really like? Were the complaints about it sprinkled throughout his correspondence due to overwork, or was there a strain of hypochondria? Was it true that his ill health around 1870 was due, as at least one commentator has argued,[19] to the profound anguish he felt over supporting Bismark as the unifier of Germany while disliking his illiberal internal policy? Was there a slight touch of antisemitism in his make up, and if so, was it merely his jealous reaction to the marriage of his favorite daughter to a Jew? The evidence is conflicting. On the one hand, his jewish son-in-law, Georg Misch, was one of his close disciples, and he had other jewish friends, too. On the other hand he did not, to my knowledge, rebuke his friend York when, after some critical remarks on Zeno, he wrote that it "was very significant that Zeno was of semitic blood" (letter of 8 March 1887). I am particularly baffled by an article on Heinrich Heine ("H. Heine," *C.W.*, Vol. XV, pp. 205–45), which shows an unsympathetic attitude to his subject that seems alien to Dilthey, and a complete lack of appreciation of Heine as a great lyric poet and pioneer of political journalism. If we had authoritative answers to these and similar questions, we could form a much more vivid picture of Dilthey as a human being.

One source of knowledge about Dilthey's life and personality that was available when I started my work has now dried up. Several of his most important disciples and friends were then alive. I met H. Nohl, G. Misch, and E. Spranger, and also Dilthey's favorite daughter Clara Misch. Some of them helped me in my first attempts at understanding Dilthey. But I was then too ignorant to ask pertinent questions, either about subtle issues in his work or about his personal life. No doubt they would have been discreet, but I might have learned something. Other scholars, the next generation of Dilthey experts, the disciples of the disciples, such as O. F. Bollnow, have some secondhand knowledge, but they have similar regrets about not having been more curious.

The bare story of Dilthey's life can be told easily enough. He was born on 19 November 1833, in Biebrich, where his father was a clergyman and court preacher to the Duke of Nassau, whose residence was Biebrich castle. In the tradition of his family, he was a liberal protestant clergyman, with a lively interest in history, politics, and even philosophy. His wife, the daughter of a conductor, was very musical, and Wilhelm inherited a lasting love of music from her. After attending local schools, he went to Heidelberg University in 1852. After a year of studying theology there, he moved on to Berlin, where he hoped to find a richer cultural life and more opportunity for listening to good music. He continued with his theology and even took some qualifying examinations for a career in the church, because his father wanted him to follow in his footsteps, but he became increasingly absorbed in history and philosophy. We know about this period because of the affectionate letters he wrote to his family. Working remarkably hard, he studied Greek, Hebrew, and English, and with groups of friends he read Shakespeare, Plato, Aristotle, and St. Augustine. He also studied composition, and for relaxation he played the piano.

He finally decided that he was not sufficiently religious to become a clergyman and continued studying with the view of becoming a university teacher. Because he continued to indulge in his wide range of interests, pursuing each subject into considerable depth, he did not submit his doctoral thesis (a short work on Schleiermacher's ethics) until 1864. Throughout this period he depended on financial help from his father, although he tried to earn some money by school teaching (which he disliked) and journalism. Soon after receiving his doctorate he qualified for the right to teach at university with a more general work on ethics.

Not long after starting his teaching career in Berlin, he was called to a chair in Basel. The young William James met him there in 1867 and wrote a vivid letter about him to his sister. He described him as a fat man, wearing "an exceedingly grimy shirt and collar and a rusty old rag of a cravat."[20] He also recounts that he talked and laughed incessantly and provided a whole history of Buddhism and other parts of the history of religion and then comments, "He is the first man I have ever met of a class of men to whom learning has become as natural as breathing."

In that same year Dilthey's father died, and a letter from his mother to his brother testifies to the continued close relationship Wilhelm retained with his family: "In our beloved Wilhelm God has given us a helper in our great need and our dear departed a most soothing and loving companion and consoler in his last days."[21]

During this year Dilthey's letters speak of overwork and ill health. He had made the same complaints during his student years, and we encounter them again in his later years. He also reported growing a beard.

In 1868 he accepted a professorship at the small University of Kiel. He had found Basel culturally and politically a backwater and was glad to return to Germany. Only three years later he moved on to Breslau. It was there, on his fortieth birthday, that he became engaged to Katharine Püttmann (Käte), whom he married a few months later. Particularly significant for his intellectual life was the friendship he formed with Graf York of Wartenburg, a landowner from an old aristocratic family, who took an active part in politics but was also a distinguished scholar with an acute philosophic mind. Dilthey admired his intelligence, moral incisiveness, and clarity. They corresponded[22] and met from time to time until York's death in 1897. Dilthey wrote to him about his ideas and plans, and York sympathized, encouraged, and, sometimes, criticized. On one occasion he robustly replied to Dilthey's complaints about his health, "the discomfort of your state is caused by constant sitting and is not a direct result of strenuous thought."

In 1877 Clara, Dilthey's favorite, who was to become his helper and confidante, was born. Max was born in 1884, and Helena in 1888. The marriage was not without troubles. One suspects that Käte, a lively woman, was a little dissatisfied with a husband who wanted to work for some 16 hours a day. According to their daughter they had severe rows, after which Dilthey was unable to work for days. Still, they stayed together. Wilhelm stayed away from the university when Käte had trouble with her lungs. She, in turn, helped him with his work.

In 1882 Dilthey returned to Berlin to occupy the chair in philosophy that Hegel had held before him. He had a charming flat and lived a comfortable middle-class life with several servants in the house. He was very content, particularly when he could concentrate on his scholarly work, but he complained about his professional duties (all this information comes from his letters). From these Berlin years we have some vivid pictures of him. I quote once again from E. Dessoir's *Buch der Erinnerungen* [Book of Memories][24]:

Small of stature, a little grown to fat, with foolish pale blue eyes in the roundish face, fingers mostly ink stained, he showed when he laughed a goldlined monolith. When he was in a bad mood he resembled a small angry monkey. When lecturing he made a strangely clumsy movement with the thumb of his closed right hand. His voice was weak, easily became hoarse and tended to break when he overstrained it; this is why he tended to speak softly and only effectively emphasised the most important sentences, sometimes by repetition. ... The complete freedom with which Dilthey was in command of his material, the perspectives which he discovered in it, was something incomparable. It was no longer an insignificant gnome who lectured from a thick exercise book, but a dwarf magician was creating a world. He, the creator of this cosmos, remained completely in the background. ...

No one of us apprentices was close enough to him to see the whole of this thinking. We had to prepare fragmentary pieces, as he needed them ... but, as it were, as a reward we were allowed the extensive right to correct the written, or even type-set, text. ...

His use of students as helpers was also described by Nohl[24] ("Wilhelm Dilthey" in *Die Grossen Deutschen*):

He had developed for some time the practice of getting individual students to come to his study as helpers; here they read to him, made excerpts for him, took dictation, added something in writing and, above all, received a curiously free brief to make corrections. We arrived in the morning towards eight and found him cheerfully sitting at his desk; then we worked without break until lunch. After the meal he lay down for an hour: we read to him until he fell asleep and then we made excerpts. He started to dictate again and went on until evening. He stood by the stove or the window and "composed" as we used to say. In between we read aloud. For the young people it was deeply exciting, particularly because they often did not know the context to which the dictations belonged and had no full view of his philosophy as a whole because Dilthey's works were not easily accessible. In the evening we plunged into the subject just dealt with, in order to keep our heads above water, and next day found ourselves with him at an entirely different spot. ...

In a sense Dilthey exploited his students for his own projects, and one might have thought that not knowing the context would be exasperating. However, the students appeared to have found an apprenticeship with a great thinker enjoyable and profitable.

Even as an old man Dilthey retained his youthful energy and enthusiasm. He was full of plans to complete his vast schemes. But while holidaying in the Tyrol, he caught an infection at the hotel where he stayed and died quite unexpectedly on 30 September 1911.

THE WRITINGS

At the beginning of this introduction I mentioned the fact that Dilthey published the first volume of *The Introduction* in 1883 and that his drafts for the completion of this work appeared a hundred years later. If we are to understand the fluctuations in Dilthey's reputation, the difficulties that beset his interpreters, and the variety of interpretations that resulted, we need to look at the long road that leads from *C.W.* Volume I to Volume XIX. I recently read in J. Hakinson's humorous introduction to philosophy[25] that Wittgenstein had published one book in his lifetime but fifteen after his death. In this respect, as in some of the content of his philosophy, Wittgenstein followed in Dilthey's footsteps. When Dilthey died, only three books had appeared under his name. The first volume of his massive Schleiermacher biography was followed ten years later by the first volume of his *Introduction,* and in the last years of his life a collection of some of his literary essays appeared.[26] As even the published part of the *Introduction* was historically slanted, it was not surprising that he was widely considered as mainly a historian of ideas rather than a "real" philosopher. In 1914, three years after his death, the first volume of his *Collected Works,* edited by some of his disciples, appeared. The edition began with the *Introduction;* other shorter works published in Dilthey's lifetime followed. *C.W.* Volume V contained a very long introduction by G. Misch, which provided the first systematic account of Dilthey's philosophic thinking, and in it quotations from unpublished writings appeared. In 1927 *C.W.* Volume VII (edited by B. Groethuysen) appeared. It combined papers only published in the proceedings of learned societies, with a substantial amount of unpublished material. These fragments were written by Dilthey in his old age and represent what are probably his most important philosophic ideas. Their publication established Dilthey's stature as a major philosopher and ensured his continued influence. By 1936, eleven volumes of the *Collected Works,* the Schleiermacher biography, the abovementioned volume of literary essays, and some selections from his letters were available in print. But then publication of his writings came to an end. Some of his closest disciples became refugees, and the climate of opinion of Nazi Germany was not favorable to Dilthey's liberal and openminded approach.

It was not until 1959 that work on the collected writings was resumed. First the eleven volumes long out of print were republished. Further volumes brought the Schleiermacher biography, and drafts for its continuation, within the compass of the *Collected Works.* A volume on moral philosophy based on his lectures and some volumes of collections of articles contributed to journals followed. *C.W.* Volumes XVIII and XIX represent his incomplete labor on the philosophy of the social sciences. Several more volumes, based, like Volumes XVIII and XIX, on the vast archives of his manuscripts and lecture notes in Berlin, are in the pipeline.[27]

The sheer bulk of Dilthey's writings—these nineteen volumes are far from slim—and the gradual way in which they became available have created a host of problems for commentators. While his contemporaries mainly knew the work of the younger Dilthey, his immediate disciples were strongly under the impression of the late writings, the composition of which they had witnessed. Few people knew in any detail the content of the archives of Dilthey's manuscripts, and so the last few volumes of the *Collected Works* produced material entirely new to most of us. Among other things, they help to bridge the gap between the early and very late writings. The same will be true of future volumes.

It was inevitable that many commentators on Dilthey, particularly those who, without being Dilthey specialists, included him in their wider considerations, gave—through little fault of their own—a partial or even false picture of Dilthey's philosophy. But the sheer bulk of the writings is daunting even to specialists. R. Makkreel's book *DILTHEY, Philosopher of the Human Studies* (1975), which claims to be a comprehensive introduction to Dilthey's philosophy, illustrates the problems such an attempt encounters. Though it contains hundreds of quotations and many more paraphrases, they come, apart from a few isolated instances, from a few of Dilthey's writings all contained within five of the volumes of the collected works.

The problem of surveying the vast body of Dilthey's writings with a close attention to nuances is daunting even to native German speakers: it is worse for English and American scholars, even if they can read German. For those who cannot, the task is hopeless. To date only a very small proportion of his writings is available in translation. Apart from a few excerpts in my *Selections,* nothing is available in English of Dilthey's extensive work on the history of ideas, which covered intellectual biographies and historical approaches to philosophic problems. The same is true of Dilthey's substantial writings on literature.

I deplore this gap, not merely, or mainly, because of the intrinsic interest of some of these writings. The important point is that they form an integral part of Dilthey's philosophic enterprises. They illustrate the use of methods he advocated, support his arguments, and, indeed, contain philosphic reflections.

2

History

Dilthey's thinking revolved very extensively around history, and his writings touch on it in a variety of ways. We cannot properly understand his work and the influence he is continuing to exercise on different areas of modern thought without tracing these concerns.

It was his interest in history that sparked off some of his most urgent original reflections on epistemology and the methodology of studying the human world. When first making his transition from theology to history, he conceived the project of a history of the early church fathers. But the religious fanaticism of these early Christians, their belief that starvation, dirt, and flagellation were conducive to holiness, struck him as strange and incomprehensible.[1] How could a modern historian enter into the minds of these people and appreciate their outlook and motives? Thus arose for Dilthey the general problem of understanding. Even as a young man, he envisaged the project of a critique of historical reason,[2] on which he still worked in old age.

Before we deal with these philosophic issues, we need to remind ourselves that Dilthey was—and remained to the end of his life—a practicing historian of ideas, pioneering, as his speciality, intellectual biography. A very considerable proportion of his writings belongs to this genre.

For various reasons, most of these writings are likely to remain untranslated. First, after some hundred years, even fine historians become outdated. Who, let us say, reads Macauley to-day? Second, the subject matter of Dilthey's biographical and historical writings is frequently only of interest to specialists, who are, in any case, likely to know German. Who else would want to read, let us say, about Frederic II's foundation of the Prussian Academy or, even, about the influence of theology on the young Hegel? The same applies to the Schleiermacher biography, even though it represents a revolutionary development of intellectual biography. Who wants to struggle through more than a thousand pages, to get only halfway in Schleiermacher's career?

However, these writings were seminal and also throw light on Dilthey's thought as a whole, and for this reason I start by listing and describing briefly this historical and biographical work.

History, in its widest sense, is the source of all empirical evidence. In *The Great Poetry of Imagination* (p. 5), Dilthey writes, "For history alone shows us what man is." There are many similar formulations to be found in his writings. In *C.W.*, Volume VII, p. 279, we find "Man knows himself only through history"; and in *The Dream, C.W.*, Volume VIII, p. 224, "What man is, history alone tells him." In other words, human nature reveals itself through the varied manifestations of its potentialities in the passage of time. This is, of course, one of the reasons for Dilthey's abiding interest in history and also the reason why, as we shall see presently, he tended to approach any problems from historical perspectives.

But history, in Dilthey's eyes, gives us more than information about ourselves. The historical consciousness liberates the mind from narrow dogmatism. It makes us aware of the historical relativity, and thus the temporally bound authority, of any system of thought. It also trains us in historical judgment—that is, the assessment of individuals and individual events in their temporal context. I shall argue that such judgments are paradigmatic of the difficult art of judging.

Finally, it needs stressing that involved in all these issues is Dilthey's analysis of our experience of time. How we experience the temporal flow, and how experience becomes meaningful in it, constitutes us as historical beings capable of making and understanding history.

THE LIFE OF SCHLEIERMACHER

It is appropriate to start an account of Dilthey's historical writings with a description of the genesis, design, and content of his Schleiermacher biography. Not only was it his first major publication that established him as a pioneer of this form of biography, but it also contains in germ all the major themes that continued to occupy him for the rest of his life.

Dilthey became first interested in Schleiermacher's work while he was still a student. Schleiermacher[3] was one of the group of thinkers—Fichte, Schelling, and Hegel were its other best-known members—who were engaged in developing and modifying Kant's philosophy into what is usually called "German Idealism." He had died a year after Dilthey's birth, and disciples of his were among the professors the young Dilthey encountered in

Berlin. Dilthey's own background and interests made him favorably disposed toward a thinker who was both theologian and philosopher, had a passionate interest in poetry, and had distinguished himself as translator and interpreter of Plato's *Dialogues*.

When one of his professors, who was editing Schleiermacher's letters, died, Dilthey was asked to take over the editorship. The knowledge he gained in his work enabled him to win two prizes for an essay on Schleiermacher's Hermeneutics. In this essay—as he claimed some fifty years later—he first formulated his basic ideas. While editing Schleiermacher's voluminous correspondence, he had also formed the intention of writing his biography.

The first volume of that biography, *The Life of Schleiermacher*, appeared in 1870. Its 700 pages, of which about 150 are given to citing and analyzing primary sources, is anything but a mere story of daily events. The work as a whole was planned on such a massive scale that its completion eluded him, though he returned to it again and again. Even the second part of Volume One had to be supplemented posthumously by manuscript notes. In preparation for Volume Two, Dilthey had collected a mass of material on Schleiermacher's philosophic and theological work. We have some poignant testimony of how this unfinished project weighed on his mind. In the last weeks of his life—over forty years after the publication of the first volume—he wrote postcards to E. Spranger, one of his most distinguished disciples, suggesting that they should work together on completing the biography.

What made the biography interesting and so difficult to complete was Dilthey's conviction that the life of a significant thinker—or, for that matter, a great poet or important political figure—powerfully reflects and, in turn, transforms the intellectual, cultural, and social forces that impinge upon him. Interacting with individuals, organizations, and institutions, he is a nodal point of history. A biography must, therefore, draw extensively on the history of the factors influencing the subject of the biography, who, in turn, becomes a building brick of history.

As he put it himself in his Preface to the first edition:

The biography of a thinker or artist has to solve the great historical question how dispersed elements of culture—given through general conditions, social and moral presuppositions and the influence of predecessors and contemporaries—are absorbed and moulded into an original whole by the individual who, in turn, influences the creative life of the community. [*C.W.*, Vol. XIII, p. xxxiii]

One after the other, Dilthey explored with great thoroughness the different contexts that had shaped Schleiermacher's life and thought. He had been brought up in the Christian sect the Herrenhuters, so Dilthey examined their beliefs and religious practices. Because Schleiermacher became a clergyman, Dilthey discussed the role of the protestant clergy in the Germany of that time. He reviewed the history and cultural atmosphere of Berlin because Schleiermacher had lived there for a time. He discussed such sociological factors as the exclusion from politics of a well-to-do middle class and notes how, having "no great goals, but no hard struggle for existence either," their energies were turned toward the acquisition of inner culture [*Bildung*].

The fact that German classical literature from Lessing to Goethe was a formative influence for every educated German provided the reason for a long chapter on that literature. In it he makes the interesting point that Germany's great poets of that time were not only entertainers, but thinkers and scholars who consciously aimed at shaping the outlook and ideals of their countrymen. Poets of the Romantic movement, which succeeded the classical period, were contemporaries of Schleiermacher, and he counted some of them among his friends. So the Romantic movement and its chief representatives required the biographer's careful attention.

As a philosopher Schleiermacher, like most of his philosophically orientated contemporaries, was profoundly influenced by Kant. Dilthey therefore found it necessary to provide a detailed study of his philosophy. We shall have to return to the fact that Dilthey was knowledgeable on this subject and sufficiently sympathetic to be described as almost a neo-Kantian.

Dilthey also discovered that Schleiermacher was inspired by Spinoza, as had been Goethe and the leading thinkers of the Romantic movement. Naturally a chapter on Spinoza had to be included. Because Schleiermacher became professor of theology at the University of Halle, Dilthey explained the genesis of this new university, created as part of the modernization of Prussia after the Napoleonic wars. At Halle Schleiermacher lectured on a topic that became of major interest to Dilthey, which we shall have to discuss in some detail—hermeneutics.

DILTHEY'S OTHER HISTORICAL WRITINGS

Dilthey's predilection for biography was deeply rooted in his whole philosophic outlook. He believed in the importance and value of individuals and the intrinsic interest their uniqueness deserved. Furthermore, history, as we shall presently see, was meaningful for him in terms of the aspirations and responses of the actors involved in it. So his historical interpretations turned on the thinking of influential individuals rather than on impersonal forces. It is not surprising that intellectual biographies and biographical sketches figure in his subsequent work.

"The Reorganisation of the Prussian State (1807–1813)," which dates from 1872 and is contained in *C.W.*, Volume XII, concentrates on the major creators of the new Prussia: Stein, Hardenberg, Humboldt, Gneisenau, and

Scharnhorst. Essays on "Giordano Bruno" and on "When Goethe Studied Spinoza" date from 1893 and 1894, respectively. They appeared in *C.W.*, Volume II. The year 1900 saw the completion of the substantial work, "Leibniz and His Age," which placed Leibniz into a wide context by discussing the origins of mathematics, German humanism, the growth of scholarly associations and academies in general, and the foundation of the German Academy in particular. The Church, music, fiction, drama, and poetry of his age are all considered.

In Volume III, together with the work on Leibniz, there also figures a long essay from the same year (1891), "Frederic the Great and the German Enlightenment," which examines Frederic's relation to Voltaire and D'Alembert, his policies and educational theories, as well as the founding of the Prussian Academy of Sciences. Even more substantial is "The History of the Young Hegel" of 1905, which was included in Volume IV. It traced the influence on his philosophy of Hegel's original training in theology. There are, in addition, numerous other essays on Niebuhr, Goethe, Thiek, Heinrich Heine, Hölderlin, Schopenhauer, J. S. Mill, and Gibbon. Some of these, such as the long essays on Goethe and Hölderlin, were revised in the last years of his life.[4]

In addition to studies that focused on one individual, or on a very small group of such individuals, Dilthey also produced works that extensively used the history of ideas as an introduction to philosophic topics he wanted to discuss. Here too, though, the emphasis on individual thinkers is evident. The first volume of *The Introduction to the Human Studies* deals exclusively with the history of the origin of the human studies, tracing their emergence over some 800 pages. Most of the book deals with the first development of social studies under the aegis of metaphysical systems in antiquity and in the Middle Ages. After a discussion of the religious roots of metaphysics, Dilthey turns to the Pre-Socratics, Plato, Aristotle, The Sceptics, St. Augustine, and the later medieval philosophers. He then traces the early beginnings of modern science and the new approaches to human studies in the hands of such thinkers as Hobbes, Spinoza, and Hume.

Volume II of the collected works contains material that supplements the account of Volume I. It discusses the concept of man as held in the Middle Ages, in the Renaissance, and in the Reformation, by examining the thoughts of Petrarch, Macchiavelli, Montaigne, Erasmus, Luther, Zwingli, and Sebastian Frank. Another part of this volume presents ideas about "The System of Nature" and "Rationalism and Pantheism" as predominantly held by thinkers of the seventeenth century, such as Herbert of Cherbury, Bacon, Charron, Bodin, Althus, and Grotius.

The essay on "The Eighteenth Century and the Historical World" (1901) deals with the development of historiography by Voltaire, Montesquieu, Turgot, Kant, Hume, Robertson, Gibbon, J. Moser, Winkelmann, and Niebuhr. It also harks back to Polybios and St. Augustine. This work, which is also in Volume III, is supplemented by early articles on Ranke, Treitschke, and Mommsen.

When Dilthey deals with educational theory—an important part of his work, which has been taken up by contemporary German philosophers of education[5]—he once again employs a historical approach, covering such topics as Greek education and educational ideas (the Heroic Age, Plato, and Sophists), Roman education, the beginnings of Christian education in the Middle Ages, the monastery schools, the development of the universities, the influence of Italian humanism, the Protestant elementary school, and the work of Commenius. All this is contained in Volume IX. The lectures on which this volume is based also examined educational theory and practice in India and China. Omitted from Volume IX, it will be replaced in due course. His writings on aesthetics have a similar historical underpinning. The title of "The Origin of Hermeneutics" speaks for itself.

In his extensive writings on literature, the historical and biographical approach equally predominates. Though he was concerned with the standards of classical literature, with style, with the psychological material contained in it and the philosophic issues raised, much of it is intellectual history. As early as 1867—in his inaugural lecture at Basel—he discussed "The Poetical and Philosophical Movement in Germany 1770–1800." In addition to his substantial writings on Goethe, he wrote on Schiller, Shakespeare, Milton, and Dickens, on Cervantes and Calderón, Corneille and Molière. Most of this is in the *Collections*, which appeared as *The Great Poetry of Imagination* and *Experience and Poetry*. His *Of German Poetry and Music* contains examinations of further German literary figures and also discussions of Bach, Handel, Hayden, Mozart, and Beethoven.

I have given space to a list of Dilthey's historically oriented writings and marshalled the numerous men whose life and thought he examined because it occupied a large proportion of his working life but is not easily accessible to English-speaking readers. It also helps to emphasize Dilthey's incredibly wide interests and breadth of scholarship. Most important of all, it precipitated many of his philosophic concerns and colored his approach to them.

HISTORICISM

Because Dilthey was a philosopher first and a historian second, he submitted the nature, aims, and methods of history to philosophic scrutiny. Not only did he reflect on his own practice, but he surveyed the history of historiography and examined the contemporary state of the discipline. His sympathy lay with the German historical school whose views are usually described as historism or historicism (but not in the sense used by K. Popper, who gave this name to a body of beliefs most of which were rejected by the scholars usually grouped under this title). The most famous figure of the movement was Leopold von Ranke (1795–1886), whose lectures Dilthey had attended at Berlin and whom he greatly admired. While agreeing with many of the aims and methods of historicism and taking its side against other approaches to history, Dilthey thought "it lacked philosophic foundations" and made it the explicit aim of his *Introduction* "to attempt a philosophic justification of the principles guiding the historical school and the specific research inspired by it" (both quotations from the Preface, *C.W.*, Vol. I, p. xvi, my translation from *Selections,* p. 160).

Some of the principles and practices pioneered by the historical school are now quite noncontroversial and others are, at least, very widely accepted, and I need do little more than list them. The first is a commitment to a rigorous scholarship, which based historical accounts on solid evidence from primary sources. These nineteenth-century historians engaged in painstaking searches among archives of state papers, collections of letters, church registers, court rulings, and the like.

Second, a set of presuppositions common in the seventeenth and eighteenth century, which Dilthey had examined in Volume I of the *Introduction* under the label "The System of Nature,"[6] came to be rejected. Instead of accepting that natural religion lay at the basis of the variety of actual religions, natural law behind the variety of legal codes, and a fixed nature of man behind varied manifestations in history, it was now claimed that such basic concepts as those of law, religion, morality, man, and many others were themselves subject to historical change.

This, in turn, meant that it was impossible to apply external standards to history and to judge different periods in general terms. The moralizing tendencies of previous history were rejected and so was the evaluation of different ages as precursors of subsequent developments, or stepping stones in a particular sequence. "All ages," as Ranke put it, "are equally near to God." In other words, they had to be treated in terms of their own values and points of view, grasped as centered upon themselves. This raised the problem of the historian's imaginative understanding of people of a different age, people vastly different from him. As it was one of Dilthey's chief concerns, we shall be returning to it in some detail.

The system of nature and history based on nonhistorical criteria such as the divine plan or the moral law were not the only targets of historicist criticism. They also rejected very sharply, in the name of an open-minded empiricism, the superimposition on the historical course of events of any kind of theoretical or metaphysical construction. In other words they rejected—as did Dilthey—the kind of philosophy of history practiced by Hegel and others. There are no speculative shortcuts to understanding the past and present or anticipating the future.

However, this empiricism did not align the historicists with the representatives of a positivist approach to history, men such as Comte, J. S. Mill, and Buckle.[7] Their mistake, in the eyes of the historical school, and in those of Dilthey, too, was to transplant dogmatically the methods of the physical sciences to the human sphere instead of exploring what methods were appropriate in that sphere.

More controversial than the contentions outlined so far is the view of reality and our cognitive access to it that underlies historicism. It is best illustrated by a number of quotations. D. E. Lee and R. N. Beck define historicism in terms of the following contentions: "the nature of anything is entirely comprehended in its development," "the truth, meaning and value of anything is to be found in its history," and "historical knowledge is a basic, or the only requirement for understanding and evaluating man's present political, social and intellectual position or problems."[8] F. Meinecke, a friend of Dilthey and historian of historicism, makes the same point. Speaking about the historian, he writes "At last it seems to him that every phenomenon of history, indeed, human existence as a whole, is determined morphologically" ("Values and Causalities in History").[9] I think that Ruggiero, too, makes—though a little obscurely—the same point when he writes, "the evaluation of reality is a historical process of spiritual formation." I conclude this particular list of quotations with F. M. Powicke's comment on a fellow historian: "Vinogradoff could never be content with philosophic exposition. He must follow the guidance of the thread of principle into the labyrinth of historical fact."[10]

It may be worthwhile underlining two aspects of these claims that stand out: First, all aspects of human life are subject to the historical process and are the proper subject matter of the historian. In fact, the rise of historicism was accompanied by historiography being extended from mainly political history to social, cultural, and intellectual history. What is even more important is that these special topics were no longer thought of as abstruse specialisms but as integral parts of historiography.

The second point to note is that the historical approach is claimed to be the main, if not the sole, road to knowledge of human reality. This raises the familiar difficulty that arguments to establish any truth must then be accepted as ultimately circular, and that all conclusions become relative. Circularity results because the presuppositions, concepts, and methods used in reaching knowledge are themselves part of and determined by the historical process, but to know about these determining processes we need to use these very concepts, methods, and assumptions, the provenance of which we are examining.

Put in terms of relativity, the argument runs: if all knowledge, all judgments are historically determined, that is, conditioned by the constellation of circumstances prevailing in a particular age, then the judgments establishing these relativities are themselves subject to the historical conditions under which they are made. This is a live issue, and that is why I want to highlight it in this book. Dilthey had a great deal to say about it, and his answer is highly complex and, in the end, not really satisfactory. He remained torn between his sympathy for historicism and his equally strong concern for valid criteria of knowledge, which was one of the difficulties in the way of completing the *Introduction,* undertaken to search for "the system of presuppositions which justifies the judgement of historians ... and provides criteria for establishing that they are true" (Preface, *C.W.,* Vol. I, p. xvii). There is no mystery, however, about the line along which he sought a solution. He clearly states it in his preface, and I shall mention it here before I return to the theme of history. It will receive more detailed attention in Chapter 4.

Dilthey anchors his justification of historicism on the recognition, which he considers universal, that "all experience is originally connected, and given validity, by our consciousness (within which it occurs), indeed by our whole nature" (Preface, *C.W.,* Vol. I) and adds, "Anthropology and Psychology are the basis of all knowledge of historical life" (p. 32). It is therefore the analysis of the way this consciousness functions, and indeed the analysis of the basic features of human nature, which provides the basis for making history, and the other human disciplines, rigorous.

There is another problem hidden in the above quotation. The transition from consciousness to our whole nature represents a deliberate challenge to the main tradition of epistemology from Descartes to Dilthey's time and remains controversial. I shall take up this issue in my last chapter.

THE "INNER" SIDE OF HISTORY

Returning to the historical approach, which represents one of the cornerstones of Dilthey's thinking, I want to take up the theme of ages being centered upon themselves and having to be grasped in their own terms. It clearly, and fairly obviously, points to a specific conception of what history is about. If it were solely or mainly about such facts as the occurrence of plagues, the date of battles, the accession and death of kings, or the growth or decline of populations, the question of seeing it in its own terms would not arise. What we must be talking about is the way in which people of a particular age interpreted their situation, defined their goals, and established their priorities. We are asked to direct our attention to the thoughts, feelings, and aspirations of human beings that underlie the sequences of observable events and to understand these events in terms of the point of view of the people involved in them. Dilthey fully shared this definition of the historian's task with the historical school, although with the qualification that this could not be the sole point of view from which the historian looks at his subject matter. Inevitably and properly, he must also see it from his own point of view and use his power of hindsight.

Once understanding what goes on in other people's minds becomes a central feature of historiography, we are landed with epistemological questions about this type of cognition. Discussion of them forms the focal, and most original, part of Dilthey's philosophizing. It will occupy us later. Now I want to show that this view of history is far from eccentric by listing the views of a number of well-established historians. Dilthey is doing much more than justifying the views of a particular school of historians. He is addressing himself to problems that arise from preoccupations widely shared by historians.

B. Niebuhr wrote in the Preface to the second edition of his *History of Rome*,[11] which appeared in 1832 (a year after his death), about considering "books ... merely as pictures of a life that was not immediately accessible. ..."

H. Taine, whose main works appeared between 1860 and 1870, makes this point more fully:[12]

What is your first remark on turning over the great stiff leaves of a folio, the yellow sheets of a manuscript, a poem, a code of law, a declaration of faith? This, you say, was not created alone. It is but a mould, like a fossil shell, an imprint like one of those shapes embossed in stone by an animal which lived and perished. Under the shell there was an animal, and behind the document there was a man. Why do you study the shell, except to represent to yourself the animal? So you study the document only in order to know the man. The shell and the document are lifeless wrecks, valuable only as a clue to the entire and living existence. We must reach back to the existence, endeavour to recreate it.

We are, of course, not just talking about books or documents. Foustel de Coulanges in *The Ancient City*[13] makes this very clear: "History does not study material facts and institutions alone, its true object of study is the human mind: it should aspire to know what this mind has believed, thought and felt in the different ages of the life of the human race." Two years earlier in his inaugural lecture, he had stated that history must probe the fables and myths, the dreams induced by man's imagination, all the old falsehoods beneath which it must discover something very real—the beliefs of man. Wherever man has lived, wherever he has left some feeble imprint of his life and his intelligence, there is history.

A more recent pronouncement, making, by implication, a similar point, is J. Huizinga's comment, ". . . an historical narrative is always dependent on the culture in which and from which it springs."[14]

If the historian needs to grasp the cultural life of the people he writes about, he must be able to call upon his own historical imagination, so Huizinga added:[15] "Historical knowledge is dead and worthless that has not as its sounding board and its measuring rod the historian's personal and spiritual life."

My final quotation documenting the historian's concern with the mental states of historical agents comes from L. B. Namier in *Avenues of History*:[16]

The subject matter of history is human affairs, men in action, things which have happened and how they happened; concrete events fixed in time and place, and their groundings in the thoughts and feelings of men—not things universal and generalised—events as complex and diversified as the men who wrought them, those rational beings whose knowledge is seldom sufficient, whose ideas are but distantly related to reality and who are never moved by reason alone.

The historian's concern—as that of the biographer—with the thoughts and feelings of human beings apportions a special place to intellectual history. Before we can deal with this, we must examine the implications of putting together this concern for the "inner" side of history and the need to grasp an age, as centered upon itself, or a person from his own point of view. History, we are told, requires us to enter into the minds of people who may not only be different from us in their natures but, certainly, looked at the world with different eyes.

MEANING IN HISTORY

The point at issue is that human beings attribute meaning to their lives. They interpret the situations they are in, the events they encounter, and even their own nature, so as to create a more or less coherent and meaningful picture. An analysis of this interpretative activity through which meaning is created figures prominently in Dilthey's philosphic justification of biography and history. It is mostly to be found in his drafts for a "Critique of Historical Reason," collected in Volume VII.

The role this analysis plays in the philosophic underpinning of historiography is plain. The historian is, traditionally, required to tell a meaningful story. Clearly he need not be warned against stringing nonsense words together. He is to tell a meaningful story by explaining events in terms of what they meant to the actors, that is, in terms of what they feared, desired, imagined, and hoped to achieve.

In case this sounds only too obvious, one should stress that it provides for Dilthey the escape from the horns of a particular dilemma. On the one hand, it has been argued that there is no meaning in history and that therefore no meaningful story can be told. We can only give a dreary account of one thing happening after another: "a tale told by an idiot, signifying nothing." If nothing more is possible, the historian is condemned to the role of a mere chronicler. On the other hand, there have been persistent attempts to superimpose a pattern of meaning on history from outside. What happens is, then, interpreted as the unfolding of the divine plan, the forward march of reason, or a progress built into the nature of reality. All these ideas were objectionable to Dilthey—as they are to the majority of practicing historians—because they preempt the labor of empirical research. In terms of Dilthey's theory, the historian looks for meaning, but not for one grand meaning—rather, the various meanings that human beings find or attribute to what they do and suffer. The same point applies to the philosopher's more general search for meaning in life.

It should be obvious that when we talk about the meaning of life, of history, or of a situation, we are not using meaning in the sense in which we talk about the meaning of a word, a sentence, or a road sign. Both usages are common in English, but the latter has received more attention in contemporary English and American philosophy. An essential feature of meaning in this latter sense is that it is constituted by the relation between "signifier" and "signified," between a sign and that to which the sign points or refers. This is, precisely, the feature that is missing in the meaning of life, history, and so on. There is, in normal usage, no suggestion that life symbolizes or refers to something that is not life. "Life does not mean something else" (*C.W.*, Vol. VII, p. 234), "behind life we cannot go" as Dilthey put it. He also uses the analogy of a melody. It is meaningful, but it does not signify anything outside itself.

There is no need, in the present context, to pursue theories of linguistic meaning. It is also unnecessary to consider the interesting point whether the use of the same word is accidental or whether—as I believe—it points to a connection. Dilthey's belief in such a connection may have been the reason why he did not even attempt a consistent terminological distinction between the two senses. It can be made easily enough. "Significance" will render the sense of nonlinguistic meaning in most cases. I shall follow Dilthey in continuing to use the term "meaning," though I am dealing here, exclusively, with nonreferential meaning.

Basically meaning arises, according to Dilthey, from the interplay between the human individual and his environment, and from the relationship the parts of one's life have to each other. It is actually the second point that is emphasized in the sections of Volume VII that deal explicitly with what Dilthey calls the "category of meaning." Stressing this aspect allows him to draw attention to one link between this kind of meaning and linguistic meaning. Just as words gain their precise meaning from their context—that is, their place in a sentence, paragraph, and so on—so an episode gains its meaning from the place it occupies in a person's life, or in the history of a nation. Equally, the meaning of a sentence, just as that of a person's life or the history of a people, is made up of its meaningful parts. He is, of course, clearly aware that linguistic meaning is essentially based on reference, and the meaning of life is not. Its place is taken by the relationship between the subject and his world.

This latter point is more complex and obscure in Dilthey's writing than is his contention that meaning is about the place of parts within a whole. One problem is that his main discussions of meaning occur in fragments dating from his last years and never published in his lifetime. It figures as a "category of life," and I must briefly explain what he means by this. Following Kant and the modern usage derived from him, he defines a category as "a concept which expresses or established a relationship" (*C.W.*, Vol. XIX, p. 360, from a draft dated 1891–1892). He then distinguished formal categories, such as identity and equality, which were "rooted in reason as such" and "designate relations which pervade the whole of reality" to the "real" categories or "categories of life" that refer to "connections in life," are not transparent to reason, and cannot be neatly sorted out. Their number and relation to each other cannot be established once and for all (ibid., p. 361).

Sometimes Dilthey contrasts meaning as the category related to the past to "value" as the category of the present. In other words, meaning arises from our being able to relate what happens to what we remember, while valuation is our immediate response to what happens in the present. At other times he lists meaning and value side by side in discussion. He also uses meaning and significance interchangeably. Furthermore, he treats meaning as a "master category," particularly in his later writings.

It is possible that Dilthey might have clarified and systematized his views on meaning if he had been able to complete and prepare for publication the drafts bearing on the subject. That these questions were on his mind in the last years of his life is beyond question. Volume V of *Selected Writings*—the first volume of the new six-volume edition in English to appear in print—provides hitherto unpublished drafts for the rewriting of his *Poetics,* dating from 1907–1908. They show that his revisions were aimed at emphasizing such concepts as "lived experience" [*Erlebnis*] and "meaning," which had gained prominence in the thinking of his later years. In fact, there are new sections entitled "Meaning as a category of life" and "Poetics considered from the perspective of the theory of meaning." However it is possible that no amount of revision of either the *Poetics* or the relevant portions of the "Critique of Historical Reason" would have produced a clear systematization, as there is evidence that he was continuing to hold the view—to which I have already referred—that the relation between the categories could not be sorted out logically and could always be seen from different, equally valid, points of view.

In my past writings I have taken a view on how the main thrust of Dilthey's argument can be most reasonably interpreted. Though it may contain an element of simplification, I summarize it here. Meaning arises from the interplay between ourselves as thinking, feeling, and willing creatures and the world that impinges upon us. Objects and events become meaningful to us insofar as they attract or repel us, give us pleasure or pain, present themselves as goals to be achieved, means to those goals, or obstacles to be overcome. Different categories, which all contribute to our experiencing life as meaningful, govern different aspects of our experience. Consciousness of being affected by the environment and in turn affecting it comes under the category of "power," our immediate responses to the present under that of "value." As we exert our wills to mold the future, we think in terms of the category of "ends and means." We interpret things as parts of wholes and wholes in terms of their parts. In the encounter with others we distinguish their "outer" behavior from the "inner" states of mind manifested in the former. This is why Dilthey speaks of the categories of "part and whole" and of "inner and outer." Experiencing and judging life in these terms constitutes its meaning.

The references to the past, present, and future underline the importance that time plays in our life. "Temporality" as the category that governs our experience of temporal succession is, clearly, of particular significance for the discussion of the way in which we make and recapture history. Dilthey's analysis of this "temporality" has been singled out as particularly influential by thinkers such as Heidegger.[17]

Meaning arises in the experience of the present, conceived not as a minute portion of clock time, but as the unit that combines with others to make up our lives. That present is complex because it contains awareness of the past and anticipation of the future. I have, let us say, the sensation of a sharp pain; that is the actual unpleasant response to a situation in the real present. My knee has collided with my desk, and I understand this because I am familiar with both from my experience (a baby would not understand the situation in this sense). I also anticipate continued pain, a swelling possibly, and interference with my plan for a walk. This triple awareness makes this small episode of my life meaningful.

These small units of meaning are, in turn, related to wider, meaningful contexts. I realize that I am accident-prone, because this kind of thing keeps on happening; or perhaps I become aware of getting clumsier as I get older, a foretaste of increasing incapacity. I may think of myself as unlucky, a victim of fate.

The above illustration refers to something that happens to me. An analogous story can be told of my doing something. At the moment of writing this, I am exerting myself to affect the environment—I am hitting the keys of my typewriter. This, as so much of my movements, is guided by a purpose. The immediate purpose is to put an idea on paper, and this is part of the wider purpose of writing a book. This, in turn, is part of wider purposes, such as making Dilthey better known, fulfilling my ambitions as a scholar, and the like. These plans and purposes and means of pursuing them have not been born this instant. They have a history, and through this alone can they be understood. Negotiations with a publisher preceded the writing of this particular book. My preoccupation with Dilthey dates back over many years. What I write now is based on many years of study, and so on. Thus the episodes of my life are strung together.

The events of my life as perceived by me, what I value and what I hate, the goals I pursue and the frustrations I meet with make up the complex pattern of meanings that constitute my life. Central to this is my awareness of temporal succession and the place of everything in it. Memory makes my experiences cumulative. I judge and evaluate things in terms of past experiences, in which I learned lessons and acquired skills. Writing one's first book is not quite like writing one's tenth.

This cumulative process constitutes the "historicity" of human life. It is the reason both for the need to understand things in historical terms and for our capacity to do so. It also explains Dilthey's starting point. Biography was important for Dilthey because in an individual, and particularly one with exceptional achievements, the meaning and pattern of his life can be traced.

THE CONSTITUENTS OF HISTORY

As meaning is rooted in the interpretations and plans that an individual superimposes on his own doings and the things that happen to him, an outside interpretation of his life must start from and take account of the meaning he has given to his own life. (A person, or, for that matter, a nation, state, or age, must be seen as centered upon itself.) This is why Dilthey starts his theoretical discussion of meaning in history with autobiography, where we get an explicit account of the meaning or meanings a person found in his life. The works of great autobiographers such as Saint Augustine or Rousseau (both called *Confessions*), are limiting cases, differing in two respects above all from the interpretations that most of us give to our lives.

First, unlike most of us who meander from purpose to purpose, focus our interest on this or that, such exceptional people organize their lives around a single overriding goal; they superimpose a global interpretation on their lives. Second, they are sharply self-conscious, whereas most of us attend only occasionally and absentmindedly to the pattern our lives assume. They have the capacity to see deeply and clearly and to write with eloquence and precision. This is what makes such autobiographies paradigmatic of the way in which meaning is constituted in human life.

The biographer attempting to tell a meaningful story about a person's life must, first of all, recapture or reconstruct how that person saw his own life. Where, as in most cases, no autobiography exists, he looks for autobiographical remarks in letters, diaries, or conversations recorded by contemporaries, which indicate what worried that person, what his viewpoint was, and what he was seeking to achieve. It is bound to remain more patchy and tentative than autobiography, for most of us do not produce comprehensive accounts of our thoughts and feelings for a future biographer and, indeed, keep many feelings deliberately private.

However, the biographer—Dilthey argued—has compensating advantages over the autobiographer. For one thing, the autobiographer can never tell the story of his own life up to the end. It is unlikely that death overtakes him as he brings his autobiography up to the preceding moment. This is more than a matter of a few months or years missing. The whole pattern changes, like a kaleidoscope reshaken, as event follows event. Ten years of happy marriage acquire quite a different meaning if followed by desertion or a further long stretch of contented married life. A young man may divide his time and interest equally between music and athletics. Only the sequel will show which of these turns out to be a hobby and which his vocation.

The biographer also has the advantage of being relatively detached. Dilthey appreciated that the bystander may, sometimes, see more of the game than the player. Precisely because of their involvement, people can remain unconscious of their motives or even deceive themselves about them, while they are transparent to a shrewd observer. This is why Dilthey agreed with Kant's assertion that it is possible to understand an author better than he understood himself.[18]

Finally—and this is the most complex and challenging issue that Dilthey confronted—there is virtue in hindsight. Here two factors are closely intertwined. First, the passage of time reveals consequences that throw new light on the original events. Luther's contemporaries saw him as a religious reformer. Later generations could appreciate his contribution to the growth of Germany as a nation, and such a topic would figure legitimately in a biography. But time not only reveals these hidden seeds in a person's activity, it also produces observers with a different outlook. Were I to write, let us say, a biography of Dilthey, I would bring, inevitably and legitimately I think, my own point of view to the work. Quite apart from the personal quirks of my personality, I am the product of a different age and therefore a different cultural climate. Matters Dilthey cared for may seem trivial and uninteresting to us, while others have become of growing importance. Features of his personality for which his contemporaries may have praised him may, today, call for apologetic explanations. Dilthey believed that the biographer or historian cannot and should not merely recapture the point of view of a person or an age of a different period. Historical judgment must also mean using the perspectives of hindsight and of the presuppositions of one's own age. After all, one is writing for one's contemporaries. Somewhere a balance needs to be struck between these two requirements. This is why history needs continually to be rewritten.

As we move from biography to history, we lose the unity that dealing with an individual person bestows on a narrative. Meaning, we say, arises from the thoughts, feelings, and aspirations that prompt human behavior, but states—Dilthey insisted—do not think, nations do not have feelings or a will like individuals, nor is their existence clearly defined in time. To talk about the birth, youth, old age, or death of collectives is a metaphor that can be variously applied. Italy seen as originating from its unification in the nineteenth century is in its youth; seen as the continuation of, and successor to, the Roman Empire, it is very old. Neither description is as significant as the ascription of an age to an individual.

There is no complete solution to the difficulty that history is not just the story of one individual or that of an innumerable number of individuals and that the sequence of events has no identifiable beginning or end, as have the lives of individuals. History must remain more confusing, impenetrable, and untidy than biography. But some comprehensibility can be salvaged by focusing attention on men—such as rulers, military leaders, political thinkers, and the like—who shaped and influenced history in significant respects, or people who eminently reflected and helped to shape the intellectual and emotional climate of their time—people such as poets and historians.

History as conceived by Dilthey must emphasize the role of "great men"—that is, it must focus on their thoughts and plans. This is why biographies can serve as the building blocks of history. However, Dilthey was not so naive as to think that history is the actualization of the ideas and purposes of leaders. He eloquently acknowledged the role played by chance and physical conditions in history. They may frustrate human goals or distort them. A battle, let us say, cannot be understood simply in terms of the strategic and tactical thinking of the opposing generals; its course might have been determined just as much by the unexpected rain that transformed the location into a quagmire. Though Dilthey clearly referred to this, it is not easy to see how this insight would translate into a methodology that did justice both to the strategies and the physical conditions. He never wrote that kind of history, and his biographies lean heavily toward intellectual biography.

There is, secondly, the vexing problem of the unintended consequences of human actions, which are not due to chance and circumstances. A million housewives buying extra sugar because they are afraid of a shortage and a price rise will produce these very results, which none of them intended. This is, of course, a familiar problem but I can recall no discussion of this in Dilthey.

There remains, finally, the fact that many of the happenings in history due to human agency cannot be attributed to individual leaders, or, for that matter, to any individual person. To my mind, Dilthey was successful in solving the problem of attributing thoughts, will, and so forth, to superindividual entities. Traditionally, two sharply contrasting views have been put forward on this matter. On one hand, there is the view that there are "real" super-individual entities—such as nations or classes—to whom thought and will can be attributed. They are the actors in history. The other view insists that only individual human beings think, will, and so on, and that collective actions can only be explained by reducing them to the actions of the individuals who make up the collective.[19] Dilthey was equally convinced that only individuals think, etc., and that history must talk about the decisions, acts, etc. of collectives. After all, it was not Chamberlain who entered into war with Hitler, nor Chamberlain plus any number of named individuals. It was Britain that commenced war on Germany. Chamberlain was elected and fulfilled a well-defined function in accordance with the British constitution. There were cabinet discussions and perhaps consultations with other people. We may or may not know what went on in these meetings and who said what. The outcome of it all—the declaration of war—can be read and understood, and in it Chamberlain spoke for Britain and not just for himself, as when, let us say, he ordered his dinner. Only individuals think, but a thought may be the result of discussion between several individuals, just as a decision may be the compromise between the wills of a number of people. It may be one person's job to speak for and act for a whole group. Whose thought or choice it was is a matter of empirical investigation, but sometimes such an investigation may be both impossible and irrelevant. Britain's declaration of war was clear in its message. We know the reason for it, and we know the consequences. We may not know whether particular formulations in it are due to particular members of the cabinet. And does it matter?

In his *Construction of the Historical World* (C.W., Vol. VII), Dilthey has quite a lot to say about the kinds of entities and contexts the historian needs to take account of, so as to subdivide the unmanageable flow of history in terms of units that can be subjected to analysis. One of these is the chain of causes and interactions concerning an identifiable event, such as the liberation of the Netherlands. Next, there are the systems of interaction focused around particular areas of human life, such as "economic life, law, politics, religions, social life, art, philosophy, science" (C.W., Vol. VII, quoted from my translation, *Pattern and Meaning in History*[20]). Unlike the state that links such various systems together, these cultural and social systems have a thematic unity.

History can also be divided into ages and periods, which is, of course, not a matter of cutting up the temporal sequences into neat parcels of thirty, fifty, or a hundred years. Nor is it a matter of the reigns of different kings. It is, rather, a question of delimiting a period "in which a unity of mental climate embracing everything from the conditions of life up to the highest ideas took shape, reached its zenith and disintegrated again" (C.W., Vol. VII, p. 164; ibid., p. 155). It is in this sense that we quite commonly speak of the "age of reason" and the like.

Explanations in history require not only identifiable, reasonably well-defined, units, but also the assumption of some regularities governing their behavior. Or, as Namier put it, "Yet in all intelligent historical quests there is, underneath, a discreet, tentative search for the typical and recurrent in the psyche and actions of man (even in his unreason) and a search for the morphology of human affairs" (*Avenues of History*).[21] Like Dilthey, he stresses the importance of underpinning the flow of history by establishing basic, relatively unchanging factors of human life, as well as an order underlying the unfolding of events. The chain of occurrences constituting a significant historical happening such as the liberation of the Netherlands, for example, consists of causally explainable sequences.

Some of the causes and effects were purely physical—for example, the water pouring through broken dykes hindering travel on land. Others were psychological—oppression producing resentment, rebellious actions anger-ing rulers, and the like. At the same time, teleological explanations of purposive behavior are available because human beings have typical goals and predictably pursue them.

Social and cultural systems can—like historical events—be explained in terms of the typical human needs and wants that they serve, and the way they function to cause these needs to be satisfied. The spirit of an age can, then, be analyzed in terms of the interaction between different social and cultural systems and the features they all share.

Thus it is basically the regularities of human nature that provide a basis for seeing any patterns in history, because they provide a constant, actually graspable factor in the flux of events. The different aspects of human nature and their role in disparate human activities form the subject matter of what Dilthey called the "systematic human studies." As early as 1875, he claimed that "The novelty of my method lies in connecting studies of man with historical studies" (quoted by Misch in his preface to *C.W.*, Vol. V).

INTELLECTUAL HISTORY

We can now return to the role intellectual history plays in illuminating history as a whole. It is not just another specialism alongside the history of politics, of fashion, of transport, or what you will. Once we recognize that thoughts, feelings, and aspirations give meaning to the course of historical events, then history, which specifically explores the life, origin, and decline of ideas and analyzes the interaction between them, becomes a central thread of all historiography. In politics and social life, in the pursuit of their ambitions and the defence of their interests, human beings are moved by and respond to ideas. The men, for example, who drafted the American Declaration of Independence, and all those who fought the War of Independence, were influenced by, and adopted for their purpose, a tradition of ideas that not only has its own history but thus affected events outside the pure interplay of ideas.

In fact, no neat separation, no specialization on facts or ideas, is really possible. Dilthey speaks of the "false ideal of a cultural history which tears the connection between circumstances and great men, between regular advances of civilisation and the power struggles of nations" (quoted in the Preface to *C.W.*, Vol. III).

This is a point that is neither outdated nor so obvious now that it scarcely needs discussion. The distinguished French historian F. Braudel, for example, has attracted a great deal of attention by putting this kind of program into practice. Echoing quite similar statements by Dilthey, he wrote in 1951,[22]

For us there are no bounded human sciences. Each of them is a door open onto the entirety of the social, each leads to all the rooms, to every floor of the house, on the condition that on his march the investigator does not draw back out of reverence for neighbouring specialists. ... [The human sciences] must deal with man, living complex, confused as he is ... man whom all the social sciences must avoid slicing up, however skillful and artistic the carving.

And again,[23]

Without the explicit will to do so, the social sciences encroach on each other; each tends to seize upon the social in its entirety ... while believing that it stays at home each moves in on its neighbour.

This suggests neither that specialization is impossible, nor that it is undesirable. It just means retaining a readiness to cross the frontiers of disciplines and also an awareness of the interdependence of different branches of learning from which the need for interdisciplinary cooperation follows. So intellectual history, though it profits from interaction with other branches of history (as well as with systematic human studies such as psychology or sociology) and in turn illuminates them, has its own distinctive features and methods. Dilthey's predilection for it was not only due to natural interest or even his realization of its key importance, but also his conviction that it possessed a number of advantages over other branches of history. B. E. Jensen, in his "The Role of Intellectual History in Dilthey's *Kritik der historischen Vernunft*,"[24] convincingly singles out a number of reasons why Dilthey believed that intellectual history was particularly suitable for "scientific" treatment. As he points out, remarks on this are scattered over Dilthey's writings.

First, he thought there was more relevant source material available in this sphere—enough, in fact, to draw valid conclusions, at least for recent periods. Purveyors of ideas write books and articles and tend to be more voluble in their correspondence. Since the introduction of the printing press, these have become readily available.

There is, second, the superior credibility of literary or philosophic writings. When people advertise goods, apply for jobs, engage in international negotiations, report on cabinet meetings, and the like, there can easily be practical reasons why the truth should be suppressed, disguised, or distorted. But what reason could there normally be for suppressing or distorting one's thought in a poem, a novel, or a philosophic treatise? (One major reason can be censorship, but that would be a publicly known factor for which we can make allowances.)

Thirdly, the transmission of ideas takes place in an inteligible way and occurs without loss. In other words we can trace the recurrence of an idea, its development, and so on. (This does not mean that we can always establish how a particular idea reached a particular person, whether he had read the original author, had received it secondhand, etc.) Furthermore, we are looking at a sphere that is teleologically ordered. In the sciences, to give the most clearcut example, there are common, well-understood purposes and cumulative achievements. Though this is not as radically true in art and literature, poets and painters, too, learn from the tradition and base themselves on it.

THE USES OF HISTORY

It may, finally, be helpful to spell out more fully the functions which, in Dilthey's view, history can fulfill.

It tell us, first, what man is, for only in the historical course of events are his various potentialities realized. It is worthwhile emphasizing the polemical point implied. In a distinct sense human nature is not unchanging and everywhere the same. Neither introspection nor experiments on forty-five psychology students will provide reliable information on human nature in general. We have generally become more alert to this issue. Traditional conceptions about the fundamental psychological characteristics of men and women, respectively, have been challenged as possibly being due to cultural factors. It has been suggested that the theories of psychoanalysis may, possibly, only apply to central European middle classes and to any group resembling them. Have we any evidence, any reason to believe, that they also apply to South Sea islanders, Russian peasants, or Californian hippies? The true empirical evidence of what is constant and what is variable in human nature is only to be found in historical records.

This also means that we cannot decide once and for all what human beings can and cannot do. There can be no final view of human nature as long as history continues. There are open possibilities, room for creativity. Surprisingly enough, this even applies, to some extent, to physiologically based achievement. It was not that long ago that we thought that human beings were not capable of running a mile in less than four minutes. Alas, we were equally surprised by the extent of pityless cruelty that a civilized nation—Dilthey's nation—displayed in the treatment of Jews and the attack on Russia.

Linked to the view that history alone reveals human nature is a second point, which is of central importance to Dilthey's whole approach but remains difficult and controversial. Dilthey believed that history, if philosophically scrutinized, can provide us with values and norms to guide personal and communal life. By insisting that the "lessons of history" require critical, philosophic scrutiny, Dilthey guarded himself against a simplistic view that what happens is right, what is believed is true, that success proves value. But while Dilthey could not accept divine revelation as the source of an absolute morality nor believe that pure reason could provide a universal moral law, he was nevertheless not prepared to accept complete moral relativism, a chaos of conflicting ethical precepts between which one cannot decide, let alone an "anything goes" philosophy. He believed, for instance, in the value of individuals and the importance of freedom. He thought such views could be supported by discovering, through the critical scrutiny of history, what human beings have consistently valued, what response to their needs sustains a rich and full human life.

The establishment of aesthetic values runs parallel to this and is, indeed, intertwined with it. Dlthey's writings on literature were designed to confirm or establish a canon of what constituted great classical literature. This in turn proved an educational norm of what should be taught in schools. Such literature, one should add, is not just an object of aesthetic enjoyment; it presents ideals of life and norms of conduct.

There is here no need to argue out the strengths and weaknesses of Dilthey's position that value judgments can be extrapolated (however indirectly) from history, as he did not himself discuss approaches to moral theory in any depth. However, I should like to adduce the support that our commonsense attitudes to these matters provide. There is, for instance, very wide-spread agreement that Shakespeare is a great dramatist—better than Eugene O'Neill, let us say. This does not mean that I, personally, prefer to watch Shakespeare rather than O'Neill, nor does it mean that the performance of a Shakespeare play would command a larger audience than would one of O'Neill's plays. Yet it is not an abstract judgment based on rational criteria. It has something to do with appreciation of the play, with the canons of playwriting developed in time, and generally with our knowledge of the history of drama.

I have already mentioned that a historical approach prevents us from drawing dogmatic, definitive conclusions, and therefore it encourages open-mindedness. Dilthey believed—and this is the third benefit we derive from history—that historical consciousness is liberating. Again and again he speaks eloquently on this. In his concluding remarks of his draft toward a "Critique of Historical Reason" (*C.W.*, Vol. VII, p. 290) he writes,

The historical consciousness of the finitude of every historical phenomenon, of every human or social condition and of the relativity of every kind of faith, is the last step toward the liberation of man. With it man achieves the sovereignty to enjoy every experience to the full and to surrender himself to it unencumbered, as if there were no system of philosophy or faith to tie him down. Life is freed from knowledge through concepts. the mind becomes sovereign over the cobwebs of dogmatic thought. Everything beautiful, everything holy, every sacrifice relived and interpreted opens perspectives which disclose some part of reality ... and, in contrast to the relativity, the continuity of creative forces asserts itself as the central historical fact.

The passage largely speaks for itself, and the matter of creativity mentioned in the last sentence has already been discussed. But perhaps a word is required on the liberation from knowledge through concepts. The wider context of Dilthey's philosophy makes it abundantly clear that it is neither possible nor desirable to escape from conceptual thought. I take it that in this passage he makes two points. The first is that immediate experience to which we open ourselves is richer than any concepts we impose on it. Secondly he has philosophic, rather than everyday, concepts in mind when he talks of liberation from them. It is dogmatic systems we are freed from. Perhaps I should add that when he speaks of "enjoying experience to the full as if there were no faith to tie him down" he does not really recommend orgies.

In a letter to Count York he writes on similar lines: "the historical world leads through self-reflection to a victorious, spontaneous aliveness, to a context in the *life of an individual* which can be analytically shown but *not formulated in thought*" (correspondence with Count York, pp. 156–57 [the italics are Dilthey's]).

JUDGMENT

From the liberating power of historical consciousness I turn to the relevance of history for judgment. Let me first pinpoint the issue by an illustration. During the Napoleonic wars, two armies of approximately equal size confronted each other in the north of the Iberian peninsula. The Duke of Wellington was afraid that with forces so evenly balanced, any engagement would be extremely costly of lives. Anxious, as always, to avoid extensive bloodshed, he began to retreat, and the French army followed. Seated on horseback, he watched the movements of the French army through his telescope while holding in the other a chicken leg which he was nibbling. Suddenly, as he saw the French extending their line to outflank him, he dropped his chicken leg, said, "This will do," and ordered his whole army to attack. It was one of the rare occasions when he fought a dashingly aggressive battle and scored a crushing victory. The Duke had made a judgment and backed it. This represented a particular ability or skill for, clearly, neither the French army leaders nor, probably, any of the soldiers about had seen the implications of the army movement of the French. This capacity had made Wellington a great general who never lost a battle.

So what is this capacity? Can we acquire it or improve it? Undoubtedly, it has something to do with knowledge. The Duke had many years of military experience, and he was remarkably well informed on the details relevant to warfare. He knew what weight an infantryman could carry, how many miles a regiment could march in a day, how long a cavalry charge could be sustained, and a thousand things of this kind. But knowledge is not enough. Thousands of blundering and incompetent commanders must have possessed the same kind of knowledge Wellington had acquired.

Immanuel Kant put his finger on this point with admirable clarity. It is pleasant to know that it was not a practical man of affairs but a cloistered academic who made the distinction so clearly. In the *Critique of Pure Reason*[25] he writes,

. . . judgement is a peculiar talent which can be practiced only, and cannot be taught. It is the specific quality of mother-wit; and its lack no school can make good. For although an abundance of rules borrowed from the insight of others may indeed be proffered to and, as it were, grafted upon a limited understanding, the power of rightly employing them must belong to the learner himself, and in the absence of such a natural gift no rule that may be prescribed to him for this purpose can assure against misuse. A physician, a judge or a ruler may have at command many excellent pathological, legal, or political rules, even to the degree that he may become a profound teacher of them and yet, none the less, may easily stumble in their application.

In a footnote Kant adds, "Deficiency in judgement is just what is ordinarily called stupidity and for such a failing there is no remedy"; he adds further that such a person could nevertheless "be trained by study, even to the extent of becoming learned." Apart from being too stupid to be able to apply to specific cases the rules he has learned, "the error may be due to his not having received, through examples and actual practice, adequate training for this particular act of judgement." Kant has some reservations about the value of examples because they might blunt the capacity for abstract understanding and encourage mechanical use of formulae. However, he concedes that "sharpening of the judgement is indeed the one great benefit of examples."

We need not pursue the specific reasons why Kant introduced these points or what conclusions he drew from them. Enough that he directed attention to the tremendous importance of making judgments in applying general rules to specific cases. We need to make such judgments constantly and do so more or less successfully. The capacity for it is quite distinct from knowledge or even abstract reasoning, and, as Kant notes, there can be no rules for applying rules because it would involve us in an infinite regress. The question remains how examples and practice can help.[26]

Dilthey did not explicitly espouse a theory of judgment, but his treatment of history contains the main ingredients for such a theory. Before spelling out this claim in detail, it may be worthwhile to underline the contemporary relevance of focusing attention on this issue. Kant's entertaining picture of a learned man whose knowledge does not help him to make intelligent judgments is, arguably, an image of our modern civilization.

The tremendous explosion of knowledge—from atomic physics to space technology, from biochemistry to electronics—has made us, collectively, more knowledgeable than any generation before. An incredible quantity of information and theoretical explanations is available for the solution of our problems, yet individuals become less and less able to deal knowledgeably with the problems that confront them because the vast store of knowledge is, inevitably, distributed among a host of experts, each master within his own small area. He, like the rest of us, needs outside help in the everyday job of living.

The point is easily illustrated by comparing life in the early nineteenth century with that of today. A housewife then had to wash or clean clothes made from a few natural materials and had learned to cope from her mother. Similarly, people learned how to light their rooms by lighting candles or adjusting oil lamps. They could, and had to, learn about horses to ride or drive them. Removing the ink stain from a ballpoint pen on a shirt is a different matter. You need to know what the shirt is made of, because different kinds of artificial fibers, and mixtures between them or with natural fibers, are used. The ink, too, is a complex chemical product. Only experts can tell you how to remove a particular stain from a particular material (though they may, of course, have provided some of that information on a printed label). Similarly, the breakdown of your electrical equipment or of your car usually calls for expert help. There is less and less scope for personal judgment in more and more areas of life. Shopping, where it gets harder to tell margarine from butter or wool from nylon, is another example. This problem is by no means confined to the products of technology. Politics, too, confronts us with problems we are not competent to deal with. Is the European Economic Community agricultural policy, on balance, a good or a bad thing? Should the provision of water, gas, and other public utilities be controlled by governments or left in private hands? Is it serious for a country to have a budget deficit? We may have some preferences in these matters in terms of feelings or general principles. We may, for example, be for or against state controls. But I must confess that I, for one, have no answers to these questions because I do not know what the implications of one or the other policy are. My only choice can be which expert to believe.

As a result, we become credulous, even gullible. If we are assured by "experts" that something or other will make our hair grow again, remove our wrinkles, or restore us to slimness in no time, who are we to challenge it? After all, science is capable of rather miraculous things. If we then discover that these experts are fallible or even phoney, we may react by becoming skeptical and even cynical. Such despair of any kind of guidance is not helpful either.

Clearly there is no alternative to accepting expert judgment in many things. It is inconceivable that one person should come to master the scientific theories behind television or computing, understand his car engine, know the chemistry of artifical fibers, and be closely familiar with the economic consequences of food tariffs and a host of similar things. At best, we may acquire some criteria for choosing reputable experts. However, prominent among our problems are human ones. Why does my wife seem discontented? Should I be more strict with my son? Will it help him to acquire self-discipline or just make him sullen? Will this applicant make a suitable secretary? How should I treat my employees? and so forth, ad infinitum.

Because most solutions in the technical field depend on applying general laws or principles, we tend to believe that the same approach will serve us with human problems. So disciplines have grown up that specialize in the theoretical knowledge relevant to answering the kind of questions I have listed, and experts emerge who develop, teach, and apply this knowledge for our benefit. So we have marriage guidance, educational counselling, industrial relations, management studies, and the like.

These disciplines, which arrive at generalizations based on the accumulation of information more comprehensive and more systematically arranged than individuals can achieve, have proved their usefulness. Yet they have serious limitations. For various reasons, including the complexity and variety of human affairs, application of their theories is often shaky and uncertain. Sometimes these theories provide salutory warnings and curbs on stupidity. But they are not really a substitute for personal judgments in situations that are ultimately unique.

This is where a counterbalance to the model of science and its application is vital. Such an alternative model is provided by history. Because of the success of science and the predominance of its applications in our lives, we have come to think that knowledge in terms of general laws, of which physics provides the outstanding example, is the paradigm of all knowledge, in comparison with which any other form of cognition is defective, uncertain, and even suspect. But we want and need and, indeed, do make, judgments about individual people and individual cases. It is surely possible to know that Shakespeare was a great poet, that your friend needs your sympathy at this moment, or that John is difficult because his parents have separated (but not that all children of broken marriages are difficult). Such knowledge is not an extrapolation from laws established by behavioral scientists and is none the worse for it. A theory that postulates that all knowledge is knowledge of laws and their applications condemns itself.

History by contrast is concerned with the individual. It must be in the business of judging how individual events are related to each other, what role individual people or things played in a situation. It is, usually, distinguished from other preoccupations with human affairs by aiming at records of the past that focus on occurrences that affected a lot of people. However, these distinguishing characteristics are not epistemologically significant. Obviously, any actual event is in the past when we give an account of it, so the fact that history usually deals with events some way back in the past is not particularly significant (although the distance in time may create methodological problems about the reliability of memories, the scarcity of records, and the like). Similarly, whether an event is "public" in the sense of having widespread effects or not is very much a matter of degree.

Once we have granted this, we can recognize everyday judgments as very like historical judgments. Dilthey appreciated this, for when he strove to formulate a "Critique of Historical Reason" he was not only concerned to lay the philosophic foundations of historical study, but he was looking for an epistemological framework for his more comprehensive and lifelong concern for understanding the human world. After all, the various systematic disciplines dealing with human life—psychology, sociology, social anthropology, economics, and so on—are based on case histories, "longitudinal studies," participant observers' accounts, and the like, which are all, essentially, historical accounts. Similarly, when I make such everyday judgments as that my wife is annoyed with me because I forgot our wedding anniversary, or that John is a delinquent because of his home background, I am reconstructing the connections between events in time in a manner characteristic of historical judgments. Something very similar takes place when I use the past to predict likely developments. (Their marriage will never work because he has been spoiled by his mother all his life.)

So history is the disciplined and organized practice of something we are all engaged in when we deal with the human problems of our everyday lives. The value of history is, therefore, not confined to giving us information about the past, valuable though knowledge of the origins of the things we have to cope with may be. It may, or may not, help us to anticipate the future.

The historical approach is intrinsically important as the training ground of judgment. The underlying reason is man's historicity, the fact that man is, essentially, a historical being whose thinking is rooted in the cumulative experience of temporal existence and who has to be understood in these terms.

To the epistemology and methodology of historical judgment we shall return later in the book. Here I wanted to emphasize the importance of this kind of approach, which is the counterpart of scientific explanation. It throws particular light on Dilthey's relevance today, if we remember that he espoused and analyzed in depth this kind of thinking. In a world that is utilitarian and pragmatic in a rather narrow sense, this is important. We know why schools and universities should teach physics, chemistry, and engineering. The development of space rockets and computers, of artificial fibers and food preservatives, of power tools and automated machines, of medicinal drugs and medical hardware makes us healthier and more comfortable, it aids national security and secures exports. Economics, psychology, and management studies can help us to select personnel, plan production, and organize workforces. But what can history do for us?

I have tried to argue that all the benefits of science can turn to dust and ashes if their use is not guided by the kind of human understanding and judgment that history helps us to achieve. To draw our attention to this and to show what was involved in historical judgment is Dilthey's special merit. It is one reason why he continues to deserve attention.

3

The Methods of the Human Studies and Hermeneutics

I would have liked to pass directly from history to anthropology so as to contrast the study of change and succession in time to that of the—at least relatively—unchanging, two approaches that are both different and interdependent. History cures us of the naive belief that human nature is always the same. Far from being just a story of external events, it provides an account of how formerly unrealized potentialities of human personality emerge in the passage of time. On the other hand, anthropology, conceived in a broad sense, pinpoints abiding features that make man man. Without assurance of such features there could be no continuity, no basis for objective judgments—indeed, no meaningful human history. "The same analysis," to give Dilthey's own words, "which makes the past of human thought its subject matter, demonstrates the relativity of every individual system at the same time it makes these systems comprehensible from the nature of man and things, it explores the laws of their formation, their common structure, their main types and their origins and forms" (C.W., Vol. VIII, p. 12).

However, too much would remain unexplained—indeed, has remained unexplained in the section on history—unless something was said next about Dilthey's methodology.[1] It is one of the vexing problems of philosophy that things are so mutually interdependent that whatever one starts with would have been clearer if one had started with something else, which in turn is not self-explanatory. As it happens, this point figures quite prominently in Dilthey's own methodology, for he rejected any absolute starting points and resigned himself to the ultimate circularity of philosophic expositions.

Dilthey's interest in methodology was serious and abiding. The empirical human studies—history, psychology, and all the rest—aim at factual knowledge of the human world. It was the special task of philosophy to examine, clarify, and justify their methods. This was not a matter of abstract logic and deductions from broad, epistemological principles. Method, he insisted, must be guided by an initial appreciation of the general nature of the subject matter. Or, as Dilthey himself put it: "The task must create its own appropriate methods" (*C.W.*, Vol. V, p. 44). Once again, we confront the hermeneutic circle: the methodology designed to show how we may know human nature must itself be guided by a prior application of that nature.

UNDERSTANDING

It is possible, by way of anticipation, to say in a few words what distinguishes the human world from the world of nature sufficiently to require and justify a distinctive method of research. Human beings talk, while the rest of nature is mute or, at least, as is the case with higher animals, inarticulate. So what we learn about human beings is based on communications from beings like us, not just on observation of objects and events. Understanding, defined as the process of grasping what is conveyed to us by words, gestures, and the like, is, therefore, an essential and distinguishing ingredient of the methodology of all the human disciplines.

The concept of understanding is commonly linked with the name of Dilthey, and rightly so. He is the philosopher of understanding. No book on him can avoid this topic, and I have discussed it in my previous books, but I cannot sidestep the issue here without leaving a gap in my account. To avoid repetition, I shall be as succinct as possible.[2]

Understanding is the translation of *verstehen*. Some commentators leave the term untranslated to convey, presumably, its distinctive flavor. I can see no reason for this. *Verstehen*, unlike other key terms used by Dilthey such as *Geist*, can be translated without loss or distortion. The meaning of the two terms and their range of application is pretty much equivalent. We must note though that the concept (in both languages) has a variety of meanings, some of which are excluded in Dilthey's usage. It is a common practice of philosophers to avoid, for the sake of clarity and consistency, the ambiguity of everyday words by narrowing their meaning to one of its normal uses. As Dilthey tried to single out a distinctive cognitive process, he had, to start with, to exclude the use of understanding for any kind of comprehension. If he had not done so, the positivists would have been justified in criticizing his discussion of understanding by asking "what is all the fuss about, as understanding is involved in all cognitive achievements?"[3] The use of "understanding" for "sympathy" also had to be excluded, for it would appear to signal an emotional rather than an intellectual response.[4] We must, thirdly, dismiss the use of understanding in phrases that indicate a special skill ("he understands how to market products").

These exclusions do not make Dilthey's use eccentric. Although clarifications and qualifications will be required, there is no mystery about what Dilthey is essentially talking about. It is the grasping of communications. If I am asked if I understood what the man across the road was shouting or understood the play I saw last night, such questions have a clear and distinct meaning. It has nothing to do with sympathy or the skill to perform in a special way, nor is it like understanding how a pulley works.

In explaining the concept, the first point to be made emphatically is that understanding is not a method.[5] Critics of Dilthey's approach have made this mistake, and I must admit that some of Dilthey's formulations can be used to support the view. But Dilthey was a careless writer. To avoid confusion, we should talk of a method based on, and aiming at, understanding rather than the method of understanding.

To start with, it is inappropriate to speak of a method because that is something we apply. We use a method, we do something. But, literally speaking, understanding is not an activity at all, not something we do, but something we accomplish. The term is, in modern terminology, an "achievement word." It is convenient, though, and saves cumbersome circumlocutions to extend the use of understanding to the immediate process that leads to the accomplishment. This still does not make it a method but, merely, a cognitive process. A cross-reference to observation and its relation to the scientific method may clarify this point. Observation is crucial in, let us say, physics or astronomy and plays an irreplaceable role in their methodologies, to the point that we may talk of observational methods. But observation is not a method. It is part of everyday life, and we may engage in it, absentmindedly or with concentrated attention, for a moment or over a period of time. It is best described as a cognitive process that, employed systematically and combined with other processes, can become part of a method, which by contrast may be defined as a systematic combination of cognitive processes.

My second point—necessary to counter assertions frequently found in the relevant literature[6]—is that there is nothing mysterious about understanding, or at least that it is no more mysterious than any other human achievement, say that of seeing or calculating. It is as common as these other achievements and no special skill; no divinatory capacity is necessarily involved. Someone says "Good day," and we understand it just as we look out of the window and observe that it is raining. Some understanding may require intelligence, imagination, experience, and hard application, but that is due to the complexity of what is to be understood, just as observation may be difficult under certain circumstances. The same is true of many human activities and accomplishments. Cooking as such is neither easy nor difficult, and it does not necessarily require consummate skill. Boiling an egg is easy; making a soufflé is not and may require experience, flair, or what you will.

As we turn to a positive account of understanding, it might be well to start with one of Dilthey's own definitions:

Understanding we call the process by which mental life comes to be known through an expression of it given to the senses. [*C.W.*, Vol. V, p. 332]

It should be made clear at the outset that this reference to coming to know "mental life" as the goal of understanding does not, as such, commit Dilthey to a psychological preoccupation. No doubt, I may, in some cases, come to understand a person's aspirations or sorrows, but very often it is something more trivial that is revealed. If someone says to me, "Look there is a cow over there," I become aware of his being aware of a cow and wishing to draw my attention to it. No more of mental life is involved if I am to understand his remark.

This initial clarification points to an ambiguity that needs to be examined more carefully. Dilthey, in conformity with common usage, refers to different types of entities as objects of understanding. The immediate object is the verbal sign, gesture, and so on, but we also speak of understanding the meaning of such signs and, finally, of understanding people. Though there is a systematic connection between them, they, by no means, boil down to the same thing.

Understanding the word or signs is a preprequisite of other forms of understanding. It is a matter of knowing the language, the idioms, the terms used, and the grammatical construction. If any of these are totally beyond our grasp, no understanding can take place. Sometimes all that is sought is understanding on that level. A man may read, for example, Sherlock Holmes stories in order to learn English. As his mastery increases, he may say "now I can understand the text." When we ask, instead, whether he had understood the meaning of the story, we are talking about the intricacies of the plot, the subtlety of the characterization, and so forth. The two forms of understanding are interdependent. You cannot properly understand the plot without understanding the words of the text, and you can hardly claim that you have understood the text if you have no idea about the story told. Yet a gulf may open between the two. My knowledge of Conan Doyle's language may be impeccable, and yet I might be puzzled why the characters act as they do. I may be a halting linguist and yet understand the plot. Thirdly, we may speak of coming to understand the author. As I read a story, I become aware of the author's sensitivity, his concern with social conditions, his desire to entertain, or his sense of humor. If I wanted to write a biography of Conan Doyle, the varied material needed would have to include—as an essential ingredient—the view to be gained from reading his works.

Understanding a text and understanding an author are, inevitably, interrelated. Unless we grasp the meaning of the text and appreciate plot, characterization, and style, we are not in the position to assess the author's intentions, let alone any of his other characteristics. Yet how can we understand a text without grasping at least something of the author's outlook and intentions? We cannot, for example, seriously understand a novel or poem if we do not realize that the author was speaking ironically, intended a parody, meant, or did not mean, to be funny. This mutual interdependence is an example of what I shall presently introduce as the "hermeneutic circle."

This connection is, however, far from simple and straightforward. It is not safe to draw hasty conclusions about the author's character and outlook from the characters portrayed and the point of view displayed in a play or novel. They might have been adopted as technical devices or as means of catering for a public taste. It is equally dangerous to interpret a text purely in terms of the author's intentions (even if we have independent evidence for them). Shakespeare may, arguably, have intended Shylock to be just the stereotype of a Jewish money-lender required by the plot of "The Merchant of Venice" and expected by his Elizabethan audience. To many readers the text conveys something different.[7]

Understanding these disparate types of objects involves, basically, different aspects of the same operation, but as we focus on one or the other of them according to the purpose of our investigation—be it the exploration of language, literature, or personality—they turn into diverse activities, as, in each case, the expressions in question are placed into different contexts. Dictionaries, phrasebooks, and texts of similar linguistic difficulty provide the context for the linguistic understanding of a text. Comparison with other detective stories, works of literary criticism, and the like would help with the meaning, and to use the text to throw light on the author, a text needs to be related to his other works and activities.

I take the view that there is no contradiction, no change of mind involved when Dilthey focused, in different writings, on one or the other form of understanding. I do not think that he rejected his earlier psychological approach in favor of a hermeneutic one, turned from the understanding of persons to that of texts. It represents, rather, a switch in interest and emphasis as he dealt successively with different aspects of a complex issue. One must admit, however, that he was not as clear as he might have been about the differences and relations between these approaches or even spelled out which he was talking about.[8]

Understanding on the purely verbal level is theoretically straightforward enough. It involves translating from one language to another, disentangling grammatical constructions that are complex, ambiguous, or have gone out of use, and replacing unfamiliar words with familiar ones. It is practically important because interpreters often have to deal with texts produced at another place and another time and addressed to a different audience.

Matters are more complex when we consider understanding the meaning of a text and its relation to understanding its author. In many cases grasping what an expression, be it a text or a gesture, means is the paramount concern. When a judge asks a jury if they have understood the point of law he has been explaining to them, he is not just asking them if some of the words he used need translating or paraphrasing. Nor, for that matter, are they asked to understand a person, except in the trivial sense that it was the judge whose words need to be understood. What the judge, personally, thinks and feels is irrelevant. He is the mouthpiece of the law, which they need to understand. Yet when we ask what the law directs us to do, what its intentions are, we are speaking metaphorically. There was a lawmaker, or lawmakers, who intended to direct our conduct in a certain way. We may not know who they were, let alone be able to discover what they were like, what they felt and thought. Nor do we need to. It is just their intention as it speaks in a legal enactment that concerns us. If someone interpreted the verbal meaning of a legal clause, it would be normal and proper, in some cases, to argue that this was not what the law *intended*.

A similar story can be told about a literary product. If one theatre-goer asked another if he understood the play they had just watched, he is unlikely to be asking if the language was familiar to the other person. Nor is he asking if the play provided a clear insight into the author's personality. The audience needs to know something of the author's intention; beyond this, any idea about the author is unnecessary and remains, if solely based on the evidence of the play, highly doubtful. A play about cowardice is not necessarily written by a coward, a description of jealousy does not always point to an author consumed by jealousy. It is, of course, safe to assume, if the descriptions are at all convincing, that the author must have known what it is like to be afraid or jealous. But that surely is the case with every human being.

Because texts, be they literary, legal, or religious, are purposeful products, we can only understand them by appreciating the intention expressed in them, but it is the texts we try to understand. We are not engaged in biography, psychology, or anthropology. These can, however, unquestionably become secondary aims of understanding a text.

Primarily, understanding an expression is a matter of grasping what is expressed—its meaning. What is in front of us—the words, signs, etc.—point to, refer to, stand for something to which we are directed. When we have grasped that a text is about the best way to feed cows, that the notice asks us to drive slowly, that the blush reveals embarassment, we have learned what these expressions mean. Here the differences between an expression or a sign, referring to an object or event, giving us instruction or revealing a mental state, need not concern us further, though they are significant for a theory of communication.

Instead, we must recall the wider context in which we are discussing understanding. Ultimately, we are talking about understanding people, understanding the human world because we are trying to get to grips with the methodology of the human disciplines. Now it is thunderously obvious that when we are trying to understand an individual, a historical event, or the working of a community, we cannot be concerned with a meaning that refers to something the person, community, or event stands for or points to. We are talking about what is pointed to or revealed about man in these expressions. Man, as we have seen, has an "inner" life. He has feelings, thoughts, desires; he has a point of view from which he looks at the world. We have no reason to assume that this is the case with the inanimate objects of the world and only very limited reasons to attribute mental states to plants and to lower animals. In any case we have no, or only marginal, access to any mental life there may be in these spheres. Even in the case of higher animals, to whom we do tend to attribute thoughts and feelings, we can proffer only tentative, probably anthropomorphically colored, interpretations of what seem to us fairly elementary expressions.

To the mental life of human beings we have access through their expressions. This is what understanding is, and this is why it is convenient to define this term so as to mark understanding as a distinctive cognitive process confined to this particular area. However, in distinguishing the understanding of expressions from the understanding of people, I am underlining the fact that expressions, in many cases, do serve purposes other than the revelation of human nature. When people lecture on orchids, write books on car maintenance, or gesture to draw attention to a hazard on the road, they present information about the outer world, and people will listen, read, and attend in order to gain that information. On other occasions people speak about their sufferings, gesture to signal their pain, or write books about their aspirations. Moreover—and this is more interesting and methodologically challenging—expressions operate on several levels. A man lecturing on orchids will, of course, convey his degree of interest in these plants, his knowledge or possible ignorance of them. Over and above that, he may quite deliberately try to convey his charm and manliness and may reveal, contrary to his intentions, his vanity, insecurity, or whatever it may be. We are helped to understand people even when their explicit communications are not about themselves. Needless to say, in such cases, the knowledge we gain may be patchy and tangential. We have to build up understanding of a person from many of his expressions culled from different contexts of his life. I shall expand on this in the chapter on psychiatry.

EXPRESSIONS

A closer look at the nature of the expressions through which "mental content" is given underlines that understanding is not a mysterious process of peeping into people's minds. What people think, feel, and want, they express by sounds we can hear or by marks and movements we can see.

People express themselves in words, gestures, and actions. The world is full of messages issuing forth from human beings, and this is what makes the human world understandable.

A great deal of what we want to know about human beings is given us through these expressions; they make up a large proportion of the empirical evidence on which the human studies must rely. Dilthey distinguished various types of expressions and suggested a number of classifications in terms of their distinct characteristics. The range of what Dilthey considered as expressions is vital to the methodology of the human studies and needs to be outlined briefly.

Basically, Dilthey distinguished three classes of expressions. First, there is language and such systems that are parasitic on language and supplement it, such as flag signals, mathematical notations, or morse codes. The development and use of conventional, complexly structured languages is one of the chief distinctions between man and other animals. It makes history, abstract thought, moral laws, intricate social arrangements, long-term planning, and science possible. The intricacies of linguistic communication have proved of great interest to sociologists, psychologists, specialists in linguistics, and last, not least, philosophers. Dilthey listed some of the chief characteristics of linguistic expressions and compared their value for understanding with other types of expressions, but he did not go very deeply into linguistic theories.

The second type of expressions that Dilthey listed are what he called "expressions of life." They are gestures, facial expressions, posture, and the like. It is, of course, a familiar fact that we express ourselves and convey our feelings by smiles and blushes, by nods and waves, even by the way we sit or walk, hold our head or place our arms. Some points that Dilthey made about these kinds of expressions are methodologically important.

First, though some of these expressions are given conventional meaning—as is the case with waves of greeting or contrived smiles—many more are natural and spontaneous and are understood beyond the frontiers of particular civilizations. We blush, laugh, weep, smile, naturally exhibiting much the same feelings, whether we are Americans or South Sea islanders.

Second, though some expressions are voluntary—i.e., under our control—others are not. We may choose to wave or not, but we cannot help blushing. Of course, some types of expressions may be either: We may choose to smile or be unable to help it.

Third, expressions may, in Dilthey's words, "lift something from unconscious depths." In other words, they may reveal something of which the author of the expression is not, or not fully, conscious.

It is easy to see how Dilthey's extension of his theory of understanding so as to cover these "expressions of life" provides a theoretical framework for lines of approach that have been widely explored in this century. Personality studies have explored the significance of how people sit, lie in sleep, or write.

Psychoanalysis treats mistakes, forgettings, and slips of the tongue as meaningful. There are obvious reasons why researchers should turn their attention to these types of expressions. Though linguistic communications can be more explicit and discriminating, they can also be untruthful and superficial. People may not wish to reveal—or may even want to conceal—what they think and feel; they may be deceiving themselves or not be conscious of their true feelings.

The third type of expressions listed by Dilthey are actions, that is, purposeful human activity such as felling trees or conducting military campaigns. Unlike words, and at least some gestures and facial expressions, actions normally do not have communication for their aim. The man swinging his axe wants to fell the tree, the general moving his troops wants to defeat the enemy. Occasionally actions are intended to express something. The axeman may want to show how strong he is, the general may wish to indicate his confidence. But this is not the primary aim of most actions. Nevertheless, "actions speak louder than words," because a person's intention is expressed pretty clearly and unambiguously by what he does. Action is meaningful behavior, and what makes it meaningful is the purpose for which it is undertaken. Incidentally, Dilthey here makes a clear and—I think—useful distinction between intentions and motives. The intention is the agent's immediate goal. The axeman's intention is to bring down the tree, and here there is little scope for error or deception. His motive, the reason why he is felling the tree, is an entirely different matter. He may want firewood, crave physical exercise, or desire to annoy his neighbor. Here (as, for example, Kant has forcefully argued in "Groundwork of the Metaphysic of Morals"[9]) we plunge into a morass of uncertainty and, possibly, self-deception. Certainly on this the act does not speak clearly; much other evidence would be required before we can even guess at motives.

THE SCIENTIFIC METHOD AND THE HUMAN WORLD

Including among expressions not only expressions of life but actions represents an important move in Dilthey's strategy of providing a methodology of the human disciplines. Understanding, as I have argued, is not a method, but it is, indeed, the cornerstone of a method, which Dilthey offers as an alternative to the scientific method as used in physics or chemistry. The opponent then, as now, was positivism. Today, though the issue may be seen in less simplistic terms, the battle is far from over.

Positivism, influenced by the tremendous theoretical and practical successes of the physical sciences and concerned for the unity of science, insisted that the scientific method was superior to any other approach and adequate to deal with any subject matter, including the human world. That the methods, techniques, and concepts of science require to be adapted to the subject matter need not be denied. Sociology cannot be conducted exactly like physics, but nor can chemistry. But basically the differences between subject matter, if not irrelevant, are not sufficient to call for radical alternatives.

So Pareto could write,[10] "My wish is to construct a system of sociology on the model of celestial mechanics, physics, chemistry." Lundberg makes the same point in greater detail. After claiming that physicists explain physical phenomena in terms of such relations as attraction and repulsion and such entities as electrons and protons, he continues,[11]

The social sciences are concerned with the behaviours of those electron–proton configurations called societal groups. It is sometimes convenient to use different words to designate behaviour mechanisms of different systems or levels of electron–proton configurations. But certain basic concepts of proton, energy and force are equally applicable to all behaviour ... from the point of view we have adopted, any situation in which we choose to observe association or disassociation is regarded a field of force. ... Societal activities are fundamentally forms of energy transformation.

Such statements as the above are literally nonsense or, looked at indulgently, no more than metaphors. Surely the notion of a field of force cannot be the same when applied to electricity and to industrial disputes. It is also methodologically useless. Who would dream of bringing the instruments measuring field forces to the boardroom where management and labor are in dispute? But even a less crass approach, which stresses such ingredients of the scientific method as careful observation, quantification, and causal explanation rather than its actual concepts and techniques, is doomed to failure. The reason is that the human world, as a human world, differs quite radically as a subject matter from the rest of reality. (I say "as a human world" because human beings as physical entities fall in space much like stones, breathe and digest like other land animals, and so forth.)

We were on the trail of the crucial and fateful difference that calls for a distinctive approach in the human disciplines when we noted that "inside view" that history, according to so many historians, must try to unearth. Human beings think, feel, and aspire; they have a point of view of their own, which we need to appreciate if we are to make sense of their behavior. This is what Dilthey's theory of understanding is about.

Dilthey's account of expressions is important because expressions represent the paramount and indispensible evidence on which students of the human world base their conclusions about that inner world of thoughts and feelings. The material to which they thus gain access has epistemologically quite a different status from the source material for scientific theorizing. Put bluntly, what confronts the historians and social scientists are messages from other human beings, while physical scientists never receive messages from their subject matter. They receive, of course, messages from other scientists and rely on their experiments and so forth, but this is quite different. The scientist's message is only a short cut. In theory you can always check it by your own observation. In the human studies there is nowhere to look beyond the message. If I were to tell someone that I frequently think of the country where I was born, he cannot check my statement by observing some behavior equivalent to these thoughts, let alone arrive at my thoughts from mere inspection of my behavior. He can only check my statement by references to other expressions (or "messages"). It is quite likely, for example, that if I frequently think of my homeland, that I would mention it sometimes in conversations, or in letters, or in my lectures. Records of such remarks would confirm, or at least give plausibility to, the original statement. I can think of no other kind of evidence that could be relevantly adduced to verify or to falsify it.

The prevalence of "messages" over other kinds of evidence in the human sciences is a plain fact, not a matter of theoretical speculation. Historians rely on eyewitness accounts, chronicles, church registers, letters, state papers, and the like. Psychologists engage in interviews, set questionnaires, seek verbal responses under experimental conditions, and evaluate stories made up by their subjects. Sociologists, too, use interviews and question-naires; they study constitutions or popular literature. Anthropologists examine folklore, myths, religious beliefs, and so on, almost ad infinitum.

This fact connot have escaped even the most rampant positivists. If they did not draw methodological conclusions from it, it must be because they thought that the difference between observing something and being told about it was trivial, as it may well be when one compares one's own experimental result with the account of an experiment by a trusted colleague. This view has a distinguished ancestry. Spinoza in his *Ethics* (Part II, prop. 50) distinguishes empirical observation and second-hand accounts of it but lumps them together as "the first kind of knowledge."

But when a verbal account is not about a publicly observable event—and most of the important and interesting communications that form the material of the human studies are not—the difference is far from negligible. Dilthey's whole methodology hinges on the claim that grasping a communication is a distinctive, intellectual process. His purpose in narrowing and refining the everyday meaning of "understanding" was to pinpoint this distinctive cognitive process.

It is not too difficult to show why expressions are not reducible to behavior that can be observed and explained in terms of theoretical frameworks such as the causal connections of mechanics. Though expressions are behavior or the products of behavior and there is always something to be seen or heard—bodily movements, marks on paper, or sounds in the air—they are more than that. When we have seen or heard them, we have yet to grasp what is there to be grasped. If someone speaks to you, it is not enough to hear the sound, nor is it sufficient to have a knowledge of psychology that explains the behavior in front of you. There is no substitute for understanding what is said, which requires such things as knowing the language in which the words are couched and the idioms and social conventions that determine usage. Analogous requirements are involved in understanding an intricate purposive activity. To know what a watchmaker is actually doing you have to know something about watchmaking.

In other words, where understanding is involved, we have to place the object to be known into a distinctive context, use special presuppositions, think in a particular way. That is why it is necessary to distinguish understanding from other cognitive processes and subject it to epistemological scrutiny.

It is hard to believe that anyone could have missed the distinction between grasping a communication and observation or, even, explaining an event. Those who ignore the distinctiveness of understanding must consider the difference so trivial that it can be dismissed or methodologically circumvented. This would be so if expressions were so transparent that you could look through them straight to the facts to which they refer. If smiles convey amusement, well, you are watching amusement. If people responding to a questionnaire say that they prefer small cars, you can count peoples' preferences. Such simplistic assumptions have, demonstrably, led to failures, for example, in opinion polls. The simple reason is that people sometimes deceive and lie, or they may be self-deceived. More seriously, a lot can go wrong in the process of communication. People can misunderstand each other through inattention, mistaken views of the presuppositions involved, or through lack of intelligence and penetration when the matter to be understood is complex. Dilthey's theory of understanding directs attention to such problems.

Positivistically inclined opponents of Dilthey's approach—while conceding most of the above—may still object that plunging into these complexities is unnecessary because we can cut the Gordian knot by attending to the behavioral equivalents of communications. Put crudely: a man who says he is hungry will eat when food is placed in front of him, and *that* we can observe.

But this is an illusion, because in many cases there are no behavioral equivalents (as when I think of my homeland), and in others there is no simple one-to-one relationship between behavior and expressions. There are, for one thing, many behaviorally quite dissimilar expressions, which are equivalent only because of their meaning (i.e., you can express that you are hungry in words or in gestures). Second, any behavior that might confirm the expression (such as eating) might be aborted, for a thousand reasons. Third, even an action is not simply the equivalent of the behavior exhibited; it only becomes recognizable as the action it is when we identify both that there is a purpose and what that purpose is.

No one would wish to ignore or underestimate the importance of observation where expressions are involved. Not only is it the only way in which they come to our notice, but often fine details are relevant: a single sound may make the difference between one word and another, the colour of the ink used may carry a meaning, and so on. But once the facts have been established, the expression still requires to be understood.

There are a number of prerequisites for understanding to become possible. The basic presupposition is that there are some basic human features we all have in common and that these common features make any expression, in principle, understandable. If we were all identical, understanding would be unnecessary, or at least easy and infallible. I would know how you feel about a play because I know how I feel about the play. One hardly needs to argue that this is not so. On the other hand, if we had nothing in common, if I could not assume that—like me—you were capable of feeling or were pursuing purposes, no understanding would be possible. The question of a constant and common human nature I shall discuss in the next section, and the final section will explore the wider epistemological implications of understanding. Now I shall pursue the issue of methodology.

HERMENEUTICS

Though epistemologically complex, understanding must be taken as a basic operation, like thinking or observing, which we take for granted as an ingredient of everyday orientation and research into the human world. Clearly, the question of its reliability arises. How do we know that we have understood correctly, gained the truth? It is important to ask this question both on the level of understanding itself and on that of any method based on understanding. Dilthey was most insistent that this question of criteria of truth should be raised, for if we resigned ourselves to treating understanding as something private, personal, and relative because it cannot be checked by observation as the conclusions of science can be, then we are driven to accept that the human disciplines are less rigorous than the sciences.

Understanding is no more infallible than is observation or reasoning, but if we do not concede a prima facie case for any of these operations yielding truth, we plunge into a skepticism from which there is no escape. If we think that our eyes deceive us, we can look again, or ask someone else to look as well, but there is no appeal beyond the testimony of our senses in such a case. Analogous points apply to doing sums and to understanding. Spinoza already made this point forcibly against Descartes' systematic doubt. At some stage we must accept that the truth must shine by its own light.

There are a number of obvious steps we tend to take in our everyday contacts with other people if we want to make sure that we understand correctly. We assure ourselves that we have attended without being distracted or otherwise hindered by the absence of conditions required for understanding (such as unfamiliarity with an idiom). Second, we may seek confirmation from another person who sees or hears the expression. Third, we relate the expression in question to other expressions of relevant contexts—that is, we ask ourselves if a particular remark, as we understand it, is consistent with other remarks in the same conversation, or made by the same person on other occasions. Checking on our understanding in the human sciences is just a refinement and systematization of this approach.

In many cases understanding is simple, quick, and unproblematic. Understanding—let us say—the greeting of a friend is virtually automatic. No skill, no application of criteria, no intellectual effort seems to be required. In such cases Dilthey speaks of "elementary understanding." In many other cases there are obstacles to understanding: the expression, or web of expressions, may be very complex, it may arise from a background unfamiliar to us such as a different age or civilization, it may presuppose some technical knowledge, and the like. In such cases where an expression presents a challenge to our understanding, we, like Dilthey, then tend to talk of interpretation. And now, indeed, we are speaking of a method.

There are marginal cases where it is not easy to draw a sharp line between a cognitive process and a method; it is a matter of degree. So when we speak of applying tests for the correctness of understanding, we are pointing to the transition from cognitive process to a methodical procedure. However, for practical purposes we can distinguish clearly enough understanding as an achievement and the immediate process leading to it from interpretation, as the more or less systematic use of various intellectual procedures in order to achieve understanding.

Interpretation is the process of disentangling the meaning of something not obviously clear. There are three spheres in particular in which interpretation has been used systematically throughout history. One is the interpretation of art and literature, another is the interpretation of sacred texts. The third area is that of interpreting the law.

The ancient Greeks who gave a prominent place to interpreting poetry in their education had a word for the art and methodology of interpretation: hermeneutics. Once Christianity became established in Europe, interpreting the Bible became a major concern, for different interpretations repeatedly divided Christianity and led to conflicts and persecutions. So hermeneutics became an adjunct to theology. This is why Schleiermacher, as a professor of theology, lectured on it, and this is how Dilthey, through his study of Schleiermacher, came to be introduced to the subject.

In Schleiermacher's hands it achieved a wider application. He did not confine it to religious texts, as he was himself a translator and interpreter of Plato's *Dialogues*. He also saw the possibility of extending this approach beyond its usual sphere of written texts to other forms of expressions. By taking this process just one step further, Dilthey could present hermeneutics as the methodology of the human studies.[12] We have already seen that the reading of texts is a very substantial part of the work of historians, sociologists, anthropologists, not to mention philologists, literary critics, and students of comparative religion. Such reading is not problem-free and requires a methodology as much as does setting up experiments and drawing conclusions from their results in the physical sciences.

Dilthey's theory of expressions extends the range of material available to the social scientist by suggesting that we can treat movements, gestures, and actions as if they were texts to be interpreted. To put Dilthey's thesis as sharply as possible: studying a person's character, the culture of a community, or the activities of a trade union is more like interpreting a poem or a law than like explaining the acceleration of falling bodies or the properties of magnetic fields.

As a result of Dilthey's influence, hermeneutics has been taken up by numerous thinkers and has, by now, become almost fashionable. In the hands of Heidegger and his followers, among whom Gadamer[13] deserves special mention, hermeneutics became a crucial philosophic approach rather than just the methodology of the social sciences. I shall not deal with this development further, except to mention that this school of thought criticizes Dilthey's approach for not being sufficiently radical and consistent. Thinkers such as Gadamer charged Dilthey with this failure. His concern with external criteria of truth was—they thought—a mistaken hangup due to his sympathy with positivist thinkers such as J. S. Mill. A hermeneutic approach, thought through to the end, should recognize that we can never step outside the culturally determined perspectives of our interpretations. This is a large issue, and to some of its aspects I shall return in the last chapter. Here an indication of why I side with Dilthey on this issue must suffice. However intellectually difficult this position may be, it represents a methodological stance which it is vital to preserve though a fine balancing act is required. It would be naive and misleading to suggest that objectivity is easily obtainable in the human studies, that its pursuit is straightforward and unproblematic, but it is fatal to the aspirations of these disciplines to give up hope for, and the effort toward, objectivity.

Philosophers outside the existentialist movement—men such as P. Ricoeur[14] and J. Habermas[15]—have taken up hermeneutics precisely because of its methodological significance. They found it a useful weapon to combat positivism and its application in the form of behaviorism in the studies of man.

The use of such a technical term as "hermeneutics" provides a rallying point for those who feel uneasy about purely behaviorist approaches or, indeed, employ methods that its methodology could not justify. It had never been very convincing when the original behaviorists disclaimed—sometimes explicitly, sometimes merely by implication—that they were conscious beings trying to communicate with us meaningfully. Modern behaviorists are more circumspect.

The aspirations of behaviorism reflect the feeling of inferiority that some social scientists experience when they compare the procedures of the human studies with the precision, rigor, theoretical sophistication, and practical usefulness of the physical sciences. Behaviorists dream that they might achieve something of the respectability of "proper" scientists if only they could confine themselves to careful observation, painstaking experimentation, statistical evaluation of quantifiable results, and the formulation of general laws.

If the result of this attitude is often arid, the reaction from it is no more helpful. Some researchers into the human world, finding that adherence to the scientific paradigm proves sterile, have reacted into an "anything goes" attitude. There is no pretence at testing theories and sifting evidence. Anecdotes and personal impressions are passed off as scholarship, isolated incidents treated, without evidence, as fair samples.

So it became important to have in hermeneutics a model or paradigm that preserved the idea that the study of man, though inevitably unlike the study of physical nature, could be methodologically rigorous and disciplined. This was Dilthey's concern, and he ceaselessly insisted that if we are to follow the example of the great pioneers of science such as Galileo, we must (like them) intelligently adjust the methods to our subject matter rather than imitate, without regard to the subject matter, the methods they had actually used. Hermeneutics, in Dilthey's view, represented a traditional methodology specifically adjusted to the study of the human world.

Some of the distinctive features of hermeneutics are the focus on individuals, the hermeneutic circle, the absence of an absolute starting point, and the direct confrontation of complexities instead of treating them, from the outset, in terms of their supposed constituents. I shall discuss and try to explain these features in turn.

THE IDEOGRAPHIC APPROACH

One of the outstanding characteristics of hermeneutics is that its subject matter is, invariably, an individual text or other kind of expression. A look at its actual practice easily confirms this. It is about interpreting Homer or the Bible—usually specific passages in them. It cannot be otherwise, because interpretation aims at understanding. What we try to understand are individual entities not classes of them, particular relationships rather than the laws governing them, the place of a part in a whole or the way a system is constituted rather than general uniformities. The object of interpretation is therefore a poem, not poetry, a person, not human nature, how A treats his wife, not marriage in general.

The German neo-Kantian philosopher, H. Rickert,[16] introduced the terms "ideographic" and "nomothetic" to mark the contrast between disciplines that have the understanding of individuals and those that have the establishment of general laws as their respective aims. He was specifically concerned to draw attention to the difference of approach between history and the systematic disciplines. His main division was based on a difference of methodology. Within each approach we can distinguish applications to the human world and to nature. In other words, there is human and natural history, just as there are systematic approaches both to the human world and to nature. It does not affect this theoretical symmetry that the historical, ideographic approach plays a larger part in the study of the human world than it does in that of the purely physical universe.

For Dilthey, the primary distinction is that determined by subject matter—namely, that between the human studies and the physical sciences. The distinction between the historical and the systematic approach represents a subdivision of each. But it is an integral part of the human studies that man's historicity makes historical perspectives relevant even to the systematic disciplines. Moreover, they are ideographic, not only because of their indebtedness to history but because of the intrinsic importance we ascribe to individuals and because of the inevitable slant toward the study of individuals that the role of understanding superimposes on the whole enterprise.

Thus the search for high-level generalizations in this sphere, for laws applicable to a wide range of cases, turns out to be will-o'-the-wisp. There are, of course, any number of such generalizations about human nature and human relationships, such as "people want to perpetuate pleasure and avoid pain," "in any complex organizations a distinction between the organizers and the organized will develop," and so forth. But these are mostly trivial, very abstract, and far from informative. Often the best we may be able to do, if we want to pass beyond the description of individual cases, is the establishment of typologies—that is, grouping a limited range of individuals within a population according to some similarities between them. The difference between typologies and classifications based on laws is that the former is deliberately designed to describe individuals and the difference between them. In other words, if we postulate that human beings can, with respect to aspects of their personality, be typed as introverts or extroverts, we are not saying that there are two classes of people with these respective characteristics. Such a typology serves to pinpoint an individual's make-up by placing him at a point on a continuous line, at either end of which there is the—possibly never realized—perfect introvert and complete extrovert. Dilthey believed that such typologies played an important part in the human studies where fruitful generalizations were unattainable. Dilthey put it as follows: "Types ... contain distillations of experience [*eine Steigerung des Erfahrenen*] but not in the direction of an empty ideality but in that of a representation of variety in something pictorial whose powerful and clear structure makes the meaning of lesser and mixed experiences of life comprehensible" (*C.W.*, Vol. VI, p. 186).

Psychology, sociology, and the other social sciences have not abandoned the aspiration to achieve laws of human behavior. Nor did Dilthey. But his stress on the implications of a hermeneutic approach is a salutory reminder of the inevitable limitations placed on such aspirations. What is more, it explains something that practitioners of these various disciplines have occasionally found painful. This is that with regard to the establishment of general laws, their achievement is rather thin. Psychology seems to have done best, but this is mostly in such areas as physiological psychology. Perhaps we need, after all, not be embarassed about this, need not excuse it by the alleged "youth" of these disciplines or turn in hope to a future "Newton of the social sciences." These goals may be unattainable in principle and irrelevant in practice. As Dilthey saw very clearly, in the human world we are intellectually and morally committed to continued interest in the individual. Freud's self-analyses, the description of Middle-town, the Hawthorne experiments, or M. Mead's accounts of some tribal societies retain their interest, irrespective of whether the theories based on them are proved to the hilt or discarded as false. The social sciences have produced a rich harvest of such material: institutional arrangements at a particular time and place, particular social movements, change in particular communities have been described carefully and illuminatingly. Even where it is possible to extract high-level laws from such material, they are no substitute for these vivid accounts and may, even, seem rather vacuous.

To contrast hermeneutic interpretation to the establishment of general laws and explanation of individual cases in terms of them is not a matter of a simple either/or. Each has its place, and, indeed, each depends on the other. A historian describing a battle—a case of ideography if ever there was one—presupposes or explicitly uses such generalizations and laws as bullets kill, heavy vehicles get stuck in the mud, human beings fear death, and so on. In turn, generalizations are derived from, tested by, and applied to individual cases.

What remains important, though, for contemporary debates is to challenge a widespread prejudice in favor of the nomothetic approach. As the intellectual respectability of ideography needs to be stressed, let us consider a model of reality that requires a reversal of our priorities.

We can make the reasonable—and, possibly, true—assumption that the universe consists of unique entities all related to each other by unique relations. True knowledge would consist of a grasp of that whole pattern of interrelated individuals, in the sense in which a man is well acquainted with the features of his wife's face. Obviously, a finite human mind could know only a tiny part of reality in this way or a slightly larger one rather hazily and imprecisely. He would then have to help himself out with generaliza-tions. He would ignore the rich uniqueness of individuals and lump them together with others under general class concepts that would be little more than what sociologists and psychologists call stereotypes. (We have become aware of the dangers of such general concepts as "blacks," "teenagers," "students," and the like, but, maybe, the same intellectual—though, of course, not moral—objections apply to terms such as "horses" or "trees"). They are merely the crutches of imperfect minds.

I have not invented this model—it is the traditional picture that nominalism gives of the world, it is the basis for the romantic's lament that all language impoverishes reality. It is, quite specifically, the account that Spinoza gives of reality (in his *Ethic*). The knowledge of the unique in its unique relationships he calls *scientia intuitiva* [intuitive science] which is for him the highest kind of knowledge. If it made sense in his philosophy to speak of God's knowledge—which it does only in a metaphorical sense—this would be the form God's knowledge would take.

A further exposition of Spinoza's philosophy is unnecessary, particularly as scientia intuitiva is nothing like hermeneutics. I have only mentioned Spinoza here because he is one of the less noted sources of the intellectual armory of modern hermeneutics, placing, as he does, the formidable weight of his arguments behind the idea that grasping individuality is a primary function of cognition.

INTERPRETATION

So what can hermeneutics accomplish, how is it to help us, what pitfalls should it protect us from? Not long ago I prefixed a paper on the subject with a story that was intended to focus the mind of the audience on the issue at hand. I repeat it here, though I run the risk—as I did at the conference—of it eclipsing the memory of my comments. It comes from a film I saw while preparing my talk ("I will, I will … for Now").

A married couple experiencing some marital difficulties attend a sex clinic in California. They are shown to accommodation in which everything is arranged to arouse sexual urges. There is a ceiling mirror above the bed, erotic pictures on the walls, and so on. In the middle of the room stands a ladder. The couple speculate on the erotic purpose and function of the ladder and arrive at various interpretations. Next morning, the electrician arrives to take away his ladder.

Though obviously meant to be funny, this is a good illustration of how interpretation is used in everyday life and how it can go wrong. A ladder, like any purposively created object, can be understood in terms of the functions it serves or the needs it satisfies. What a ladder is normally for we have usually learned from childhood, but if, by chance, we have not, we may well be able to work it out in terms of what its distinctive features enable us to do. But we also interpret an expression—and in this sense a ladder can be described as an expression of a human purpose—in terms of the context in which we encounter it. Even if we have encountered the expression in the past and grasped its meaning, we may want to revise it in a new context. The couple in the film had—correctly—interpreted the context in which they encountered the ladder: it was an environment designed for sexual stimulation. So they tried to interpret the function of the ladder in this light. They were ludicrously mistaken because the ladder, in fact, belonged to a different context, which they did not know about.

Successes and failures of interpretation of this type—though usually less bizarre—occur constantly in everyday life. A man returning from work finds that his wife, instead of welcoming him, snaps at him and generally seems moody. He assumes that she is angry with him and considers possible reasons for it. Has he forgotten an important date? Does she suspect him of infidelity? After a while it emerges that his wife has heard from her sister and is worried about her health. In this new context a new and more adequate interpretation of her behavior becomes easy. Analogous illustrations can be given from the sphere of the social sciences. Take, for example, the famous, often quoted Hawthorne experiment.[17] The investigators were concerned with the optimal conditions for improving work in a factory making telephone equipment. In conformity with good scientific practice, they successively varied the conditions—introduced extra breaks, provided snacks, and so forth—and observed the effect on production. They noted that the women workers responded positively to the measures taken, and production rose cumulatively. It seemed a reasonable interpretation that the changes introduced encouraged and enabled the workers to improve their performance. Then the investigators made—in conformity with good scientific practice—a final test. They canceled all the changes made and returned the workforce to its original working conditions. Production soared to new heights. It seemed that, after all, it was not the soup or the extra breaks that put up production. Had the experiment failed? Certainly not. Now what was needed was a look at the context in which the experiments had taken place.

The answer with which the researchers came up is history and, in fact, tallies with common sense. It was the fact of being involved in an experiment that made the job more interesting and motivated harder work. The investigation had stumbled on the discovery that as important, probably more important, than the physical conditions was the social climate of production. I have deliberately phrased the conclusion very cautiously because to say that this investigation established or confirmed a law of industrial psychology would be to overstate the case. Workers may not invariably respond positively to being studied. In some work the spacing of rest periods may be extremely important. What we have is an extremely suggestive case study of what happened in a particular case.

I have stressed and illustrated at some length this type of elucidation because modern philosophy of science—and, indeed, the general intellectual climate—has tended to emphasize explanation in terms of bringing the individual case under a covering law. This is why it is important to give methodical attention to questions such as what is involved in knowing individual objects and their relationship to each other? What are we looking for, and under what conditions can we be intellectually satisfied? What operations of the mind are involved in seeking and gaining a cognitive goal?

To avoid confusion, I shall try to speak of explanation only when reference to general laws plays a prominent role in accounting for an event. Where the constituent parts of individuals and their relation to other individuals are mainly at issue, we shall speak of interpretation. We have seen that in the human world such individual relations are more accessible and more certain than laws and cannot be replaced or accounted for by them. These relationships are—as we have seen—accessible to us through expressions that we have to interpret.

It is therefore convenient to use the interpretation of a verbal utterance, let us say a sentence, as paradigmatic. How do I work out what a particular word in a sentence means? How do I come to realize that a word or sentence is part of a larger pattern? The answers are all familiar and shatteringly obvious. They need to be given because they provide a model of the hermeneutic approach.

THE CONTEMPORARY IMPORTANCE OF HERMENEUTICS

Naturally, we do not think of our attempts at making sense of utterances as hermeneutics. Like the Molière character who was surprised to learn that he had been speaking prose all along, we practice the hermeneutic art without knowing it. To apply it rigorously and systematically is of the utmost practical importance. Of course, some of our interpretative efforts are trivial—what does this newspaper article try to say?—or personal—does Aunt Mary really want me to come, or is she just polite?—but other cases are of the utmost public importance. I have mentioned before the importance traditionally attached to the interpretation of theological statements and the educational interest in disentangling the meaning of literary or philosophic texts. If these seem less urgent now, the interpretation of the law remains important.

But there is something of wider and more urgent importance than private concerns, religious disputes, legal niceties, or academic clarifications that requires the attention of hermeneutics. This is the area of public agreements: international settlements, trade pacts, compromises between management and labor. There are, also, public commitments such as the policy statements of governments, the manifestos of political parties, or the rule books of trade unions. It is astonishing how widely politicians, trade union leaders, journalists, broadcasters, and pundits of all kinds readily disagree on what—presumably—carefully drafted and readily available written statements actually mean. This is not only intellectually frustrating but fuels destructive disputes.

Not long ago a bitter, prolonged miners' strike occurred in Great Britain, and centrally involved were a number of issues of the kind I have just referred to. Had there been a change in the Coal Board's declared policy? Were there breaches of agreements? Had the miners' union broken its own regulations by calling a strike without a ballot? In boardrooms, congresses, international meetings, as well as in the press, these types of questions were debated constantly.

No one would wish to deny that in such cases substantial differences of interest—partly veiled by these disputes over interpretations—are really at issue. Nevertheless, it is strange that documents produced by skilled experts can be given totally different interpretations by intelligent and literate protagonists. Cynics may argue that such documents are ambiguous precisely because they have been drawn up by clever experts. But surely it would be more difficult for ambiguities to appear—by design or inadvertently—in documents and harder for negotiators to insist on eccentric interpretation if more explicit attention were given to the principles and practice of hermeneutics.

CONTEXTS AND THE HERMENEUTIC CIRCLE

Getting the precise meaning of an international agreement or of a difficult philosophic text is a matter of refining and using in a more systematic way procedures used in everyday life. So what is involved in understanding anything but the simplest communication—say, a complicated sentence or article? The first thing is to read quickly through the whole of it to get a feel of the pattern, the thrust of the argument, the main point being made, for without it one cannot appreciate the purpose of qualifying clauses or even the sense of individual words, the meaning of which in isolation may be obscure or ambiguous. Only the context can make clear what "this," "the latter," "the author," etc. refer to. Only within a sentence does it become clear if we are talking about a social "club," a blunt instrument, or a card suit.

But the reverse is equally true. We cannot understand a sentence, let alone a larger piece of writing, if we have not understood the individual words of which it is made up. So clarification of a text takes the form of a kind of to-and-fro movement between attending to the parts and attending to the whole. This movement, which is an essential characteristic of all interpretation, is called the hermeneutic circle. Of course, a spiral would be a better description, as a circle does not get anywhere, but this is the traditional name given to this process.

This circular movement of interpretation is, however, not self-contained. The sentence, the paragraph, even a whole book is part of a wider context. In some cases the main aim of interpretation is to clarify the internal structure of the unit under scrutiny and to pinpoint the meaning of its parts. But it is usually also important to refer to a wider context: the role of the sentence in the paragraph, the chapter in the book, or the book in the total output of an author and the literature of the time. Here, too, the circle applies, as the book is made up of chapters, the literature of an age of the individual books.

Other types of contexts are relevant too. Words may have to be looked up in dictionaries, names in books of reference, and so forth. We may have to refer to changing speech habits and social conventions. For example, until quite recently, in most places addressing someone by his first name used to indicate (and does still in such countries as Germany) a considerable degree of intimacy. Today in the English-speaking countries it means very little, because near-strangers do so. An illustration of how changing conventions change the meaning of phrases comes from Dilthey's own pen. In a letter to his wife, he says "I'll never forget the day when you gave yourself to me in ..." and he mentions a public park. If this were written today, one would tend to conclude that the couple had engaged in sexual intercourse on a park bench. Written in the late nineteenth century, it meant nothing of the sort. They became engaged on that day.

Hermeneutics functions very similarly in the sphere of nonlinguistic expressions. Experiments have confirmed what we really know from common sense. A facial expression is difficult to interpret if we only see part of the face. Interpretation becomes easier and more reliable as we progress to seeing the whole face, the whole person, and finally not just a picture but the person in movement. With each step the context for interpretation is enriched; the meaning of the smile or the frown becomes clear as part of a wider whole. Yet, obviously the meaning of that whole must, somehow, be recognized by piecing together the meaning of the parts.

Illustrations could be multiplied endlessly across the different human disciplines. I must add one more. How does the anthropologist establish the meaning of a particular ritual dance encountered in the tribe he is studying? Clearly it must be seen as part of the tribe's religion, social life, and struggle with its environment. It may also be necessary to compare it with similar dances found in other communities. The reverse equally applies. The whole pattern of culture of a tribe or the traditions of tribal dances in a variety of communities are made up of ingredients like that particular dance. It has to be studied and interpreted as an element from which the whole picture can be put together.

The hermeneutic circle also applies to a wider sphere, of which we have already had a glimpse. It is one of the central themes of this book that the historical approach and a systematic study of human nature are interdependent. Without historical accounts, the systematic studies would be without material; without systematic knowledge, the links between historical events could not be understood properly. History provides us with the rich variety of human life, which makes understanding a challenge. The systematic studies point to common and abiding features by means of which we can meet that challenge. Similar relationships of mutual interdependence can be demonstrated in the case of individual disciplines—say psychology and sociology. To a discussion of the relationships that bind the different human disciplines together, I shall turn in my next chapter.

THE ABSENCE OF A STARTING POINT

When Archimedes discovered the principle of the lever, he is supposed to have said: "Give me a point to rest the lever on, and I can lift the earth from its path." Many philosophers have looked for the equivalent of such a point, an Archimedean point, as the firm basis of certainty on which to build their philosophic systems. Empiricists consider experience—interpreted, in the case of the British empiricists and the positivists, usually as receiving sense data—as such a firm basis. Rationalists rely on rational self-evident truths. Descartes is particularly associated with the explicit, epistemologically self-conscious quest for a certain starting point, which he claimed to have found in his *cogito ergo sum*, the certainty of consciousness of its own existence, which defied the possibility of doubt.

The hermeneutic circle leaves no room for an absolute starting point. Whether we start from the parts or from the whole, our knowledge can only be provisional and awaits correction by a switch to the other angle. This applies not only to the interpretation of texts, the original subject matter of hermeneutics, but, by extension, to all knowledge. Unless we accept the data that reach us through the senses as reasonably reliable, we could never build up a body of knowledge about the world. Yet quite obviously we are often mistaken. This is no grounds for complete skepticism, for we know how to correct such errors. In the wider context of experience—though it is, of course, itself made up of individual impressions—we may decide that a particular impression deceived us. "It could not have been Smith I saw." "The light must have been red, though I saw it amber."

Though clearly intended as a joke, a remark from a French farce makes this point forcefully. A girl finds her fiancé in a highly compromising situation in a hotel room. He gets his friends to swear to her that he was with them elsewhere at the time. When the friend presents the alibi to the girl, she replies "but I saw him with my own eyes." "What does this prove?" the friend replies. So much for naive positivism.

All cognitive achievements must be treated prima facie as provisional and corrigible. At best they are facets of the truth, which mislead if we forget that their truth is partial. If this is intellectually unsatisfactory, well, this is just too bad because we have to live with it. I have raised this matter here because no account of hermeneutics would be complete without mentioning the rejection of an epistemological starting point. But I shall discuss this matter more fully in my final chapter (on epistemology).

The same point about the absence of a starting point can be made about the distinct but interdependent objectives of understanding. Is understanding the actual sign, the basis and proper starting point of other forms of understanding? Well, it can be. But the reverse may be the case. We may know first that a man is angry and only gradually disentangle what precisely he is saying and doing.

The interdependence of different disciplines shows the same absence of an absolute starting point. In some of his writings Dilthey stressed the central importance of psychology for all the other human studies. But he had also emphasized the basic, irreplaceable role of history, and in his later years he returned to the subject of hermeneutics, on which he had written his doctoral thesis, and now treated it as the key discipline of the human studies. Philosophy, or more precisely epistemology, while playing a fundamental part as the arbiter of all truth-claims, has to qualify its claim to priority by accepting the inevitability of the hermeneutic circle. Though having the claims to truth of psychology among its subject matter, it is psychologically grounded. But, unlike Kant, who to avoid this based his epistemological conclusions on transcendental arguments, Dilthey did not think that such a circle was vicious.

The full philosophic implications of this rejection of any absolute starting point we shall consider later, but in methodology it demands flexibility and tentativeness from practitioners of the social sciences. This is what is implied in the hermeneutic approach, and, as I mentioned earlier, the logical conclusions from it were drawn by thinkers such as Gadamer. Dilthey was uneasy about pushing the disclaimer of any objective certainty to its extreme and was, therefore, accused of a positivist hang-up. He did try to break out of the hermeneutic circle, and men like Habermas followed him in this.

STARTING FROM COMPLEXITY

Dilthey's practice reflects his determination to confront any problem on the level of complexity on which it presents itself. It should be obvious that this, like the rejection of absolute starting points, is closely related to the hermeneutic circle. When we have a text in front of us, obviously we cannot begin by sorting out the meaning of one word after another and then reconstruct the text from these building blocks. This applies to everything. It is not safe, let alone adequate, for a psychologist concerned with the human imagination, intelligence, or, let us say, the capacity for composing music, either to assume some elementary capacities from which these more complex abilities are made up, or to look for such elementary capacities in the behavior of lower animals. We may, of course, learn something about intelligence from the way rats learn to run mazes, or dogs solve problems, but these will never take us all the way to a proper understanding of how an able man's mind works. For that we must look for painstaking descriptions of how such minds solve problems. Or if we are seeking to understand the nature of imagination we must use—as Dilthey actually did—the testimony of great poets and artists.[18]

What is openly challenged is the Cartesian approach of dividing each problem "into as many parts as possible, starting with what was simplest and easiest to know and rising little by little to the knowledge of the most complex."[19] In hermeneutics, distinguishing the parts of a situation is not just a preliminary exercise but part of the journey toward a solution. Hermeneutics is, here too, a corrective to a predominant paradigm. Physics has developed most successfully on the global acceptance of the basic premises of the atomic theory (though these are not its only assumption, field theory may bring it closer to hermeneutics) and psychology has operated extensively with primitive urges or instinct, with simple reflexes and elementary capacities, with mechanisms such as association and conditioning.

Dilthey argued that, at the very least, we were not ready to explain mental phenomena in terms of such elementary entities and processes. There is a danger of misunderstanding and misrepresenting complex phenomena when we treat them from the outset as made up and, therefore, explainable in terms of simple reflexes, drives, or capacities. The mind has an innate structure—different tendencies, capacities, feelings, and the like are structurally related to each other and affect each other dynamically. Cumulative experience superimposes on this original structure, in the course of life, an acquired structure. We develop skills and attitudes, and these color our experiences, influence our actions, and are reflected in the things we produce. These structural links make us capable of appreciating life as meaningful. Only a hermeneutic approach starting with an overview of complex wholes and then moving to and fro in the hermeneutic circle between the whole and its parts can do justice to human beings or their higher achievements, such as their poetry, science, legal systems, philosophies, and the like.

THE USE OF DILTHEY'S METHODOLOGY

Despite Dilthey's proverbial inconclusiveness and the fragmentary nature of so much of his writing on the subject, a fairly coherent methodology emerges from his discussions on understanding, experience, meaning, and expressions, his examination of interpretation and his revival of hermeneutics. Beyond question it is important and useful, but what precisely is the range of its methodological relevance and what precisely is it useful for?

The original and primary subject matter of hermeneutics was—as we have seen—texts. Its object was traditionally to review the obstacles to their being understood and to provide means of overcoming them. Hermeneutics, even if taken in its original narrow sense, is of the utmost importance today. The traditional subject matters of hermeneutics have not faded from view. The law will always need interpreting, and interpretation in theology and literature has produced heated debates of late. Theologians are divided on the question of demythologizing the sacred texts,[20] and in England there has been, quite recently, angry debate about a bishop who refused to take the resurrection literally. Literary criticism has produced a rich variety of views on what the job of interpreting and evaluating literary works entails. At one extreme, thinkers such as Hirsch[21] maintain that the main job of literary scholars is to give a true account of what the author intended to say. At the other extreme, poststructuralists such as Derrida seem to suggest that the artistic product is just the raw material for the critic's new creation.[22] In-between there are different views of how far the critic might pass beyond the author's intentions. These controversies have caused flutters in the academic dovecots far beyond the literary establishment.

But the problem of interpreting texts is a much wider one. The world has never been so full of communications. Texts were not plentiful in antiquity or in the middle ages, and their quantity has only gradually increased until the explosion of our own time. Their rapid dissemination is also a recent development. I have mentioned earlier the growing importance of interpreting treaties, contracts ("read the small print!"), agreements, and rules. No less in need of interpretation is the constant flood of newspapers and journals, which, we are told, shape public opinion and may win or lose elections for those they favor or reject. There are party platforms, manifestos, press conference hand-outs, press releases, and advertisements. It often matters very much that we should be able to assess them fairly and critically, but we all need help to sort it all out so that we are not tricked, deceived, confused, or left in ignorance.

In the different disciplines concerned with the study of man, the need to interpret texts is no less than in the public sphere. Opinion polls and any research—psychological or sociological—based on questionnaires can go disastrously wrong if the meaning of both questions and answers and the way they could possibly be misunderstood are not painstakingly scrutinized.[23] Management schools need to warn their students that conflict between workers and management is not only a matter of conflicting interests, but one of different languages. History now, as in the past, needs to scrutinize its material for traces of bias and must use every means of the interpretative art to recreate the life of the past from the written word. It is hardly necessary to add that philosophers and philologists, students of comparative religion or comparative literature, need to pore over texts.

So far the case for hermeneutics is neither revolutionary nor controversial. We are deluged with texts, which we need to understand. Hermeneutics, as the traditional discipline concerned with the interpretation of texts, can give us systematic help. The point is only saved from being trivial by reminding us that understanding is often difficult and cannot be taken for granted. Texts can be vague, obscure, misleading, and—by accident or by design—ambiguous. Something I heard on the radio on the day of writing these pages will serve as an example. Respectable and prominent members of parliament from Britain's two main parties commented on a recent announcement of a fall in unemployment. The opposition spokesman said that these figures were phoney. The government was merely hiding the unemployed in training schemes. The minister replied that the number of unemployed had, over a given period, fallen by 80,000, whereas the number of those in training schemes had remained the same. I do not believe that either of them was flatly lying, because, for one thing, this could only too easily be brought home to him. But clearly the official reports on the movements in unemployment allow different interpretations. Listeners have little choice but to accept one or the other version, according to their party allegiance or the esteem in which they hold a particular interpreter. An objective assessment is outside their scope, as it would require evidence, expertise, and, above all, time. Is an objective interpretation even theoretically possible? How deeply rooted are the ambiguities of the reports on employment trends? A detached hermeneutic approach might help to throw light, but something is already gained once we are aware of being confronted by contested interpretations and not the gospel truth.

The second step in establishing the relevance of hermeneutics to contemporary problems was Dilthey's move—partly anticipated by Schleiermacher—of extending the application of hermeneutics beyond actual texts. Speech, facial expressions, pictures, actions, and their products can be treated as texts insofar as they convey a meaning that can and needs to be interpreted, and the techniques of hermeneutics can be applied to doing so. We can recognize the use of these techniques in social psychology, personality study, social anthropology, archaeology, in psychoanalysis or other approaches to mental illness.

Though this approach runs counter to traditional behaviorism, it is hardly controversial today. Only the common name for cognitive approaches well established in different disciplines is new to many. It is the next step that brings us to the crux of the matter and into an area of continuing controversy. The question is, how far can hermeneutics be represented as the methodology of the human studies. After all, human beings and associations of human beings such as tribes, families, nations, trade unions, or what you will are neither texts nor text-like. True, texts in the narrower and the wider sense of the term give us access to their thinking and feeling, their aspirations and plans, but that is, clearly, not what all the human studies such as psychology, sociology, or economics are all about.

Dilthey had not overlooked that human beings were physical entities— animals that need food, warmth, and sleep, that want sex and are vulnerable to illness and injury. To him Kierkegaard's ironic picture of the philosopher in cosmic absentmindedness forgetting that he was a living individual certainly did not apply.[24] (Kierkegaard was actually attacking idealist philosophers such as Hegel). We noted earlier that Dilthey qualified his use of the term "*Geisteswissenschaften*" by reminding us that man and his works only partly belonged to the realm of the mind, and that these disciplines were at times about "mind" only insofar as it had affected, organized, or used and become embroiled in the material sphere. Elsewhere he stresses that from a certain point of view mind was only a tiny insertion in a vast material universe. He had a strong, tragic sense of human life being exposed to chance and accident in the form of external physical forces such as earthquakes, plagues—today it is AIDS—hurricanes, and avalanches. He speaks of the random, meaningless way in which historiography is affected by manuscripts and all kind of artifacts from the past becoming victims to fire or mold. He was seriously interested in physiological psychology and inveighed against philosophers who did not treat man as a creature of flesh and blood. He makes it plain that battles are determined as much by rain or mud and the lay of the land as by the plans of generals and the morale of soldiers.

The fact remains that a methodology that pivots on understanding cannot but focus on the mental states of human beings rather than on physical facts and events. There is, however, a plausible course by which Dilthey accommodated physical factors in his approach. The kinds of physical factors that can be diagnosed as relevant present themselves to human consciousness. If weakness due to illness prevents me from doing the work I planned, I am aware of it. The general conducting a battle takes the rain and the mud into account in his tactics, or, if he has failed to do so, can retrospectively reconstruct the reasons for the outcome in terms of the climatic interference with his plans.

When circumstances affect our actions, we tend to be aware of them. (But this is not always the case, and this raises a crucial problem, which we shall have to take up.) Indeed, it may be awareness of circumstances, rather than the circumstances directly, which affects our action. People do not become communists because they are poor, underprivileged, and proletarians. They may do so because they consider themselves poor, are aware of lacking privileges extended to others, and accept the label of proletarian. Whether or not their judgments rest on objective criteria for describing themselves as they do is irrelevant to the present case. Being objectively poor in terms of income without being aware of it would not affect my political allegiance. (For some purposes it is, of course, important to know how realistic a man's judgment is. I shall presently return to this issue.)

So we see the world around us as something to be taken account of and to be reacted to. We experience objects and events as obstacles that frustrate our aims or as means to serve our plans. The link between a man's idea of himself as poor and his allegiance to the communist party, between a general's plans and his expectation or knowledge of particular climatic conditions, between being aware of the money in your pocket and the purchases you make, all fall comfortably within the hermeneutic sphere, because they can be described as relations between parts of a meaningful whole.

But then we encounter the first snag. It is surely relevant for understanding a person to know that he thinks himself poor, though he has a comfortable home and a large bank balance, or that the general was culpably mistaken in his assessment of the climate. We need to be able to tell if a person is realistic or paranoid in his elaborate precautions against burglaries. But to know these things, we must use methods that are anything but hermeneutic. We have to assess a person's physical environment, his income and capital. We have to establish the normal climate of the scene of battle or learn about the rate of burglaries in the area where the cautious householder lives.

The need to move from hermeneutic interpretation to factual inquiry actually occurs throughout the hermeneutic sphere. We might discount the reliability of an "eyewitness" report by establishing the person's bias from what he says or his untruthfulness from contradictions in his story. We might equally discount his alleged observations when we learn that he is extremely shortsighted. We may dismiss a supposedly historical document either from internal evidence or because it is written on paper from a later period.

All this is plain common sense. Dilthey took up these kinds of points as a matter of course, and many practitioners of hermeneutics have done the same. I have lingered over this point for two reasons. First, even when hermeneutics is on its own home ground, the interpretation of texts, without assuming the role of the methodology of the human studies, tends to rely on evidence not provided by hermeneutics but by everyday observation or scientific research. Before we can establish what a statement means, in any but the trivial sense of its verbal meaning, we may need to know if the author was drunk, or his recollections factually wrong.

My second reason for discussing this particular issue is that it illustrates the needs for cooperation between science and hermeneutics in areas in which it is methodologically unproblematic. I have, in fact, mentioned two types of cases that I have so far not specifically distinguished. One concerns the material manifestation of the text or expression. The paper it is written on, the unevenness of the writing suggesting a trembling hand is relevant for the understanding of the text. The other case was that of assessing a statement by relating it to the objective situation to which it refers or responds. We want to know if it is fantasy or description, plan or wishful thinking.

There is no mystery about the observational and scientific methods we may need to employ. We can weigh the gold bars in the cellar of the man who thinks he is poor. We can submit paper to chemical tests. We can measure the average rainfall in a particular area. Is there any problem about relating and coordinating the two methods? Surely not, because the lines of contact are clearly marked. We are asking, first, what light the physical characteristics of a message may throw on its contents, and, second, what corresponds in the outer world to the content of the message.

Insofar as hermeneutics, as I presented it—and as Dilthey understood it—has cooperation with factual research built into its approach, it meets some of the criticism that the claim of hermeneutics to be more than a methodology of textual interpretation has aroused. However, it does not meet all of them, and we are entering territory where Dilthey remains vulnerable. The point I brushed aside earlier and must now confront is the possibility that our actions, our thoughts and words, our feelings and aspirations may be affected by circumstances of which we are not aware. I may be irritable because my glands are not functioning properly, and far from being aware of it I attribute my bad temper to my friend's exasperating ways. I may not realize and, indeed, may hotly deny that my political views are due to my economic status, or that it is the wine that makes me amorous, and not my partner's endearing charms.

We accept that such causation is possible and often occurs. But can we ever pinpoint their occurrence? If these hidden factors are effective, they are so because—and as long as—they remain hidden. I cannot remain angry with my friend once I realize that it is my spleen that makes me peevish. I could not remain an enthusiastic communist if I realize that I am motivated by hidden envy. Would I still feel in love once I knew it was the wine that was arousing me? It might be argued that the observer may know what is going on even if the actor does not, but when we are talking about feelings and motives the superiority of the observer's interpretation over that of the person who thinks, feels, and desires is eminently challengeable. These difficulties are not insurmountable; we do think sometimes that we know that a person is deceiving himself, that he is confused or mistaken about his own motives. To see through such error and self-deception is part of "understanding the author better than he understood himself." How it can be achieved is a crucial issue of hermeneutics.

Another problem presented for hermeneutics by the possibility of unconscious motivation requires attention. We have the text or text-like phenomenon—the abusive letter to my friend, the declaration of love to my partner, or the revolutionary tract—in front of us. I interpret it, and there is no problem about establishing that one text is abusive, the other romantic, but does it really mean abuse if there is nothing I have against my friend, is it really love that is expressed if it is my intoxication that speaks? Put brutally—I cannot intepret the text because it is determined by something that is neither text nor text-like and, what is worse, is not even accessible to me. Opponents of hermeneutics might then drive the knife in: could it be that we are always in this predicament, that texts can never be interpreted adequately in their own terms or in terms of their contexts?

Probably the most widely known contemporary thinker who leveled this type of criticism against hermeneutics is J. Habermas.[25] He primarily raised it in terms of psychoanalysis, but he had the Marxist view about ideas being distorted by economics and political features specifically in mind. He recognized psychoanalysis as, to some extent, a hermeneutic discipline, as it is in the business of interpreting dreams, mistakes, verbal accounts, and forms of behavior. It has, however, a peculiar feature that distinguishes it, he thought, from a practice of hermeneutics as normally understood. Psychoanalysis is—according to Habermas—based on theories about physiologically based factors such as the libido and models of causal interaction, which are matters of scientific theory rather than hermeneutic interpretation. In other words, when we interpret, let us say, a dream, we cannot do so merely by relating its parts to the whole or even by placing it into the context of other expressions such as the patient's free associations. The meaning of the dream is determined by, and can only be understood through, psychological or, even, physiological laws at work in the production of the dream. Habermas thought that this model of a hermeneutic approach, limited, corrected, and underpinned by a scientific one, corrects both a positivistic scientific and a purely hermeneutic approach and can be given wide application in the study of man.

Underlying his approach there are two assumptions that are both questionable. The first is that psychoanalytical theory and practice is as he describes it. In fact, a good deal of controversy as to the way it should be interpreted and its status as an interpretative or scientific discipline continues. The second assumption, which many scholars do not share, is that psychoanalysis is a significant, successful, and epistemologically respectable discipline.

These two assumptions are, obviously, essential for Habermas' argument as it stands. The case of psychoanalysis as a model for research would hardly be persuasive if Habermas had misunderstood its nature or if it were intrinsically unsound. I suspect that there is a case for skepticism about Habermas' two assumptions, but very substantial arguments would be needed to make good my suspicions. It is more to the point to look at the model irrespective of its supposed derivation from psychoanalysis. After all, Habermas' ultimate concern was not the psychoanalytic treatment of neurotics but the way in which intellectual debate was conditioned by social structures. Following essentially the revised Marxism of the Frankfurth school but adapting it originally to his purposes, he argued that the way in which economic, social, and political conditions affected debate and exchange of information in a society determined success or failure in the pursuit of the truth. I feel that the conflation of social/political and epistemological categories is confusing and not adequately justified, but it is not easy to pin down a subtle and sophisticated writer who has expressed his view voluminously and somewhat obscurely.

However, we are still left with the model and its challenge to hermeneutics. Not that every one of its functions is challenged. We have seen that human beings have ideas and intentions, and it is the unquestionable job of hermeneutics to understand these by interpreting their expressions. We have, secondly, noted that external circumstances become subjects of our mental attitude and in this way figure unproblematically in our interpretations. We mentioned, thirdly, that the physical form as well as references to physical factors may need checking by nonhermeneutic means if the hermeneutic process is to function properly. I suggested that this created no major methodological problem because the expressions themselves clearly indicated the direction any investigation should take. It is a more intractable issue—whether illustrated by everyday examples or the supposed practice of psychoanalysis—if interpretation is inadequate, flawed, and misleading because what is being interpreted is significantly affected by factors accessible to factual investigation but hidden, unreachable, and even unsuspected within the perspective of any interpretative approach. This would, clearly, set severe limits to the claim of hermeneutics to represent the methodology of the human studies.

The problem can be stated somewhat more generally. A hermeneutic approach inevitably views historical events, the behavior of individuals, and the life of society in terms of the thought and intentions of the actors. The student of the human world attempts a meaningful account of the occurrences he studies by relating them to mental states. Of course, such accounts need to be given—but are they the only story, are they the most appropriate and useful account of human affairs that can be rendered? It can be argued that the emphasis on the "subjective" can be misleading because sometimes what happens has nothing to do with what goes on in people's minds.

The central relevance of explaining human affairs in terms of human intentions can be challenged in several ways. There is, to start with, the peculiarity of intentions that are unconscius. Psychoanalysis extensively assumes the presence of such unconscious factors, and Dilthey anticipated it by his belief that expressions can lift mental content from unconscious depth. But what can an intention, a motive, or, indeed, anything mental be when it is not conscious? If we take, philosophically, a hard line on this issue, we must dismiss explanations of human behavior in terms of unconscious mental activities as pseudoexplanations of what must be attributed to chance, biology, or reflexes. But not only psychoanalysts— even if they overstate their case by believing that *all* slips of the tongue, mistakes, and the like are caused by hidden motives—and other psychotherapists, but also novelists and shrewd observers of human affairs explain what people do by referring to unconscious forces. The case can be put with epistemological caution. I break, let us say, an expensive ornament but deny that I did it intentionally. It was just an accident. To salvage the Freudian model, it may, then, be argued that the theory that I acted "as if" I had done it intentionally fits the case better than any explanations in physical terms such as the slipperiness of the vase or the clumsiness of my fingers. This hypothesis can, so the argument continues, be supported by my being made aware that I really disliked the ornament or its donor and therefore—in some way—wanted to break it. Even this modest formulation salvages the hermeneutic paradigm and, indeed, extends it traditional application. What on the surface requires a factual, scientific explanation turns out to be a kind of meaningful communication accessible to interpretation.

Another challenge to the hermeneutic approach concerns the unintended consequences of purposeful action. People act intentionally when they press for wage increases or go on spending-sprees, but no one intended the inflation that results. If the free market contributes to the public good, it is not due to any of the traders having that good in mind. In a panic everyone wants to get out of the plane or building, and as a consequence nobody does. Explanations of the mechanisms at work in producing inflation, prosperity, or a panic are possible but, unlike explanations of the intended consequences of purposeful actions of individuals or groups acting in concert, do not fit the hermeneutic mold because gauging the purposes from their expressions does not account for what happens.

There is no complete escape from this argument, and Dilthey never confronted it squarely. At the most, one can argue that the model I have just presented is an oversimplification. People do not stockpile goods, bargain for pay increases, or rush to the exit in total unawareness of what others are doing. To various degrees they may consciously discount, respond to, or even manipulate the actions of others. So it is possible to push a hermeneutic analysis into this tangle of mutual expectations and anticipation. However, in many cases it will not take us all the way. The majority of inflationary spirals, panics, and the like are not contrived.

Thirdly, there are facts and sequences of events that affect human life and consciousness but are themselves not, or only marginally, affected by human purposes. Take the case of ageing. Quite obviously, it affects almost every aspect of human life. As a baby, I am helpless, and—quite apart from the human help I receive—I become less helpless, more able to cope, to learn, and so on simply by growing older. Later on, this process of ageing will affect my energy for work or sport, my sexual attractiveness, my memory and span of attention. Eventually, my chance of completing work in hand becomes questionable. I need not expand on this theme, which has been the subject of numerous dirges. The process is explainable in physiological terms and is largely out of our control, though we may affect the process marginally by our mental attitudes, by exercise and diet. Once again, we have come up against limits to a purely hermeneutic approach, even in the case of purposive actions. Commenting on a book we think poor, we may say, "he did not plan his argument well enough" but also "he is getting old and, perhaps, senile." From the hermeneutic point of view we might try to save the situation by thinking of the body as a tool or means, the nature of which affects our intentions. However, in some cases an explanation of a person's age, health, or the like *is* what we require.

I am not, however, talking merely about the obvious fact that we have bodies that need accounting for in studies of human life. Entirely different examples can be given. Dilthey notes—as many other writers must have done—that the fate of Germany has been seriously affected by being the country of the middle, of being surrounded by numerous neighbors. Fears of being attacked, desire to expand its frontiers, openness to cultural influences from East and West, North and South all are connected with this geographical fact. As in the previous illustration, some of this can be construed in terms of conditions of which the Germans and their neighbors were aware, which they had to cope with and adjust to. But not everything fits into this scheme. Not all Germans, influenced by Italian culture, reflected that this was due to their being nearer to Italy than was, for instance, Russia. A few may not even have known it. Many more never gave it a thought but were influenced irrespective of this.

I am not suggesting that the points I have listed cause insurmountable problems to a methodology of the human studies. Historians, sociologists, and psychologists are accustomed to coping with a variety of factors requiring a variety of approaches. Dilthey never intended to replace what these various scholars did by his hermeneutic approach. He must be seen as having pursued, by and large, the more modest aim of reminding them of an approach that was sometimes neglected, or, if not neglected, practiced absentmindedly and not as purposefully and systematically as possible.

This list of issues of the human studies that do not easily fit into the pattern of hermeneutic interpretation makes it clear that hermeneutics does not provide a complete, comprehensive methodology of all the disciplines concerned with man (even if we discount the studies of man as a purely physical being). What it does is to contribute an indispensible approach, one that modifies and affects any other approach.

A second point follows directly from this. A kind of dialectic has been at work in the relation between hermeneutics and the scientific method. Before science had properly taken root, people tended to approach all reality hermeneutically because they thought of natural events as the expressions of animate beings—such as gods, nymphs, and the like. Science had to assert itself against this animism and triumphed to the extent that even conscious human beings came to be explained as if they were natural objects and nothing else. Dilthey and his followers provided a corrective, or, at least, a philosophically sophisticated basis for the reaction against this "scientism." We have yet to produce a new "synthesis." Put more simply: we need to give further thought to the way in which we can systematically relate our different approaches—the scientific and the hermeneutic one—in the fruitful study of man.

4

The Systematic
Human Studies

As we saw in Chapter 3, Dilthey believed that methodology must be guided by the nature of the subject matter. What makes this more than a platitude is that this effect on method is conceived of as central, not marginal. The kind of circularity that Dilthey not only accepted but considered inevitable is involved here. The aim of a methodology is to consider how a subject—in this case man and his works—can come to be known. Yet Dilthey demands that this methodology should itself be guided by an idea of what man is like.

Such an idea of what man is like must, in Dilthey's view, provide the starting point for all reflections on human life. Thus, talking about his moral philosophy, he writes to Count York in January 1890:[1]

I start from the structure of mental life, from the system of urges. The point at which I plant my feet in the flow of evolution and its vague possibilities to which today's modern thinkers have abandoned themselves, is the psychologically knowable nature of man, as it constitutes our human mental life, consciousness of self, etc. The mental structure which we find in ourselves I consider a fixed standpoint.

Before turning to the distinctly psychological slant in the consideration of human nature that is exhibited in this quotation, I want to consider the whole range of human studies dedicated to the elucidation of man's nature from different points of view. Dilthey's collective name for them was *Die Geisteswissenschaften*. One of them, history, I have already discussed separately because its relation to the other—systematic—human studies represents one of the tensions in Dilthey's work. Now I turn to the systematic human studies. While the former deals with change, the latter have the permanent for their subject matter. First, however, Dilthey's conception of the *Geisteswissenschaften* needs explaining.

THE IDEA OF THE HUMAN STUDIES

Dilthey's work contains lengthy discussions of separate disciplines—particularly psychology, history, and philosophy—but it revolves, ultimately, around the group to which these belong and which constitutes the study of man as a whole. The one major work—apart from the Schleiermacher biography—that appeared in his lifetime was the first volume of his introduction to the *Geisteswissenschaften* (i.e., human studies). During the rest of his life—another 28 years—he repeatedly tried to complete this work.

A list of disciplines comprised within the human studies will provide an initial idea of their nature. To complete such a list is impossible, as new disciplines can and are being developed, but fortunately it is not necessary. A selective list will indicate the range covered, and this is what matters. History, psychology, geography, economics, philology, comparative religion, jurisprudence, and the study of art and literature are all human studies in Dilthey's classification. Dilthey also includes philosophy, and this requires separate discussion. He does not mention sociology, because what he knew under this name—Comte's work—was too speculative for his taste. However, some of his own discussions and proposals for the study of topics such as the cultural and social systems[2] would come under the heading of sociology as conceived today.

Dilthey originally introduced the term *Geisteswissenschaften* as a translation of J. S. Mill's "moral sciences," but it would not be helpful to retranslate it this way as the term has largely gone out of use. A literal translation would be downright misleading, for who would recognize economics or philology, in fact anything except branches of psychology, as "mental" sciences or "sciences of mind." The term "social sciences" has too narrow a meaning; while covering sociology, economics, and the like, it is not expected to include philology and history, let alone philosophy. "The humanities" include the latter but not sociology, social anthropology, and the like. Such a term as the behavioral sciences is, if anything, even narrower in its meaning than "social sciences." The usual solution to this problem of nomenclature is to abandon any attempt at translation or alignment with common classifications in the English-speaking world and call the group of subjects Dilthey was referring to "the human studies" or "human sciences." This gives the intended meaning quite accurately but loses the transparent relationship between *Geist, geistig,* and *Geisteswissenschaften.* The choice between "sciences" and "studies" is relatively trivial. "Science" is, of course, the literal translation of the German term, but one has to remember that it is used more widely for any form of scholarship. In English we do not naturally expect a man described as a scientist to turn out to be a historian or philosopher. There is something of a courtesy title about the label "social science." This is why I tend toward the use of "human studies."

It would not have been worthwhile spending even a paragraph on this matter if it were merely a question of translating an awkward term. The substantial claim that merits attention is that such a large number of diverse disciplines naturally forms a single group that it is profitable to treat as a unitary whole.

Of course, we cannot go back on specialization. Not only must there be specialists who concentrate on psychology while others spend their time on sociology, but there must even be division of labor between, let us say, industrial, educational, and social psychology, between political sociology and the sociology of religion. Yet it is well to be reminded that these disciplines are dealing with abstractions, with aspects of situations, with isolated spheres of human experience, whereas in life we are always confronted with whole human beings and complex multidimensional situations.

Man is a historical being, but he is also a social, economic, political being; he is a thinking creature and a tool-using animal. When we turn our attention to one of these aspects, we cannot safely ignore that he is all the other things as well. Similarly, the problems he faces are not just economic or social or psychological ones. These are only aspects of human problems selected for treatment by different disciplines. Delinquency, unemployment, industrial relations are multidimensional and therefore not the preserve of any one discipline.

Problem-centered, essentially interdisciplinary studies such as criminology, management studies, peace studies, and the like have been developed in response to practical needs, but it is questionable how far integration in terms of a genuinely interdisciplinary strategy has advanced in them. This issue of interdisciplinary cooperation is theoretically interesting and practically important today. What we need to understand is man, his works, and his world. It was Dilthey's virtue—and constitutes some of his relevance for us—that he saw this very clearly and promoted this goal by treating the human studies as a group of interdependent disciplines that needed to cooperate in the pursuit of knowledge of social, historical reality and shared a common epistemological basis, which, in turn, gave rise to a common methodology.

Even apart from the question of the common theoretical basis of these disparate disciplines, grouping them together has proved practically stimulating. As yet, we have no schools or departments of the human studies in Dilthey's sense, but the value of looking over departmental fences is increasingly recognized. More use is made of literature as source material for psychology and sociology, just as psychological and sociological concepts and theories are applied to the interpretation and evaluation of literature. Philology, statistics, and demography are put into the service of history. These are fruitful developments, and their systematic use at least is relatively new.

Dilthey's conception of the *Geisteswissenschaften* becomes clearer when we remind ourselves that he contrasted it to the *Naturwisschenschaften*. This represents a bifurcation of all scholarly disciplines into those dealing with man and those dealing with nature.

It may occur to the reader that there is something odd and misleading about the contrast. As a matter of fact, Dilthey was fully aware of, and indeed draws attention to it when he introduces his terms (*C.W.*, Vol. I, p. 14). The contrast between mind and nature is appropriate when we speak of, let us say, the study of law or literature on the one side, that of electrical phenomena on the other. But if we read the *Geisteswissenschaften*—as Dilthey intended—as the studies of man, the contrast is misleading. It would only be clear and neat if men were disembodied spirits.

Man, as we noted in the previous chapter, is embedded in nature. He is a physical creature with a biological makeup and physiological needs. He expresses himself by physical means and confronts a physical world. Psychology cannot ignore the working of his nerves, brain, and glands, philology may have to take account of the way his speech organs work, the fact that mathematics predominantly works to a base of ten may be connected with our having ten fingers (the above illustrations, apart from the last, are given by Dilthey himself). History, sociology, and economics all deal with the interplay between ideas and physical facts—people shaping their environment according to their purposes, which, in turn, are affected by their environment and physical needs. Social anthropology has for its counterpart physical anthropology.

MIND

When we refer to *Geist* as the subject of the human studies, what we are talking about is a sphere that is embodied and rooted in nature but permeated, affected, and shaped by mind. As long as we are talking, for example, about the human digestive system—how it functions, what it can absorb, and how it is related to other bodily functions—we are moving purely in the realm of nature, and its study is a physical science. When we consider, instead, what people actually eat, when they eat, what they consider good for them and what disgusting, we are in the sphere of traditions, conventions, prejudices—in short, we are in the sphere of mind.

The two spheres of mind and nature are closely interlinked. Not only is the desire to eat and our choice of food physiologically conditioned, the reverse is equally true. A man who has eaten a tasty stew which in no way can harm his stomach is—at least if he is an American or European—most likely to be sick if you tell him that the meat had come from sewer rats or a cat. Similarly, it is training and habit rather than a purely bodily process that make us ready for food at accustomed times of the day. It is hardly necessary to elaborate this illustration further to show how the intake of food becomes the subject matter of the human studies.

The same story can be told of other areas of life. Sex is a biologically grounded urge, but it is transformed and channeled by moral rules, patterns of courtship, marriage customs, and changing fashions in taste, which make different aspects of people appear sexually attractive. For example, views as to whether the ideal woman should be slim or have a fuller figure have varied through the ages and from civilization to civilization.

Or take housing. Houses are made of physical materials and basically serve physical needs for shelter and warmth. But what the houses look like, how they are arranged, how much space is considered desirable, and the like are all matters of our ideas.

In the sense indicated by the above illustrations, mind permeates our environment insofar as it is created or changed by human beings and their activities, whether it be work, play, social interaction, or art. Indeed, it affects every aspect of human life. This is why the "studies of mind" are the human studies.

In a sense Dilthey means nothing more mysterious than that areas of reality are affected by human thought, feeling, and aspirations, whereas the rest of nature is not, and that this makes a difference as to how these things need to be studied. However, Dilthey's use of the term "mind" needs a little elucidation. I shall be brief, as this is well-trodden ground.

The literal translation of *Geist* is "mind," "spirit," or "ghost." The last sense is, of course, irrelevant, but either of the other two have been used. I do not like to use "spirit" in this context because it suggests something more solemn and elevated than is implied in the German. A dirty joke is obviously a product of mind, but to call it spiritual sounds odd. But in using "mind" one must remind oneself of a difference of usage between the English word and *Geist*. Mind is often used for an individual's consciousness ("What's on your mind?" "My mind has gone blank," etc.). "*Geist*" is usually used in the sense in which we use "mind" in such phrases as "Mind over matter," "Mind arises only at a late stage of evolution." It is an attribute of man rather than the totality of an individual's mental life that is referred to.

What the mind has created—that is, the products of conscious human activity, be it languages, institutions, works of art, buildings, laid-out gardens, and the like—constitutes what Dilthey called objective mind, "the objectification of mind" or "the objectification of life." In this use of "mind" he followed Hegel, but he was anxious to strip the concept of any metaphysical connotation. He had no wish to argue that mind constituted the whole, or even part, of ultimate reality, but only to map out a sphere that can be usefully distinguished from such other spheres as that of physical objects and events on the one hand and that of psychological states on the other. If I say, "In bridge the ace can take any other card of the same suit," or, "January comes before February," or "Five plus seven makes twelve," we are not talking about physical facts or events. Nor are we talking about someone's state of mind or mental process.

It is, of course, true that bridge cards, mathematical signs, and periods of the year have a physical, observable existence, just as it is true that games, mathematics, and the calendar have been produced by mental processes and are used in them. In the usual sense of existence, mathematics only exists as marks on paper and as mental operations of mathematicians. Yet the three statements I have given as illustrations are not about either. Bridge is a game, the names of the months are part of our language. We play these games, we use that language, and this presupposes that there is something to be played or used. These entities affect us. I can, let us say, be driven insane by bridge, or be influenced in my thinking by the idioms of English. We, in turn, operate on them. I can give up bridge, misuse the English language, and so forth. It would be very hard to express these very ordinary statements while talking about nothing but physical entities or mental processes. So we talk about mind, the world of mind, objective mind, and so on. I shall briefly return to the concept of mind in my chapter on psychiatry, and there I shall provide a couple of Dilthey quotations that illustrate his view on the subject.

Equally innocuous and metaphysically neutral is Dilthey's contrast between mind and matter. He does not, like Descartes, assume that these represent two distinct substances, or, like idealists and materialists, that one or the other sphere is merely an epiphenomenon of the other. Experience— even ordinary, everyday experience—is highly complex, and we abstract from it different features. For Dilthey the distinction between the mental and the physical, between mind and matter, marks prominent features of this kind. This abstraction underlies the basic distinction between sciences and human studies. Further acts of abstraction give rise to the various disciplines within these main categories. Psychology and sociology (or, for that matter, physics and chemistry) are mostly not about entirely different things, but look at the same things from a different angle or focus on different features. I am, let us say, sitting in a room having a conversation with some friends. This one situation can serve as subject matter for physicists, chemists, biologists, linguists, psychologists, sociologists, and so on.

PHILOSOPHY AND THE HUMAN STUDIES

The final point to be made about the human studies—once we have explained the disciplines embraced by them, the contrast to the sciences and the concept of mind on the basis of which they are grouped—is to consider the role of philosophy in them. The very fact of placing philosophy into the same class with disciplines such as psychology is a little surprising to most people. We tend to contrast philosophy to all empirical disciplines—be they sciences or human studies such as philology or sociology—and disciplines that are purely formal, such as the various branches of mathematics.

To explain why Dilthey included philosophy among the human sciences involves examining the two terms and considering the distinctive status of different branches of philosophy. Science is the rigorous and systematic search for knowledge based on the careful sifting of evidence. I deliberately avoid specifying what kind of evidence, as the German term for "science" does not narrow it down to physical science, and it is in this sense we must use the term if the label "human sciences" is to make any sense. Philosophy is, essentially, man's reflection on himself and his doing, his place and role within reality. It is clearly "human," but can it qualify as a "science"? Can it, in other words, meet the two main criteria of scientific respectability of being, first, rigorous in its approach and in its use of concepts and arguments and, second, solidly based on experience?

Dilthey thought that some but not all branches of philosophy could meet these criteria. Metaphysics as knowledge of the ultimate nature of reality and the *Weltanschauungen* [world views] related to them, which combined a picture of reality with human ideals and moral precepts, could not qualify as scientific. They cater for a metaphysical need that is universal but are—as Dilthey argued at some length in his "The Types of World Views and Their Development in Metaphysical Systems"[3]—reflections of different temperaments and points of view. They illuminated—he thought—facets of a many-faceted truth but could not be combined into an adequate system that objectively represented reality.

On the other hand, epistemology and logic—which for Dilthey, as for many nineteenth-century philosophers, was not just a formal discipline but overlapped with epistemology and extended into methodology—could be treated rigorously, because of their multiple links to empirical knowledge. First, because they had human knowledge for their subject matter, they need not engage in free-floating speculation but, by attending to the conditions presupposed and operations involved in cognition, could engage in cogent analysis and argument. Second, these analyses provided the criteria for the rigor and scientific objectivity of the sciences. Science and epistemology had to sink or swim together. So if we wanted to accept the physical and empirical human sciences as reliable, we could not reject the equal reliability of philosophic disciplines that had laid bare the reasons for that reliability.

Dilthey, thirdly, thought that epistemology and logic, far from being purely formal, rational disciplines, themselves depend on the findings of empirical disciplines. Intellectual operations, including logical processes, were mental events that could and needed to be explained in psychological terms. The categories in which man thought were rooted in his nature and affected by historical developments. So epistemology had to look not only to anthropology but to history. As has been noted before, this involves a circle, because psychological and historical research must itself be based on cognitive activities and logical operations. On the whole, Dilthey believed that this circularity was inevitable, an inescapable feature of human cognition and so nothing to worry about. There is, however, some evidence that he occasionally shrank—possibly through the influence of Husserl— from such "psychologism" and "historicism." Personally, I think that he was right to do so, and I shall discuss this matter more fully in my last chapter.

Dilthey's view of ethics ran closely parallel to that on epistemology. Man's ideals, norms, and valuations are relevant to the understanding of man's mental life and to the interpretation of history. On the other hand, the facts of human nature and the history of human ideas provide the material, not, indeed, for straightforward deductions of moral codes, but for critical reflection from which ethical conclusions follow. He writes:

Ethics cannot define the goal of life with universal validity. This can be known from the history of morality. What man is and what he wants he only discovers in the development of his nature through the millenia and never to the last word, never in universally valid concepts, but only in significant experiences which spring from the depth of his whole being. As against this every meaningful formula about the final aim of human life has proved itself to be historically conditioned. To date no moral system has been able to achieve universal recognition. [C.W., Vol. VI, p. 57]

Ever since Hume stressed the logical gap between "is" and "ought," a view that assumes that a passage from facts to injunctions can be legitimate has been suspect. Moore labeled this assumption "The Naturalistic Fallacy"[4] and criticized it in detail. Yet the belief that we could pass from conceptions about man and reality to a view of how man should live has a respectable ancestry. Both Plato and Aristotle thought that man had a function that could be extrapolated from his essential nature and place within reality. Fulfilling that function and, so, being what a human being was meant to be, was virtue and at the same time self-fulfillment.[5] How man should act followed from what he was. Two thousand years later and arguing from different premises, Spinoza reached the same conclusion.[6] We could rationally determine the nature of reality and our place in it. Norms of how we should live directly followed from it.

Utilitarianism, which enjoyed a recent revival, is also committed to the "naturalistic fallacy." Utilitarians based judgments of right and wrong on the amount of pleasure or pain an action causes. J. S. Mill produced the widely criticized argument that something must be desirable if it was generally desired.[7]

It would be frivolous to attempt to do even an element of justice to these issues in anything but a full-length book on the topic. In any case, a lengthy treatment in a work on Dilthey would present an "overkill," as he himself did not deal with the issue in any depth nor examined the pros and cons of different philosophic positions on it in any detail. Suffice it that he thought that our moral conclusions are based on evidence from history and the other human sciences of what people have valued through the ages, what they commonly agreed on, and what has sustained human life and social harmony. I am, myself, not easy about his approach, and this is all the more reason to mention that this point of view has an eminently respectable ancestry.

There is no need to pursue the matter further, as I merely want to explain why Dilthey not only treated moral philosophy as one of the human studies but considered that it enjoyed a close two-way relationship with the empirical human disciplines. But nothing would be further from the truth than to think that this indebtedness to empirical studies in any way detracted from the importance of moral philosophy. On the contrary, philosophy's moral role, its function of placing ideals and moral rules before human beings, gave philosophy much of its practical importance. Fulfilling this function is the main service the philosopher can perform for his nation or society. This is why philosophy is not just an academic subject but must be taken out of the schoolroom to reach a wider public. To do so effectively, philosophy must look to common human experience and its systematic exploration by various human disciplines. But facts do not speak for themselves—philosophy is necessary because they must be interpreted and evaluated.

What I have said about the relations between specific branches of philosphy and the empirical human studies applies to the relation of philosophy as a whole to human experience. Dilthey shared the traditional view that in philosophy man reflects on, aims at becoming critically aware of, himself, his nature, his potentialities and his place within the scheme of things. This idea is as old as the very beginnings of philosophy in Ancient Greece, for it was then—though not exclusively, as it was fairly broadly defined—a response to the Delphic injunction, "Know thyself."

It tallies equally with modern conceptions of philosophy as a meta-activity: Man is engaged in a multitude of activities—he uses language, gets involved in politics, explores the world scientifically, records the past, introduces moral and legal rules into social life, and worships gods. In political, religious, and moral philosophy, the philosophies of history, of science and of language, he reflects critically on what he is doing in these different spheres by analyzing the concepts and methods used, the presuppositions applied in them.

The idea of philosophy as second-order reflection on what we do and what we know, on our beliefs and aspirations, is widely accepted. Though Dilthey does not express himself in such terms as "second order" or "meta-activity," the thrust of his argument is in this direction. It is, however, a characteristic feature of his approach that he tends to slur over distinctions.

His tentativeness, open-mindedness, and carelessness about technical terms has its appealing side but can also be irritating. It would have been more helpful if he had pinpointed and examined more incisively the differences between analyzing concepts, speculating, stipulating postulates, and tracing presuppositions on the one hand, and empirical research on the other. It is most probably his failure to outline his intellectual positions more sharply that militated against a wider and earlier appreciation of so dedicated and original a thinker.

These imprecisions are partly due to the style of thinking of a man who wrote and dictated rapidly a vast body of work. It is also true, though, that he did not believe in sharp distinctions between philosophy and science, between epistemology and psychology. I quoted Bollnow in defence of this elusiveness (p. xii), but think it confusing and wrong-headed in these cases and shall return to this criticism in my last chapter. It has, however, a positive side. Though the point could have been made equally, and even more forcefully, in terms of sharper distinctions, Dilthey's stress on the close interrelation and interdependence of these various intellectual activities and various human disciplines is of the utmost value.

Specialization is inevitable, but we only too easily take the existence of watertight compartments of knowledge and inquiry for granted. Psychologists, linguists, and philosophers are only too often content to stick to their "own subject." But looking over the fence is intellectually stimulating and has, in fact, often proved practically fruitful. The interdependence between philosophy and the human and scientific disciplines is not Dilthey's discovery. In a book like Plato's *Republic* the lines between what we would still recognize as philosophy and psychology, political sociology and educational theory are constantly crossed. Kant, to give just one more example, was well schooled in mathematics and science and responded in his *Critique of Pure Reason* to Newtonian science. He also lectured on anthropology and military engineering. It is Dilthey's distinction that his whole work is dedicated to and colored by this commerce between philosophy and the empirical human studies. The point can be put most neatly by paraphrasing—as has been done before for this type of purpose—a rightly famous Kantian pronouncement (*Critique of Pure Reason*, B75): the human studies without philosophy are blind, philosophy without the human studies is empty.

ANTHROPOLOGY

The study of man that the different human studies divide between themselves has, traditionally, a general name of Greek coinage: anthropology. Dilthey used it in this broad sense, and his work raises the question that crystallizes the issue about the relationships within the human studies, as to how an empirical anthropology is related to its philosophic treatment. To my knowledge Dilthey never used the term "philosophic anthropology," which was brought into use by M. Scheler, H. Plessner,[8] and their followers. However, the agenda of this discipline was set by Dilthey.[9]

In modern usage, anthropology usually figures as one discipline among other human studies. As social anthropology, it came to be associated with the study of societies, often described as "primitive," but its methods were later applied to more complex modern societies. There is also physical anthropology, which is, according to our definition, not properly a human study at all, as it deals with physical characteristics, such as size of skull, pigmentation, and so on, of groups of human beings in different ages and different parts of the world. The global claim of anthropology has, however, not been abandoned. The American Anthropological Association, in a pamphlet published in 1982, contends "Nothing is alien to anthropology, and of the many sciences that study certain aspects of our species, only anthropology attempts to understand the whole panorama, in time and space, of the human condition." The pamphlet goes on to distinguish four main branches of anthropology—"cultural anthropology, linguistic anthropology, archaeology, and physical anthropology"—but it also refers to "economic anthropology, psychological anthropology, ethnomusicology, medical anthropology, educational anthropology," and many others. It is not clear if these are intended to replace psychology, economics, and the like. There is clearly, as Dilthey envisaged, a case for such a unification, but it must be said, in passing, that this case has as yet not been widely accepted. University departments of sociology, psychology, or economics are not usually part of a faculty of anthropology. (Are they anywhere?)

Dilthey's references to anthropology and anthropological reflection are not very numerous. Nor are they systematic. His usage, not sharply defined, also appears to have changed. Sometimes he identified anthropology with psychology or, more specifically, social and cultural psychology. As such, he thought of it as a key discipline of the human studies rather than a culminating systematization of all the human disciplines, which, to his mind, would have destroyed the rich variety of life reflected in the separate disciplines. So he writes, for example:[10]

All the human studies presuppose a type of human nature in order to develop their truths. This type is something different and is more than psychology has developed to date. A theoretical development of it I call anthropology.

In other passages, particularly in his later writings, Dilthey seems to reject this identification; he lines up anthropology with a hermeneutic rather than with a psychological approach and asserts that it is about "meaning and value of life." It is an extenuating circumstance and a further complication that Dilthey was developing a conception of psychology that diverged from what went under this title in his time and, indeed, diverges from much of what is called psychology today.

His proposals for a special kind of psychology were developed more fully and systematically than his references to anthropology, and they require specific discussion. Adhering to the terms of reference that I set for this book, which is not intended as a historical portrait of a thinker, I shall pursue the subject of anthropology a little further. The title *Dilthey Today* is meant to suggest the inclusion of discussions of how we might use and develop his ideas and follow paths to which he pointed. Looking critically at Dilthey's basic approach and using the hindsight of knowing how the subject of philosophic anthropology was developed after him, I want to explore what a philosophic anthropology can and should be. Put very crudely, I shall attempt to suggest, from my own point of view, what Dilthey should have said on this subject.

Philosophic anthropology, though not Dilthey's own term, describes something that was certainly his aim, namely the systematic philosophic reflection on what it is to be human as it is revealed to us through inner awareness and the findings of the human disciplines. It must include consideration of the presuppositions and methods we employ in gaining knowledge of man and must encompass elements of speculation that take our conceptions beyond what is simply given by experience. It is the nature of this combination I want to explore, not only because it provides a clearer view of the tangled connection between philosophy and the empirical studies so central to Dilthey's approach, but also because I consider it intrinsically important.

There is something shocking about the title, because it seems to suggest a speculative alternative to acquiring knowledge normally based on experience. While social anthropologists travel to distant communities to observe, pencil at the ready, to listen to the stories of the elders and to participate in ceremonies, the philosophic anthropologist speculates in his armchair. It is, alas, the philosopher's fate that his working posture can look all too much like the position in which others rest. The question is, however, what can thus be achieved by speculation.

The new label highlights the problems of demarcations between empirical research and philosophy and points to specific functions that philosophy is acquiring with the development of the social sciences. Before I deal with this aspect, however, I want to recall that the newly labeled subject matter is, in fact, traditional to philosophy. I have already mentioned in passing that philosophy in general has man's reflection on his nature and doings as its goal. What is in fact a natural human preoccupation thus becomes a task of philosophy. As philosophy deals with the many topics on which each of its different branches concentrates, it makes sense to introduce philosophic anthropology as one of these branches. However, the topic of man is central to all of them. As L. Landgrebe put it, "In every philosophic question man himself is implicitly or explicitly put in question."[10] When Socrates questioned his fellow citizens on justice, courage, and political wisdom, or when Aristotle lectured on the soul and on virtue, questions of human nature were prominently involved. In fact, it is in these very discussions that they invented (the term is used deliberately by Scheler in this context) the definition of man as a rational animal.

The thinkers—from the church fathers and St. Augustine to the scholastic philosophers of the Middle Ages—who tried to explain and justify Christian dogma in philosophic terms were, similarly, concerned with man's nature and destiny as a major theme of Christian teaching. At the very outset of the modern age, philosophy, and with it the concern with man, took a new turn. Descartes precipitated the development of modern philosophy by making the certain knowledge of the "I," of the indubitable existence of a conscious, thinking mind, the cornerstone of his whole philosophy. His emphasis on the theory of knowledge placed the knowing subject into the center of the picture and thus gave an explicitly anthropocentric twist to philosophy. Most subsequent thinkers—both empiricists and rationalists—followed the epistemological path mapped out by Descartes and therefore turned their attention to the cognitive capacities of man: his powers of perception, the scope and limitations of reason, the relevance of imagination, and the like. However much they differed in their presuppositions and conclusions, they were at one in the priority they gave to the study of man's mind.

The tendency, starting with Descartes and culminating with Kant or, as some would argue, Hegel, to focus attention on a pure, disembodied, cognitive subject raised critical issues, and the problems of reuniting the mind conceived as pure consciousness with its body received various familiar solutions in the seventeenth and eighteenth centuries. In the nineteenth century more radical solutions, rejecting the original premise, arose. The general thrust of this attack was that it is human beings we must look at, not pure consciousness, even when we are discussing thought. Kierkegaard stressed that man was, first and foremost, a unique individual making choices, Nietzsche that he was basically an animal, Marx that he was a worker using and molding his environment. Dilthey was part of this reaction, and I shall revert to his contribution. Here I am only illustrating the persistent and indeed progressively accentuated theme of human nature.

In the twentieth century, the philosophic interest in man has continued. In the English-speaking world it is often indulged in as the philosophy of mind, a title misleading because it covers behavioristic accounts or discussions of the mind/body relationship. The frequent emphasis on the topic of language focuses attention on a uniquely human development and has also led some of the exponents of linguistic philosophy such as Wittgenstein and his followers to follow Dilthey into seeing language as part of a way of life. (I have no idea if Wittgenstein knew Dilthey's work and was consciously influenced by him.) In fact, there has been some convergence—only noticed fairly recently—between Anglo–American and continental philosophy, both in the interest in language and in the broader concern with what I call anthropology.[12]

We can see an internal dynamic at work within the ongoing debate that makes up the history of philosophy through which cosmic concerns have receded as the abiding interest in man shifted to the center of attention. There were, however, outside forces at work to strengthen and accelerate this process. Intensely practical reasons for understanding human nature have always existed. For success in any field, we need to assess our own capacities and the reliability of our friends, or the resolution of our opponents. In business, war, or love we must learn to evaluate human situations. Social changes, precipitated, shaped, and accelerated by technological developments, have made these needs more urgent. Old rules or conventions lose their application in changing circumstances. Even moral values become questionable. What price thrift when there is constant inflation, or hard work in a world of high unemployment and automated production? We have achieved enormous powers over nature—will we use them for good or for ill? We have the knowledge to produce a flood of useful goods—do we have the knowledge to safeguard industrial relations so as to keep that flood going? We have, quite literally, the power to destroy mankind—have we the knowledge of each other to keep the peace? Many questions of this kind are thrust at us. They all point to the overwhelming need to understand ourselves.

Various social sciences have developed rapidly or have even been newly created to meet this need. But it is, unfortunately, a plain fact that these disciplines are not as theoretically well developed and practically successful as one might expect and wish. This is where Dilthey wanted to make a contribution as a philosopher, and this is where philosophy can still hope to be useful.

Quite apart from practical problems such as lack of funding, moral restraints on experiments, and the like, a number of theoretical and methodological problems stand in the way of progress.

First, there is no consensus on concepts, theoretical presuppositions, and methods, even within individual disciplines. In psychology and psychiatry, in sociology and economics there are different schools that are in irreconcilable conflict with each other on these issues. Behaviorists and cognitive psychologists, psychiatrists and psychoanalysts, conflict theorists and structuralists can barely talk to each other, let alone cooperate, test each other's findings, or utilize each other's conclusions.

The situation is aggravated when we turn from internal squabbles to the relationships between disciplines. Cooperation, indeed some kind of integration, is made desirable by the fact, already noted, that practical problems, such as delinquency, have economic, political, psychological, and sociological aspects. This is not news, and cooperation and exchanges of views are often attempted. It is, however, not enough to move different specialists into a common building or place them around the same table. Though one should not minimize the usefulness of this, we ultimately need a theoretical framework that will accommodate the points of view and findings of different disciplines. We are back with the immediate subject in hand—a conception of man that makes sense of all the different approaches used.

Each discipline—or perhaps, in the light of the above, one should say sometimes each school within a discipline—uses an image of man, a schema or model that incorporates the essential assumptions about human nature and conduct on which that discipline bases its approach. Dahrendorf[13] compares several such models in his essay "Homo Sociologicus," and a few quotations will make the point I am concerned with. He defines homo economicus as "the consumer who carefully weighs utilities and cost before purchases and compares hundreds of prices before he makes his decision . . . the perfectly informed, thoroughly rational man." Psychological man is, for Dahrendorf, "the man who even if he always does good may also want to do evil—the man of invisible motives . . ." and homo sociologicus is, for him, "man as the bearer of socially predetermined roles." Dahrendorf is a highly regarded scholar, so his definitions will do well enough as illustrations of these models. There is no need to examine here whether they accurately represent the assumptions and practice of the respective disciplines, which would require a detailed examination of each discipline, though his definition of homo psychologicus seems, even at a glance, to fit only some psychological approaches.

What we need to look at is the status and nature of these models. They are not descriptions or even aspects of actual people. We can never meet them, because they do not exist. They are ideal types embodying in a pure form qualities or tendencies that actual human behavior is supposed to approximate to various degrees. The human beings we meet at business or in the streets are nothing like homo economicus, because they are concerned not only with buying and selling, but also with lovemaking, saving their souls, making a good impression, or fighting for political rights. The important point is that not only is their time and energy divided among these different pursuits, but they color and modify each other. For example, I may not buy at the best price, because I have political objections to buying Polish goods or because I find a particular saleswoman attractive. Because of this—as Dahrendorf makes clear—these homunculi must be seen as artificial constructions whose value lies in their providing hypotheses for research. As long as we are warned against taking these types as portraits, there is no problem. Plato already used such constructions, and they are familiar in modern physical science, which uses, for example, the notion of "unimpeded fall," which in practice never occurs.

The real problem appreciated but not dealt with at any length by Dahrendorf is the relation between these models. Do we not also need a general conception, or model, of what man is as a whole, and how would this be related to the one-sided models used by different disciplines? If the homunculi are to have some predictive value, they must somehow relate to, be relevant to, real multidimensional people. Yet the different images cannot be simply combined, for they may contradict each other. If, for instance, economics presupposes a conception of man as motivated by rational considerations while psychology insists that man's choices are largely swayed by irrational motives, or if sociology assumes human nature to be almost infinitely malleable while psychology stipulates fixed characteristics, it is intellectually unsatisfactory, and perhaps even practically disadvantageous, to leave each discipline to its own devices as long as they can deliver the goods, that is, offer explanations and predictions in their own sphere.

There is, surely, something rather remarkable about the possibility of successfully making predictions about actual human behavior based on contradictory assumptions about his nature.

Even if we were able to explain away the grosser contradictions as only apparent, because they deal with different aspects or levels of human life, we would still be left with a large array of assumptions and findings that do not add up to a coherent and meaningful picture of man. We cannot make up that picture from an endless list of human characteristics, even if they did uniquely distinguish man from other creatures (as for instance the twin characteristics of being featherless bipeds). We need a unitary conception of man, which provides strategic guidance for understanding him and deciding what is important, significant, and valuable. Clearly traditional definitions of man, as rational animal or spiritual being made in the image of god, or as dual creatures in which reason and passion are in conflict, take us beyond the sphere of factual assertion. They involve judgments and evaluations. We are supposed to live up to our rationality, to the image of god within us, or whatever is stipulated in the original definition.

This is not an abstruse technical requirement, not a need of academic philosophy. An all-round evaluative conception of man is involved in our dealings with each other. What can I expect from my wife, and what do I owe her? What is the road to a happy marriage? What are we trying to achieve in education? How should we set about it, and what chance of success do we have? What are the goals of politics, and what means are appropriate to achieve them? Answers to these and many similar questions depend on our having a conception of man.

DILTHEY'S IDEA OF MAN

So what can a philosophic anthropology be like if we approach the matter in the spirit of Dilthey's philosophy? It cannot be a compendium of the empirical findings and theoretical conclusions of all the separate disciplines. Such a compendium would be endless and constantly shifting. It could not provide the value accents to which I have just referred. It might not even be able to eliminate inconsistencies. After all, one might ask: who is to put all these bricks together into an adequate edifice? It is too much to expect this from a philosopher. No single man could collect and review all the evidence. Still less would any man be competent to judge the reliability and importance of the findings of such a wide range of disparate disciplines (not to mention the schools within disciplines, which are in conflict with each other). If, on the other hand, it were the job of a committee or of an editor delegating subject areas to specialists, Kierkegaard's ironic comment on "the system," by which he meant Hegelian philosophy, would apply—"when the book is bound the system is complete."[14] We would have a kind of directory instead of a philosophy of man.

On the other hand, philosophic anthropology cannot be the product of pure speculation. Dilthey did not believe—and few people today would believe—that purely rational reflection could unveil the structure of reality and with it the nature of man.

What Dilthey is actually doing can be described in different ways that gain credence from the philosophies known to have influenced Dilthey. One must think, above all, of that of Kant, but Husserl's phenomenology is also a candidate as Dilthey in his last years was impressed by the work of the younger man, who in turn expressed his indebtedness to him. It must be stressed, though, that Dilthey did not apply their approach either explicitly or consistently.

What Dilthey does can be described as an examination or analysis of what experience is. He writes,

Nearest to life, is the method which describes and analyses the sequence and coexistence of concrete mental states. ... So the anthropological method describes and analyses the sequence of concrete mental states.

Anthropological research is neighbour to poetry. Here experience is developed in imagination according to its inherent meaning and thus the relation of a mental event toward surrounding life is described in its concrete reality. [C.W., Vol. VI, p. 305]

The analysis of experience is closely linked to an examination of the presuppositions about the judgments we make about experience of the human world, because experience involves judgment and analyzing it includes looking at what is presupposed in it.

In my chapter on Dilthey's approach to history I gave a brief account of the way in which he attributes meaning to human life and of the categories in terms of which meaning arises in, or can be attributed to, our experiences. This constitutes part of Dilthey's attempt to lay bare some unchanging features of human existence.

Man is a historical being in the sense of not only experiencing the passage of time but experiencing it in terms of the links between past, present, and future. He is the creature who gives to or finds meaning in his experiences in terms of this temporal structure, responding to the present in terms of the value things have for him, interpreting it by relating it to past experiences, and anticipating the future in terms of his purposes. He appreciates things as means that serve his goals or as forces helping or frustrating him.

Man is, secondly, a dual creature of mind and body in whom the mental finds constant expression in physical manifestations. We become aware of these fundamental aspects of being human when we look beyond the specific experiences to their characteristic patterns. Without difficulty, and without giving special thought to such matters, we assert in everyday conversation such things as "He showed his anger," "He went for a walk to get some exercise," "He was exhausted by the heat and put on the fan," "The cocktail bar is part of his ostentatious style of life."

All these statements are, clearly, empirical statements; we arrive at them through the encounter with people and situations. But we do not arrive at the idea that a frown has a mental equivalent, that the walking has a purpose, that we are affected by and affect the environment, or see things in terms of parts and wholes, by inspecting individual cases. We presuppose the general judgments, and they make the individual judgments possible. As Dilthey chose to follow Kant's usage and speaks of categories, I constructed them in the sense in which Kant used the term. "The fire burned my pants" is an empirical statement. But "every event has a cause" is a categorial judgment, which we presuppose as we make the specific judgment about fire causing the burn on my trousers.

A social anthropologist arriving newly at the homes of an alien tribe has much to learn. There is much he does not understand. But because it is human beings he is observing, he takes it for granted that most of their movements are purposeful, that the noises they utter are language, that they are capable of suffering and try to manipulate the environment. He will also assume that recognition of a situation may give rise to feelings, and those feelings precipitate purposeful action. In other words, he understands, before he has learned their language and communicated with them, that, let us say, an earthquake arouses fear, which in turn will suggest flight. Things of this kind are necessary conditions for his coming to understand these people, to learn their language, and to appreciate why they act in particular ways. Without these presuppositions, he could not even begin. A Martian visitor, however intelligent, who, let us say, could not conceive what it was to have feelings and be motivated by them, would lack the necessary clues to understand the human community confronting him. He might possibly, at the most, develop a kind of behaviorist account, observing regularities and constructing hypothetical laws to account for them, much in the way in which physicists account for the behavior of material objects.

We might say—and, indeed, Dilthey maintained this—that we know these things because we are human ourselves, we are kin to the subject matter we study, we are moving within a world that is ours. We are aware, from looking into ourselves, what it is like to want something, to be anxious, and so on, as we can never know what it is like to be an electric charge repelled by another electric charge. This is the line or argument that obscured for Dilthey the distinction between epistemology and a descriptive psychology.

As in other cases, it did not worry Dilthey that a circle was involved if experience provided the categorial presuppositions that made experience accessible. But a problem remains. I am, let us say, aware within myself of enjoying wine or abhorring violence. I find it natural to think before I make a decision. Can I presuppose any of this when I try to understand other human beings? Quite obviously not. If, for a moment, I entertained this notion, I would be quickly disabused. Human beings are very different from each other, and we have to be very cautious about what we can assume as features common to all.

The question what we can and what we cannot accept as common human nature is of great practical importance. It gives rise to endless personal problems and misunderstandings. I find it natural and easy to be punctual, so what fiendish motives, what hypocrisy in her protestations of love, lie behind my girlfriend's persistent unpunctuality? My mother was content, indeed proud, to be a housewife, so is it unnatural and unfeminine for my new bride to want a career? I have given up smoking, why does my friend make such a pathetic fuss about doing the same?

The same applies to attitudes that divide groups, nations, and so on. The habit of fox hunting among the English upper classes, the popularity of bullfighting in Spain, the fascination for cricket shared by many nations of the British Commonwealth, appear odd, and even reprehensible, to outsiders. The fact that people are different from us is forcibly thrust upon our notice, but we are not content to accept it. As likely as not we attribute it to stupidity, mental aberration, or moral depravity.

The issue raises equally serious theoretical problems—problems that take us to the heart of Dilthey's position and its difficulties. What it is like to be human we know, because we are human ourselves. Without such direct acquaintance and experience, any knowledge of man would be incomplete and hypothetical. Yet such immediate knowledge is itself incomplete and, indeed, flawed. Our self-knowledge can be defective and we may even deceive ourselves; above all, introspection gives us no clue as to what reflects common human nature and what is peculiar to an individual.

We can correct such egocentric and defective views by understanding others and by relating our views to our cultural heritage, that is, to the sphere of objective mind. But such correction is itself subject to the limitation that all this understanding itself hinges on our initial familiarity with human nature. The relationship between philosophy and the empirical studies of man reproduces this predicament, which we have identified as that of the hermeneutic circle. As we have already seen, the acceptance of a close but ill-defined interrelationship between philosophy and the empirical studies of man is an integral part of Dilthey's whole approach. But it also represents a weakness in his philosophy, which leaves crucial issues undecided.

Once we have posed the question about what philosophy can add about human nature beyond what we know from common sense or research, we cannot fudge the issue by generalities such as the "critical evaluation" of information or "analysis" of concepts. One possible way out with which Dilthey was thoroughly familiar, but which he did not use as explicitly and consistently as one could have wished, is that of Kant's transcendental deductions.

PRESUPPOSITIONS ABOUT MAN

Kant started his major works by accepting from the outset that such achievement as gaining empirical knowledge and making binding and universal moral judgments were within our grasp. He then asked what made these achievements possible, what was involved and presupposed in our confidence in factual knowledge and moral principles. To answer *this* question he considered the philosopher's proper job. If it were possible—as he believed it was—to pinpoint necessary presuppositions of what we actually accomplished, then the former could be validly deduced from the existence of the latter. Of course, if the difficult task of showing something to be a necessary presupposition were impossible, the step from the one to the other would still be possible, but would yield a hypothesis or theory rather than a logical conclusion.

The kinds of things Kant thus deduced—for example, the unity of the knowing "I" as the condition of experiencing unitary objects or events, or causality as the condition of connecting particular sequences of events—could not be reached by observation or by generalizations from experience. Even if they could, this would be totally irrelevant, because trying to explain the possibility of empirical knowledge in terms of empirical knowledge constituted for Kant a vicious circle. Judgments merely based on experience would also lack universality and authority. If experience showed that A was the condition of B, the next experience may show something quite different. Kant in his epistemology was emphatically not in the business of psychology, sociology, or the like.

Dilthey, who did not mind circles, believed that what served as presupposition in one case was given in experience in another. The psychological makeup of our cognitive faculty and common-sense knowledge based on experience produced the presuppositional framework of cognition. In my last chapter I shall consider if this position is really tenable and if Dilthey was quite consistent in maintaining it. Here I am concerned with another aspect.

But even if what is presupposed in one case is also empirically given, the fact that something figures as a necessary or even just as an actual presupposition or precondition lends it a special status in argument. It would also help to distinguish clearly the empirical study of facts from the philosophic consideration of presuppositions. While highlighting the relation between experience and philosophy, it would also single out the distinctive task of the latter. Dilthey did not make full use of this possibility. If he had it in mind, he did not make it explicit. However, his own conclusions can be fitted pretty neatly into this kind of framework.

Some of the things we know through whatever sources about human nature are presupposed in what we think, believe, and value. Our intellectual and moral life is anchored in them, and so they are not dispensable or easily corrigible, even if they derive originally from experience.

In the field of cognition, two sets of presuppositions about man are involved. They, in fact, overlap in content, but they arise from different contexts. The first set of presuppositions represents the answer to the question: what is generally involved in our being cognitive subjects? It is impossible that I should ever consider myself as not being one. Once I am conscious, I am also aware of knowing all kind of things, both about myself and about a world around me. Though I may be mistaken about much that I think I know, I cannot be wholly mistaken about what is involved in my knowing at all. I take in things through my senses, experience events as continuing in time, can direct my attention, use concepts, and make judgments. These and other things I cannot but attribute to myself.

So if our possession of knowledge, be it the knowledge that it rains outside or that uncle Fred is sad today, not to mention all the knowledge we are convinced we possess in physics, astronomy, psychology, and all the other disciplines, actually presuppose certain human features that make us capable of such knowledge, we have the germs of a philosophic anthropology.

If we turn, then, to the more specific presuppositions involved in the knowledge of the human world, we find, to start with, that the general presuppositions of knowledge apply as well and, what is more, in two ways. They apply, quite obviously, because knowledge of man is a form of knowledge, but the general assumption of common sense that excludes solipsism—that I live among other human beings who operate fundamentally in the same way, however much they may differ in the specific views they hold, the pleasures they prefer, and so on—now becomes a crucial and heuristic principle. Other people—the social scientist's subject matter—are fundamentally cognitive subjects like him, and his knowledge of them must take account of this. It would be arrogant, intellectually self-defeating, and, incidentally, morally invidious to think of other people just as objects given to the senses and not as cognitive subjects fundamentally like oneself. This is a criticism not only of any form of behaviorism, but also of theories that attribute inevitable class bias, ideological distortion, or what you will to others without conceding that the theory attributing such bias is itself a product of such bias.

A second set of presuppositions involved in the knowledge of the human world has a somewhat wider scope. How far these presuppositions overlap with those involved in being a cognitive subject is a matter of fine analysis not required for our present purpose. From looking at the knowing subject, we turn to what is involved in the judgments we make about human beings. The form these judgments basically take is determined by such categories as "purpose," "value," "means and ends," "expressiveness," and the like, which we have already encountered. They function as presuppositions—that is, they spell out assumptions as to what form our judgments must take. Treating them merely as generalizations from experience would not properly reflect the role they actually play in our thinking. When I see a man waving his arms or hear him shouting, I do not speculate if he, like other human beings I have previously encountered, is a purposive being, I do not frame the tentative hypothesis that his shouts may be intentional. I immediately assume that he is trying to communicate and address myself to understanding what he is trying to convey.

There is no need to deny that we know these basic human characteristics from experience and that we can confirm by experience that they are present in a particular case. But because the presence of these fundamental characteristics is presupposed in our judgments about human beings, we cannot even imagine them being proved false by experience. We do not entertain the idea that tomorrow we might meet a person devoid of purposes or incapable of having preferences. This is why we can treat these categories—Dilthey's "categories of life"—as a contribution toward a philosophic anthropology.

As Dilthey emphatically believed that we must look at man as a willing, feeling, and acting creature and not only as a pure cognitive subject, it is in the spirit of his whole approach to extend our consideration of presuppositions to areas of life beside cognition. The moral life is an obvious candidate because making moral judgments is a universal feature of human existence.

By the universality of morality I do not mean to imply the universality of uniform moral standards. Manifestly, moral codes vary enormously from age to age, from civilization to civilization, and, indeed, from individual to individual. It is arguable that this diversity does not indicate complete moral relativity as some of it, at least, is undoubtedly due to differences in what is believed to be true about the world rather than disagreement on basic principles. A much-quoted example of moral divergence is the fact that members of some communities considered it right to eat their grandparents, whereas this is frowned upon in the United States. It appears, however, that there is no disagreement on the morality of showing love, care, and respect to one's grandmother. The difference lies in the belief of those who eat grandmothers that it serves their interest to be incorporated in their offspring rather than in worms or jackals. There are many less bizarre cases where differences in the interpretation of facts look like moral disagreements. Disagreements on the rightness of the death penalty, for example, may not always hinge on moral considerations but instead on different interpretations of statistics about its deterrent power.

However, it does not really matter for my case whether this is or is not absolute agreement on fundamental principles, once we have made allowances for different factual or religious beliefs and varying circumstances. All I need for my case is that all human beings tend to make moral judgments of one kind or another.

People not only value objects, approve or disapprove of actions or events, find things to their taste or distasteful, but they also make moral judgments that are different from personal preferences because they are intended as authoritative guides to action applying not only to oneself but to everyone else. Failure to comply with them we condemn in ourselves and others.

Moral codes, thus defined, vary considerably. Some may appear to us narrow, bigoted, selfish, or cruel, but they are held recognizably as moral codes distinguishable from merely pragmatic guides to action. Even people we consider depraved—say, convicts serving prison sentences for serious crimes—have their principles. There are things they would consider wrong, things they condemn in others. They may, for example, give a child molester a hard time.

So what have we got as basis for our argument once we have abandoned, as too controversial for this purpose, any claim to the universality of moral principles? If we cannot rely on the content of any moral principle, we cannot hope to argue toward such preconditions of morality as sympathy, sense of fairness, desire for happiness, or anything of the kind. However, the very form of moral law leaves us with substantial grounds for accepting presuppositions required for it.

First and foremost among these is the traditional assumption that man is free. Incontrovertibly, "ought implies can." It is both futile and—on any moral code—unfair to ask a child to work harder at his lessons, or to blame him for not doing so, if he is incapacitated by serious illness. It only makes sense to urge the child to do better, or to blame him if he does not, on the assumption that he can make a decision to this effect and then make an effort to implement it. What freedom means and how it is possible is a notorious problem of philosophy because it appears to conflict with the universal belief that our behavior is conditioned by natural endowment, nurture, and the circumstances around us and can therefore be explained in causal terms, much as any other event. What is more, morality itself presupposes a predictable causal order, for what would be the point of making a moral decision about punishing little Johnny if there were no way of telling how this punishment would affect him.

However, we can specify quite clearly what is actually presupposed in the moral life without going into these wider philosophic issues. We must assume that the outcome of reflections on one's own principles or the moral persuasion of others can affect a person's line of action, irrespective of the forces of heredity and upbringing or the pressure of circumstances.

The fact that people propound moral codes, feel guilty when they break them, engage in moral arguments, attribute—justifiably or not—moral reasons to their political allegiances, exhort their children to be good, blame each other for breaches of moral codes—all these palpable facts testify to our presupposition that man is free in the sense indicated. Otherwise it would all be illusion, hypocrisy, and waste of breath.

My description of the minimal conditions for freedom involved more specific presuppositions. Our instincts must be restrainable and malleable; we must be able to resist impulses of the moment. We must be able to reflect on principles and weigh alternative courses of action, which presupposes mental capacities much like those required in the purely cognitive sphere. Unless, for example, we could entertain ideas of what was not present in front of us, there would be no choices, or at the very least they would be confined within very narrow limits. We must also be capable of foresight and planning.

Similar extrapolations can be made from other spheres of life. Social and political organizations and the activities sustaining them are as universal as morality, though probably even more varied. It reflects the fact that man is a social and political animal, one that tends toward and is indeed dependent on associating with others, cooperating with them, and submitting himself to common restraints.

The fact that education is going on, and more or less elaborate educational systems exist in any human community, presupposes that human beings can and need to be educated and molded, that they are capable of learning and require discipline. There is no need to continue the list of illustrations, which could certainly be extended. Nor is it necessary to document and argue the points I have made. It is enough to survey the kinds of bricks from which a philosophic anthropology can be built up.

We certainly do not need to assume some mysterious process of intuition, a priori reasoning, or philosophic reflection through which we come to know that man is a political animal, that he is capable of abstract thinking, acts on the assumption that he is free, and so forth. We know it and constantly confirm it through experience. We are talking of things that are observable or can easily be extrapolated from what we observe. They become the constituents of a philosophic anthropology when we survey them broadly and critically, sift the universal from what is merely the product of chance and circumstance, and consider how far they constitute the framework for specific research and practical action. As we engage in a particular psychological or sociological investigation or experiment with an educational innovation, we do not expect these to shatter this presuppositional framework and will not lightly accept results that appear to do so. This does not mean that such frameworks are wholly incorrigible, not subject to revision. This would be quite alien to the spirit in which Dilthey conducted philosophy.

Dilthey's chief contribution to a future philosophic anthropology was his persistent concern with the close interrelationship between philosophy and the empirical studies of man. His sketchy theory of categories of life took the project a step further, and his contributions to psychology pinpointed fundamental features of human nature, such as the establishment of acquired structures in mental life, which affect individual mental acts. He also pioneered the use of literature as source material for the understanding of basic human features. A younger generation of German philosophers took the subject further.

THE DEVELOPMENT OF PHILOSOPHIC ANTHROPOLOGY

The most influential thinker who followed Dilthey's lead toward a kind of philosophic anthropology—though he, like Dilthey, did not use the term—was Martin Heidegger. In *Being and Time*,[15] his avowed aim is not philosophic anthropology but an elucidation of "Being." As a rough indication of it, one might identify it with the traditional ontological quest for knowledge of ultimate reality. It is by now well known that he got side-tracked, or to put it more precisely, that he felt that before he could tackle his ultimate objective, a preliminary task needed accomplishing. It is this clearing of the ground that is the outstanding feature of the work and made it so extremely influential.

Man is the being in whom "Being" becomes conscious of itself. Reality shows itself within the human perspective. The preliminary task that Heidegger had to accomplish was an analysis of the human situation, the crucial features of human existence in and through which reality becomes visible. This examination of what it fundamentally means to be human became a source of inspiration for existentialism; its main features have become widely known. Man finds himself in a world and among other human beings. His attitude to this world of people and things becomes one of care in all the three senses in common use. It means looking after things (as in "caretaker"), showing an affectionate interest (as in the complaint that someone "does not care"), and worry (as in "careworn"). He has a sense of having been flung into a situation without rhyme and reason. He sees himself as a maker and doer, perceiving part of the world around him as tools. He is sharply certain of his own finitude, the inevitability of death. This certainty of death fills him with dread but also calls him to a resolute and authentic grasping of his own self, which is in constant danger of slipping into the safety of the impersonal collectivity of the social.

There is no need to continue and expand on this list of basic characteristics of the human situation or the way it illuminates "Being." One thing is clear, though—like Dilthey, Heidegger rejects a purely cognitive subject as the starting point of what might be called, though he does not, a way into a theory of knowledge. The sober, even tragic, coloring of this "anthropology" chimed in well with the temper of the time and became characteristic of existentialism. It is not a necessary feature of a philosophic anthropology and is not prominent in Dilthey.

E. Cassierer, a contemporary of Heidegger usually classed as a neo-Kantian, spoke of "anthropological philosophy" instead of philosophic anthropology and stressed that man's effort toward self-knowledge was a central theme of all philosophy. Like Dilthey, he was concerned with the necessity of coordinating the findings of the different empirical sciences of man, which cannot be accomplished by simple addition. He pinpointed man's capacity for using and developing systems of symbols as his most characteristic feature, which provided a focal point for the different human disciplines.[16]

The name "philosophic anthropology" was actually introduced by Max Scheler, who emphatically stressed its importance and proposed a comprehensive program for this new discipline. In *Man and History* (1926)[17] he wrote:

If there is a philosophic task required by our age, with unique urgency, it is philosophic anthropology. By this I mean a fundamental discipline about man's nature and its structure, about his relation to the realm of nature (the inorganic, plants and animals) and the ground of all things; about his metaphysical origin and his physical, psychological and spiritual beginning in the world; about the forces and powers which move him and which he moves; about the basic tendencies and laws of his biological, psychological, cultural [*geistesgeschichtlich*] and social development; about its essential possibilities and realities. The psychophysical problems about mind and body, the problem about the cognitive and the vital are contained in it. Only such an anthropology can give a final philosophic foundation and, at the same time, determinate and ascertainable goals for research to all the human disciplines, be it the scientific and medical ones or the prehistorical, ethnological, historical and social disciplines, normal and developmental psychology and characterology.

This is quite a mouthful, and we need to look more closely at what this program contains and involves. The beginning and end of the quotation spells out the need for a common framework covering the different human disciplines to which I have already referred. Noteworthy is only the inclusion of scientific and medical disciplines, implying that even the study of human physiology or of human diseases involves a distinctive conception of man. Interesting, too, is the specific mention of prehistory. I suppose here the question is how far we can identify human nature without verbal records.

We have already encountered the need for a philosophic clarification of the twin problems of the body/mind relationship and of the way cognition is or is not dependent on the whole personality of living being. Here, and even more explicitly in the preceding specifications, Scheler moves into metaphysics. If some phrases could be interpreted as merely stipulating epistemological clarifications of crucial concepts and approaches, such phrases as "the ground of all things" (by which he means God), "metaphysical origin," and "essential . . . realities" put his intentions beyond doubt. The project as such is not new. Plato, Aristotle, Spinoza—to give only a few, though outstanding, examples—attempted precisely this: they tried to show what man is and can be in terms of his role and function within reality and his relation to the rest of creation. Evolutionary accounts of man's nature and social life are not new either, but I am not sure what "metaphysical origin" means.

At issue here is the status and value of such an enterprise and not the specifics of Scheler's philosophy. For Dilthey metaphysics, though a natural preoccupation, could never amount to a science, never be the source of objectively demonstrable truths. Most of today's philosophers share this skepticism, but this does not dispose of philosophic anthropology as proposed by Scheler. It is more in line with the intellectual temper of our time to describe speculation as conceptual creation, the exploration of how the universe might be conveniently and usefully described and explained. It is meaningless to ask if such speculation, which boldly reaches out with generalizations beyond what can conceivably be verified, is true or false; instead, we must ask what guidance and inspiration such a theory gives to disciplines that are concerned with verifiable results. I suppose the most spectacularly successful case of speculation that anticipated and guided the subsequent development of scientific theories is the philosophic theory of atomism, which preceded any scientific, testable formulation of atomism by some two thousand years. On the basis of such pragmatic criteria we can accept highly speculative accounts of man as part of a philosophic anthropology.

H. Plessner,[18] who shares with Scheler the distinction of having introduced the concept of philosophic anthropology, also shared with him an interest in the biological aspects of man and the philosophic implications that can be drawn from them. The same interest combined with interest in modern sociology and psychology characterized the work of a whole group of modern thinkers, most of them German, who can be described as philosophic anthropologists.[19] To my mind the main interest of their theories lies not in the details of their interpretations but in their effort to extrapolate a rounded and normative conception of man from different findings of the empirical disciplines concerned with human nature, to guide research by this general image of man, and specifically to encourage and direct interdisciplinary approaches.

THE LIMITS OF PHILOSOPHIC ANTHROPOLOGY

It did not prove too dificult to point to universal features of man that we can presuppose in any consideration of him. Purposiveness, capacity for choice, the use of language and symbols are features of this kind. But can they be knit together into a unified picture of man? We have already seen some of the difficulties that militate against it. First, we cannot accept some of the presuppositions that underpin the different human disciplines as sacred or logically unassailable, though pragmatic criteria take us some of the way toward assent. The theoretical adequacy and practical usefulness of a theory encourages acceptance of the presuppositions on which it rests. But the case is fragile. Astrology, even if logically structured and occasionally predictive, is most probably nonsense. Faith-healing, witchcraft, and acupuncture all seem to achieve cures, even though they do not fit into the presuppositional framework of Western medicine. Different approaches to psychiatry—though at odds on their presuppositions—all explain and alleviate mental disorders.

Undoubtedly the presuppositions on which theories and whole disciplines rest are historical products. Most modern philosophers of science believe that it involves the superimposition of conceptual schemes rather than merely the discovery and recording of how things are. This allows for the scientist's approach being colored by the beliefs and circumstances of his age, his background, his predilections and experience.

This does not mean, of course, that presuppositions are arbitrary. They must fit the evidence that needs explaining and also be reasonably consistent with the bulk of our other presuppositions. The reason, for example, why we tend to feel uneasy about telepathy and related phenomena is not that there is no evidence for it, though needless to say it requires most painstaking checking, but that it does not appear to yield to explanations that fit our paradigms. We have, not unreasonably, a deep-seated preference for intellectual unity.

The fact that presuppositions cannot be fully justified by the theoretical or practical success of the theories they underpin and that they contain an element of arbitrariness[20] makes conflict between them more tolerable. However, as the same human beings are the subject matter of economics and of psychology, we cannot be entirely happy if for the economist they are rational while they are irrational in the eyes of the psychologist. Inevitably we look for and work toward a coherent image of man.

It is, however, not entirely unfortunate that a consistent, let alone a complete, conception of man eludes philosophic anthropology. After all, as conceived by Dilthey and the explicit exponents of this discipline, it is there to serve and interact with the empirical studies of man. But if conceived as complete and definitive, it would close the door on further empirical research, which would be at best, superfluous, at worst, subversive. But no one believes today that we are at the end of all enquiries, that the results of our researches are complete and incorrigible. Any idea of completing once and for all a philosophic anthropology would not only conflict with, and therefore inhibit, future open-minded research but also contradict our recognition that a philosophic anthropology cannot but use, incorporate, and draw lessons from corrigible empirical research.

The same conclusions follow from looking at philosophic anthropology from the point of view of its implications for morality, politics, or education. A definitive conception of man carrying definitive answers for these spheres of life would leave no leeway for creative effort.

It remains important to struggle toward a clear and coherent conception of man, based both on our reflections on experience and on generalizations from it, and designed to guide our study of man as well as our conduct to each other. But it may be as well that we cannot finalize this project. Here Dilthey's tentativeness, his sense of being on the way rather than at his goal, is not a fault.

PSYCHOLOGY

A good many things so far discussed in this book—man's nature, the temporal structure of human life, the way meaning arises, and so on—can be described as subject matters of psychology, and this would have been in Dilthey's spirit as he considered—at one period of his life particularly—psychology the key discipline of the human studies. I have referred explicitly to Dilthey's views on psychology. Here I want to address myself squarely to this topic and take the opportunity of providing a few quotations that illustrate Dilthey's approach.

Well known is Dilthey's attack on the methodology of psychology predominant in his time. He calls it "explanatory psychology," and his description fits much that goes under the name of psychology today. It "establishes a causal nexus which claims to explain all mental phenomena, it tries to explain the constitution of the mental world according to its constituents, forces and laws, in the same way as physics and chemistry explain the physical world".[21] Explanation is seen by him—as it still is by philosophers of science—as subsuming individual cases (analyzed into their elements) under general (causal) laws.

To this he constrasts what he calls "descriptive psychology" and marks its chief difference—which it shares with the other human studies—from the sciences, as follows:

The human studies differ from the sciences because the latter deal with facts which present themselves to consciousness as separate phenomena, while the former deal with the living connections of reality experienced in the mind. It follows that the sciences arrive at connections within nature through inferences by means of a combination of hypotheses while the human sciences are based on directly given mental connections. We explain nature but we understand mental life. [*C.W.* Vol. V, pp. 143–44[22]]

In other words, because in the world of mind the connections are given in experience, description *is* explanation. If I say, "When I heard his remarks I felt a hot flush of anger and I hit him," the description of what I heard and felt is the explanation of what I did.

Closely linked to this descriptive approach is the hermeneutic principle of tackling issues on the level of complexity at which they occur. Thus Dilthey writes, "We must start from the culturally shaped human being" (*C.W.*, Vol. V, p. 157[23]). "Psychology must start with developed mental life, not deduce it from elementary processes" (*C.W.*, Vol. V, pp. 168–69) and "This acquired mental structure [about which more presently] is given to us most directly in a developed human being, particularly in ourselves." He goes on to assert, "We can study the vigorous working of particular forms of mental activity in the works of men of genius" (both quotations *C.W.*, Vol. V, pp. 180–81[24]). In other words, what we encounter in life and what we need to understand are such things as how two people adjust in marriage, how a shrewd politician assesses the situations he has to cope with, how a poet's imagination works, and so forth. Dilthey did not think that we would get very far by starting with reflexes or the behavior of rats in mazes and build up from there to the more complex behavior of human beings. On the contrary, it is better to look for help in understanding such complex but everyday phenomena by studying fully developed human beings rather than babies, good poets rather than bad ones, successful rather than unsuccessful politicians.

To tackle this complex subject matter, psychology needs to combine different approaches ". . . compensating for each other's defects. It combines awareness and observation of ourselves, understanding of other people, comparative procedure, experiment and the study of anomalous phenomena" (*C.W.*, Vol. V, p. 199[25]).

He goes on to distinguish specifically the study of processes, that is, mental events, and that of their products, what he called "the objectifications of mind." The processes we observe (first of all in ourselves or in others, to which we are introduced through historical accounts). The products we learn to interpret. "Language, myth," he says, "religious tradition, custom, law and outer organisations are products of the collective mind in which human consciousness, to use Hegel's phrase, has become objectified and so open to analysis" (*C.W.*, Vol, V, p. 181[26]). He continues in the same passage,

> Dissection of the products of the human mind which is designed to give us insight into the origin, forms and function of the mental structure, must combine the analysis of historical products with the observation and collection of every available part of the *historical process* by which they were produced. The whole historical study of the origin, forms and working of man's mental structure depends on the combination of these two methods. ... In order to study the nature of imagination we must compare the remarks of genuine poets about their inner processes with poetical works.

It must strike the reader—and this is, indeed, the purpose of these quotations—that what is said here specifically about psychology is very much what Dilthey more generally claims for the human studies as a whole. And this is no accident, because on the one hand his psychology is more like hermeneutics than like conventional psychology, and on the other hand it is, in his view, the heart and core of the human studies. "Each of them [the human studies] requires psychological insight. So every factual analysis of religion involves concepts like feeling, will, dependence, freedom, motive, which can only be explained in a psychological context. It must deal with the context of mental life because in it alone the consciousness of God originates and gains strength. But it is conditioned by general, regular, mental connections and can only be understood through them." He goes on to make analogous points about law and politics and concludes ". . . the systems of culture, commerce, law, religion, art and scholarship and the outer organisation of society in family, community, church and state originate from the living context of the human mind and, ultimately, can only be understood through it. Mental facts form their most important constituents so they cannot be grasped without psychological analysis" (*C.W.*, Vol. V, pp. 147–48[27]).

The crucial role of psychology even extends to the theory of knowledge. "Positively at issue," he writes, "is the progress from self-awareness to hermeneutics on to knowledge of nature. However, all these relations have for their most general basis the relation of life to knowledge, of inner experience to thought. ... We must therefore submit the whole of inner reality to an explicit description of inner states" (*C.W.*, Vol. VIII, pp. 178–79). In other words, the processes by which we can gain knowledge are rooted in our mental life as a whole and can be illuminated by psychological analysis. More specifically, our whole cognitive apparatus and the categories we use are conditioned by mental life so that epistemology is rooted in and merges with psychology. Thus he can write,

The material [*inhaltlichen*] categories: whole, substance, causality, essence, the real connections given in them, which find expression in classification [*Urteilsform von Zusammengehörigkeit*], in aesthetic grasp of the whole, and the practical one of value, can only derive from the context which as mental structure provides the unavoidable conditions under which a coherent reality [*Realzusammenhang*] ... is there for us. [*C.W.*, Vol. VIII, p. 186]

The two points I have stressed so far, namely that Dilthey advocated a descriptive, hermeneutic, or "understanding" approach to psychology and that he thought of psychology as a key discipline of the human studies, are obviously linked. A historian who asked for the help of psychology in understanding, let us say, Hitler's appeal to the German people would get little benefit from experimental or animal psychology. What is relevant is a tangle of hopes, fears, and resentments tied in with the meaning Germany's situation had for its citizens, and not anything accountable for in terms of conditioned reflexes. Analogous points, which scarcely need elaborating, can be made about the kind of psychology of use to literary critics or students of politics. Dilthey writes, for example:[28]

Shall we ever find the means of describing scientifically the impact which the imagination of an epoch receives through a work of art? Literary history has not even seen the problem clearly; its solution lies in the future of psychology which today is still far from insight into the laws of imagination.

There is little doubt that different disciplines can profit from cooperation with psychology. Much has been done on these lines since Dilthey's proposal of it. It is equally clear that only certain kinds of psychology will prove serviceable in this role. This does not mean denying the legitimacy and usefulness of other forms of psychology, and Dilthey would not have dreamed of doing so.

It clearly follows that a psychology that can serve other disciplines must, in turn, be dependent on them. Unless we can envisage man, from the outset, as a historical, social, or economic being, a creature capable of using language and creating art, the study of him could not really illuminate the different spheres in which he is active. "What can be considered certain in psychology," Dilthey writes, "is insufficient for an explanation of the deepest manifestations of the human mind. We must rather expect the founding of the 'content' psychology which alone can serve history, from a combination of psychological description and analysis with the dissection of historical facts" (*C.W.*, Vol. VIII, p. 15). The fact that man is a biological creature, an animal with desires, needs, and inherent capabilities, is not irrelevant, but it is not sufficient to account for poetry or political organizations. So historical, social, and other dimensions have to be introduced if we are to understand how human beings actually "tick."

The Authoritarian Personality (Adorno et al.)[29] is a famous example of these relationships. It is essentially a massive psychological study based on questionnaires and interviews, of the psychological factors that dispose people to be authoritarian, both in personal life and in politics. It was designed to throw light on the rise of Hitler and was later used for the screening of suspected Nazis.[30] In a subsequent volume of comments on this work some of its limitations were attributed to the inadequate political analysis on which the concept of authoritarianism was based.[31] Basically, the authors of *The Authoritarian Personality* thought primarily of right-wing authoritarians, but, in fact, there are authoritarians on the left and their personality structure appears to be similar.

Apart from advocating a special kind of psychology and stressing its interdisciplinary role, Dilthey also made points of substance about the human mind. I can be brief because some relevant points have cropped up elsewhere in this book. Furthermore, Dilthey's points are fairly general and not based on systematic empirical study. Today some of these ideas figure in psychological theories in which they are elaborated and applied.

Dilthey's central concern was the unity of the mind. He never tires of insisting that it functions as a whole and provides a context in which individual mental acts take their place. It must be studied as a structure. "Here ['in the structure of fully developed mental life'] analysis must deal with the architectonic structuring of the complete edifice; it does not inquire about the stones, the mortar and the labour first but about the inner connection of the parts. It must discover the structural law which links intelligence, instinctive and emotional life and acts of will into the whole of mental life" (*C.W.*, Vol. VIII, p. 176[32]). He goes on to emphasize, "The decisive fact for the study of mental structure is that the *transitions from one state to another, the effect of one on another are part of inner experience. We experience this structure*" (*C.W.*, Vol. VIII, p. 206[33]). In the same passage he adds, "who has not experienced how images thrusting themselves on the imagination suddenly arouse strong desire which confronted with great difficulties, urge us towards an act of will," and concludes, "The process of mental life in all its forms, from the lowest to the highest, is from the beginning a unified whole. Mental life does not arise from parts growing together; it is not compounded of elementary units; it does not result from interacting particles of sensation or feeling; it is always an encompassing unity. Mental functions have been differentiated in it but they remain tied to their context. This has reached its highest form of development in the unity of consciousness and the unity of the person and completely distinguishes mental life from the whole physical world."

Three points that clarify and expand the general thesis of structure remain: First, some of the structure—that is, the way different aspects of mental life, such as thinking, feeling, and willing, are related to each other—is innate and cannot be further explained. It just happens that human nature is like that. "There is no compelling reason why ideas should give rise to feelings: one can imagine a creature which only has ideas and which, in the tumult of battle, remains the indifferent, passive spectator of its own destruction. Nor do feelings necessarily give rise to acts of will" (C.W., Vol. V, p. 208[34]). Having thus invented Mr. Spock,[35] he insists that the relation between these mental factors is *sui generis*. People vary in what they fear or want and how they react to such feelings. But though their motives and actions can be causally explained, the basic relationships within mental life cannot be further accounted for. They represent aspects of a common human nature.

Second, in Dilthey's own words, "the inner mental structure is conditioned by the person's situation within an environment. The person interacts with the external world; the form this takes can be represented as an adjustment between the person and the conditions of his life. ... In this adjustment chains of sensations and motor-activities are linked to each other" (C.W., Vol. V, p. 208).

The third point is that as a result of this interaction between the environment, the cultural atmosphere that envelops the person, and the historical factors working on him, an acquired structure is superimposed on the original structural relations of the mind. It is that total, partly acquired structure that affects all of a person's thinking and doing. "The whole acquired structure of mental life acts in these processes of formation" (C.W., Vol. VI, p. 143).

Today none of this will strike the reader as wildly revolutionary and new. One must remember, though, that at the time these things were written, they helped us to direct the relatively young science of psychology into fruitful channels. Even now there are schools of psychology that can profit from the kind of corrective Dilthey's line of thought provides.

5

The Epistemological Basis
of Psychiatry

To test the continued relevance of Dilthey's philosophy, I shall consider what bearing it has on the presuppositional framework of psychiatry. As a branch of the human studies in which the emphasis clearly lies on practical application, it is of undoubted importance today. One needs hardly argue that our modern world contains many people who suffer from mental disorders, depression, phobias, persistent anxiety, and similar mental states, which interfere with their work, enjoyment, and human relationships. The number of people actually under psychiatric treatment or being counseled for marital difficulties, suicide statistics, and court evidence of emotionally conditioned crimes provides ample evidence. In addition, many people who seek medical advice have mental rather than physical problems.

How successful is psychiatry in coping with these problems? Certainly it has not eliminated forms of mental disorder in the way in which medicine has virtually eliminated formerly deadly diseases, but then, even medicine has not done very well with others such as the common cold. The difficulty of answering this question about success highlights general problems psychiatry has to face. It is sometimes unclear or even controversial what counts as mental illness and what can be considered success in treatment. We certainly hear stories of people having been wrongfully confined in institutions, just as we hear of cases of patients being released as fit for life in the outside world and having relapses with dangerous consequences. This is not intended as an outsider's snide sneer. Thoughtful psychiatrists themselves worry about such problems in this intrinsically difficult sphere. Have they classified a case correctly, or indeed, is the classification available to them adequate? Does the disorder they confront have physical or psychological roots? Does the problem lie outside the patient, in his family situation or in society at large? Conscientious therapists are bound to ask questions such as these.

The continued existence of rival theories and conflicting schools of psychiatry adds to the uncertainty. Methods remain controversial, and concepts are contested. This is where the need for philosophic reflection arises. Not that the philosopher can come and wave a magic wand and thereby dissolve all the psychiatrist's problems. As is the case with problems in other spheres, those of psychiatry have to be tackled—and are being tackled—by the common sense and intellectual penetration of experts with the appropriate experience. But philosophy can help in the review. Its expertise in developing, analyzing, and systematizing ideas would be a futile accomplishment if it could not be put to the service of solving problems outside its own specialist sphere.

DILTHEY AND JASPERS

Dilthey was interested in psychiatry because he appreciated the relevance of its findings to psychology and anthropology, but in none of his writings did he address himself explicitly to the philosophic basis of psychiatry. There is, however, an indirect way of showing how his ideas can serve as such a basis. This is by looking at a philosopher who explicitly mapped out a philosophic framework of psychotherapy and in doing so reproduced many of the salient features of Dilthey's philosophy.

Karl Jaspers (1883–1969) was predominantly a philosopher, known particularly as one of the founders of existentialism, but he had originally studied medicine and worked as a psychiatric assistant. His first major work was *General Psychopathology*,[1] which appeared in 1913. It was intended, and indeed successfully served, as a textbook of psychiatry. As such it is undoubtedly now out of date, as Jaspers acknowledged in the new preface to the book of 1959. But it also contains extensive reflections on such philosophic issues as the relation between body and mind, the historicity of consciousness, and the epistemological accessibility of consciousness. Coming under the last heading there are, specifically, discussions of understanding, meaning, and expressions that provide philosophic backing for his methodological views. These discussions are not very systematic and painstaking and, in consequence, are sometimes a little obscure. However, they very largely follow Dilthey's ideas on these matters. So while providing a bridge between Dilthey's philosophy and psychiatry, they can themselves be illuminated by relating them to Dilthey's more sustained discussions.

That Jaspers' view on understanding, expressions, and related subjects are virtually identical to those of Dilthey can be proved to the hilt by simply placing quotations of the two philosophers side by side. Had Jaspers taken them directly from Dilthey's writings? Had he heard about them from a third source? Had they both drawn the same conclusions from shared older sources? It is difficult to answer such questions and fortunately is not required for the present purpose.

Jaspers knew some of Dilthey's work. His *Psychology of World Views,*[2] for example, is undoubtedly indebted to Dilthey's *Typology of World Views.* In his single reference to Dilthey in the *General Psychopathology,* Jaspers acknowledges the link between his own ideas and those formulated in Dilthey's essay, *Ideas towards Descriptive and Explanatory Psychology,* which was published when Jaspers was a child. In a rather curious formulation he writes, "My ideas were then carried further by Dilthey." However, *C.W.,* Volume VII, which contained Dilthey's most sustained discussions of understanding, had not appeared in print when Jaspers wrote his *General Psychopathology.*

PHILOSOPHIC PROBLEMS OF PSYCHIATRY

Before I take up the salient points of Jaspers' exposition and link them to Dilthey's views, I want to review briefly some of the crucial philosophic questions raised by psychiatry. As the subject matter is mental problems and disorders, the access to mental states is clearly at issue, whatever view we take of the ultimate status of mind or the factors producing mental illness. This question of access arises at different stages and on different levels, because it alone puts the psychiatrist in possession of his subject matter. Theoretically, the possibility of gaining evidence of mental states is a necessary condition for conceptualizing mental illness. On the practical side, access is involved in diagnosis and treatment.

Even in the case of physical disease, diagnosis is usually based on, or at least greatly aided by, listening to the patient and attending to such expressive behavior as cries of pain or clenched teeth. However, such information is normally combined with physical examinations—X-rays, chemical tests, and the like—which can take the place of communication altogether if necessary, for example if the patient is unconscious. In the case of mental disorders, there is no substitute for communicating with the patient. There is nothing to observe except expressions.

Communication, above all linguistic communication, is important for almost every aspect of human life. Here its importance is demonstrated in the psychiatrist's need to understand his patients. If understanding people by interpreting expressions were significantly less reliable, less subject to objective criteria, then knowing the physical world by observation, experiment, and reflection on their findings, the treatment of the mentally ill would rest on extremely shaky foundations.

It cannot be said often enough that no methodology and no epistemology can guarantee freedom from error. Historians, psychologists, and psychiatrists, like the rest of us, make mistakes. Physicists, astronomers, and mathematicians have no immunity either. Indeed, the history of science plainly shows that theories believed to be true by the best scholars of an age were later abandoned. Today it is widely accepted that all scientific theories are corrigible and have to be treated as provisional.[3]

However, research and scholarship, indeed any investigation, would be pointless unless we retained the idea that there was a truth toward which we can approach. Some theories are better than others, some interpretations more plausible, more acceptable than others. What would otherwise be the point of the scientist's labor, of the historian's painstaking work, or of the psychiatrist's probing? Epistemology, and following from it basic methodology, is concerned with the grounds on which we can claim knowledge. Of course, methodology is not an engine that produced knowledge nor even a gauge for deciding on the ultimate truth of conclusions. But it does provide criteria by which to judge the soundness of our procedures. In other words, it tells us that unless we proceed in certain ways, we have no justification for our claims to truth. It provides us with pointers as to where and how to look and what we neglect at our peril.

Psychiatry is an area in which the reliability of communication can be literally a matter of life and death. In history or art criticism, we might allow ourselves—as some recent exponents of hermeneutics tend to do—a free-floating perspectivism, a skeptical cultural relativism. But not here. Surely Dilthey was right, and not merely hung up on an outdated positivism he had imbibed in his youth, when he persisted in his search for criteria for the soundness of understanding.

The requirements of psychiatry bring a number of themes we have already encountered into sharp focus and highlight particular aspects of the problems. There is, to start with, the ideographic approach. Hermeneutics, we saw, is essentially concerned with individual entities: a particular text, a specific pattern of expressions. But when we treat hermeneutics as a key discipline of the human studies, the edges of this approach are inevitably blurred. However much the individual matters and continues to hold the center of the stage, we are also looking and hoping for generalizations to help us; where generalizations are elusive or tend to be too vague or trivial, we at least hope to arrive at typologies as an aid to organizing our material and arriving at explanations. Of course, psychiatry hopes for help from valid generalizations and uses typologies. A great deal of effort is put into classifying mental disturbances. Yet what obviously matters is the individual patient. The psychiatrist confronts human beings who need to be understood and helped. All theory is just an aid to this, something to be applied in the service of one person's problems.

We are also reminded that a particular aspect of understanding is un-ambiguously at issue. We noted earlier that understanding is directed toward three interrelated goals: the literal meaning of an expression, its reference, and the author. Circumstances and our interest determine which of these is treated as focal. If, let us say, we want to appreciate Othello, we need to grasp the language, take in what we are told about jealousy, and gain a glimpse of Shakespeare's outlook and intentions. We need all three but may be particularly interested in one or the other and orientate our attention and intellectual efforts accordingly.

In psychiatry we have the limiting case in which one of these goals of understanding is at the center of attention. So the philosophic exploration of how understanding operates and what it can achieve, the evaluation of different forms of expressions, and the assessment of the resources of hermeneutics must all clearly subserve the aim of understanding a person through his expressions.

Before going into any details, it is worth emphasizing a crucial point: In this sphere it becomes of utmost importance to relate a person's different expressions to each other. The point is best illustrated negatively by the absence of this necessity in other spheres. I want to learn about geology and read a book about it. There is nothing about the author I need to know except his competence as a geologist. The fact that I do not hear his voice or see his gestures is no loss. I need not and probably do not know about his other activities. For all I care, he may be a champion sprinter or be in prison for having murdered his wife. All I need is the text and, perhaps, other texts to supplement it. As I read I may, incidentally, get glimpses of the author's personality, his or her enthusiasm, sense of humor, pedantry, or whatever. This may be pleasant or irritating but is essentially irrelevant. If instead of reading a book I attend a lecture, I will be exposed to expressions superimposed on the purely linguistic communication. Gestures, facial expressions, the raising or lowering of the voice may augment and clarify what is said. It may drive home what is important and what is marginal, what is meant seriously or is merely a joke. On the other hand, the lecturer's mannerisms and fidgets may irritate and distract. (Whether it is the one or the other is, at least partly, a matter of the speaker's skill and self-control).

In psychiatry, by contrast, the very things the student of geology wants to discard, can do without, or at most finds of minor help become crucial. As the person is the focus of interest, all expressions need to be evaluated in terms of what they tell us about the author rather than about any object referred to. So the most diverse expressions—books on geology, nervous habits, hobbies, and the like—are linked together by their common authorship. We have a natural and obvious context into which they fit.

With this point in view we can now look more closely at Dilthey's classification of expressions and his suggestions about the respective advantages and limitations of each. How revealing and reliable particular types of expressions turn out to be becomes more than a matter of philosophic curiosity. They assume the utmost practical importance for psychiatrists.

Dilthey's first class of expressions was linguistic communication, and clearly a lot of talking goes on in the psychiatrist's consulting room. At the outset the patient, or perhaps his relatives, have to explain what is troubling or worrying him. Though various kinds of physical tests may follow, in many cases the verbal communication provides the main initial evidence. The therapy may also consist primarily of the patient talking to the therapist and the therapist responding, encouraging, and explaining. It is widely understood that giving people the opportunity to talk about their lives and problems is itself therapeutic. After all, most of us gain satisfaction and relief from talking about ourselves and our worries to friends, wives, or sweethearts. No doubt one of the services psychiatrists provide is listening to the lonely or to those who have exhausted the patience of their relatives. The value of this service is increased by the professional listener not being emotionally involved and trained not to obtrude his own problems and need for self-expression into the therapeutic situation. But this can, obviously, not be the whole, or even the main, function of psychiatrists. Otherwise any benevolent-looking and patient person could do the job. In fact, the patient's urge to express himself is put to the use of providing the material for understanding and treating him.

It then becomes important to be aware of the numerous pitfalls encountered in verbal communication. The function of hermeneutics is to alert us to the presence of such pitfalls and help us to avoid them. We must believe that understanding is possible, and psychiatry rests on that belief. But we must also remember that it can be difficult. If we take success for granted, it may easily elude us.

Misunderstandings occur on the purely linguistic level—that is, in the use of vocabulary and idioms, even though people speak the same language. A difference of national background can be one reason an Austrian-born psychoanalyst may miss the implications of English idioms, an Israeli doctor who has learned Hebrew as a second language may misunderstand a patient who grew up in the language. An American with an Italian background may talk past one of Irish descent.

Even more important because, probably, more frequent and less obvious are the potential misunderstandings due to differences in linguistic usage of different generations and social classes. I gather that the young use the word "love" with less discrimination than did my generation. I am still not absolutely clear what my young friends mean when they say that they "freaked out." The use of circumlocutions and preferences for under- or overstatements differentiate speakers of different social classes and complicate communication.

In addition to misunderstanding due to differing backgrounds and ignorance of idioms or conventions, there are other reasons for failures in communication. For one thing, people may lie. To do so to your psychiatrist may seem silly, however useful it may have proved in some social situations. Yet people lie even in this situation, because they are ashamed, embarrassed, or afraid. They may present a fancied image of themselves, suppress or hide something they do not want to face. Behind the misrepresentation may lie anything from failure in self-analysis to downright self-deception, from defective linguistic skill to skilful evasion.

To penetrate such defences is, obviously, part of the psychiatrist's stock in trade. The philosopher's job is not to teach others how to do their job but only to reflect on, and provide a systematic framework for, successful practice. Such a framework also places it into a wider context in which psychiatry can profit from the experience of other disciplines. Hermeneutics provides such a framework. It was not designed for, and has not been applied until recently to, the diagnosis and treatment of the mentally disturbed; indeed, its application to talk, instead of texts, is relatively new. However it has dealt traditionally with the kind of difficulties of communication also encountered in psychiatry.

The texts that historians, theologians, philologists, or literary critics try to interpret are, frequently, not in the scholars' mother tongue and were produced in a different age. So the interpreter has to recapture unfamiliar assumptions and ways of thinking the authors took for granted. He has to guard against "lies" too because the eyewitnesses of history may have been biased, the historians propagandists of one side in a war or dispute. Nor are chroniclers free from self-deception and wishful thinking. Letter writers are sometimes confused, ignorant, or hypocritical.

Hermeneutics is about being prepared for such problems. It has systematized the precautions taken by good sense. Texts have to be read against the background of the life in the midst of which they were written. Not dictionaries by themselves but only a knowledge of contemporary literature can give us an accurate sense of what the words of the text mean. Only by learning about the author, his personality, allegiances, financial position, and the like can we assess his reliability.

Dealing with a person is, of course, different from evaluating a text but the principles of gaining understanding, the methodology of interpretation, is much the same. However, the contexts needed and available are somewhat different when a living person, in front of you, both provides the information and is the goal of inquiry. It is here that the importance of relating the different expressions of one person to each other becomes evident. Hermeneutic issues have here a direct bearing on the psychological understanding of the patient. Indeed, it would be a mistake to think that we can sharply distinguish a preliminary stage of hermeneutic clarification from the proper psychological study of the material thus provided. The distortion and disguises, as well as the relationships between different forms of expressions, are an integral part of the problems the psychiatrist has to deal with.

To supplement and correct the verbal messages he receives, the psychiatrist takes account of the blushes and fidgets, the pauses and facial expressions that accompany them. They have a meaning that can be interpreted just like the mistakes, slips of the tongue, or physical fumbles that Freud explored. In everyday life, as in psychiatric sessions, verbal and nonverbal communications closely intertwine. The words we hear are emphasized, modified, sometimes even contradicted by their intonation, the smiles or frowns that accompany them, the body language of leaning forward or cringing, of raising a hand or swinging a leg. What sounds like an insult is recognized as a joke because a smile accompanies it. A girl may say "no" but be understood as meaning "yes" from the way she says it, or the way she acts as she says it. A man may deny being worried but give every sign of worry.

In situations in which we are not concerned to understand a person but seek information or wait to be given instructions, these meanings superimposed on language can just be a nuisance. In psychiatry they are a lifeline.

Having stressed the importance of attending to these different dimensions of communication as a corrective to verbal misunderstanding, untruth, and self-deception, I want to add the more general point that no single expression, nor any one type of expression, can, in principle, adequately represent or reveal the personality of the author. Though obvious, this needs emphasizing as a prelude to spelling out the one-sidedness of different types of expressions.

The fact that various types of expressions are subject to conventions limits their power to reveal mental contents. Some phrases are so obviously conventional that we have virtually forgotten that they have a literal meaning. People greeting us with a "How are you?" do not expect to hear about your health. Strangers responding to an introduction with a "glad to meet you" feel no joy. The people I address as "Dear Sir" are not really dear to me. Other cases are not quite as obvious. I have exchanged good-night kisses with girls I had first met that evening at a social gathering. A few years ago I would have taken it as an encouraging sign of affection. A person from another country might think so now. I know, however, that social kissing has become quite common in the circles I move in. Similarly, a person eating slowly and moderately at a dinner party cannot be assumed to lack appetite, or be free of gluttony. He may simply have been brought up to behave that way in public. Individuals, and indeed members of particular civilizations, appear to be less emotional than other individuals, or members of a different civilization, and this may be due to a person's upbringing or to the conventions of a culture that discourages emotional display. In some cases such conditioning by conventions may itself be a significant aspect of a person's make-up and problems. In other cases it may be just a thin veneer.

In psychiatry, as in everyday life and, with some modifications, in historical research or literary criticisms, we try—in order not to be misled—to be aware of the conventions that govern a particular expression. Only thus can we learn if a greeting is a standard response or an expression of affection, if the poet of a different age is as passionate and as eternally committed as he sounds, if a person's composure is rooted in a well-balanced personality or merely a pose required from members of his class. Though some of this is merely common sense, it points to the need for interdisciplinary cooperation. To understand a person, it is not enough for the psychologist or psychiatrist to examine him and his life history. He or she needs to know—from history or sociology—about the social forces that have shaped the patient and the social situations to which he or she is responding. The literary critic needs to look beyond the poem being interpreted, beyond its purely literary contexts, to the social and intellectual background that historians can provide.

The second line of defence against being misled by the conventionality of an expression is to relate it to other expressions. Even if these other expressions are themselves governed by conventions, they may convey a divergent message, for only a very skilled social actor can produce a complete unity of conventional expressions. Such divergences ring storm bells for the psychiatrist. If my friendliness comes from the heart, if my greeting is genuinely felt, my friendly smile will match my friendly words. But conventions do not command as much. The friendly word may be socially obligatory, but my smile may be half-hearted without breaking with the convention.

Even more helpful toward genuine understanding are expressions that are not, or only marginally, governed by conventions. Blinks and blushes cannot be conventional because we cannot control them at all. Laughing and crying can be conventional, but more often than not they are beyond our control. Absent-minded movements with hands or feet may or may not be controllable, but we usually do not even think of doing so. In this lies the diagnostic advantage of face-to-face encounters, but even a text might contain stylistic and grammatical quirks that are neither conventional nor consciously controlled.

Expressions are not only governed by conventions, they also tend, in many cases, to be colored by the situations in which they occur and to which they respond. This is particularly the case with actions, and their advantages and limitations as sources of information need to be considered. We have seen, when I discussed Dilthey's classification of expressions, that actions give particularly reliable information of a person's intentions. If I travel a long distance to see a girl or spend many hours helping with her with her work, I may or may not do so to convey to her that I care. My main intention is probably to see her or to help her, but it may convey to her my concern more reliably than a letter or a speech. However, when we ask how much about a person's inner life we can tell from an action and how far we can rely on it, we come up against the fact that such actions are extensively colored by circumstances. I do not take my girlfriend to expensive restaurants, the rare presents I give her are cheap. Does it mean that I do not care for her, or that I am by nature mean? Neither may follow if I am extremely poor. Coming into some money, I may show myself incredibly generous.

It is not only actions that are determined by circumstances as much as by the actor's personality and mental attitudes. Dilthey noted, when considering methodological problems confronting the biographer, that letters written by a person at the same time and referring to the same matter may be very different according to the correspondent to whom they are addressed. In other words, I may write factually, humorously, or romantically according to my assessment of the person to whom the letter is directed, and of the relationship between us. Only by collating different kinds of evidence could a biographer establish to what extent I am actually down-to-earth, humorous, or romantic.

Similar qualifications apply to gestures and facial expressions. I may put on a poker face because I am playing poker, I may be unusually restrained in my movements when among strangers. I will repress my natural jollity among mourners. I shall try to be unusually dignified and business-like at an interview or a business conference. This appears obvious enough, but there is sometimes insufficient methodological awareness of how the interviewing situation and the personality of the interviewer, and similarly, the trappings of therapy and the therapist's personality, limit or distort the interviewee's or the patient's responses.

Expressions, furthermore, give one-sided information about their author because they are mainly directed toward something other than self-revelation. Any interpretation of them must take account of this. We have seen this already in the case of actions that normally serve a purpose that has nothing to do with communicating anything. But the point applies more generally. A lot of language is simply used to convey information. A book on car maintenance will inform us about cars but may tell us little about its author. We cannot even be sure that he is interested in car engines, as he may have undertaken the job for many reasons: to oblige a friend, to earn money, and so on. The same applies to gestures. We may readily understand that a man is waving down my car. He may do so for many reasons, but by itself it tells me little about him.

Understanding a person means putting together the relevant aspects of his different expressions into a kind of jigsaw puzzle. As we consider how this putting-together is done, I must correct an impression that focusing on individual expressions may have given. We have noted that many expressions—I suppose one could say most—are governed by conventions ranging from the rules of grammar to social conventions and cultural habits. They are also codetermined by the different physical, social, and cultural contexts in which they occur. I argued that this limits and qualifies the insights they afford into their authors' personalities. This is one reason—though a negative one—to give them careful consideration, if only to discard as unrevealing what is purely conventional or determined from outside.

However, knowledge of the conventions governing a conventional expression and of the circumstances in which they occurred is required for positive understanding as well as for avoiding misunderstanding. It is needed if we are to draw conclusions from deviations from the norms and uncharacteristic responses to circumstances. If a man swears who does not do so habitually or swears in circumstances in which he would no normally do so (say, during a church service), it is likely to be significant.

Such knowledge of conventions, circumstances, and the like is not only a necessary condition for understanding, it also colors and enriches the meaning the communication has for us. If, for example, someone says "I am in love," we understand this not only in terms of feelings we guess at or behavior we observe, but in terms of the way the phrase is used by other people, by the meaning that poets and playwrights have given to the phrase. How much of the echoes of what we have read and heard we can attribute to the speaker is, then, a matter for investigation.

This public sphere, consisting of language, conventions, cultural habits, and the like, which we have already encountered as constituting for Dilthey the sphere of objective mind, not only determines the range and richness of the meaning of expressions but also shapes the attitudes expressed in them. The sphere of *Geist* is a constitutive factor of human personality.

The fact that personality is shaped by and therefore needs to be understood in terms of social and cultural factors is not new. Plato discusses it in *The Republic* when he explains how potential philosophers are corrupted by having their values distorted by the values of a corrupt society. He also produced a typology of personalities, which are the products of different cultural values, reflect them, and support the political systems based on these cultural values. The links between social and cultural setups and personality structure have become familiar topics of modern anthropology, social psychology, personality study, and, last but not least, psychiatry. Dilthey approached this issue in terms of a theory of objective mind created by individuals, and, in turn, affecting and molding them, a theory also found—as we shall see—in Jaspers.

Put concretely, in terms of my example, a person has learned from his cultural background what it means to fall in love, how valuable an experience it is, what its dangers are, and how one should properly respond to it. For example, in some circles it not only justifies sex but may be the only justification for it. Such attitudes form part of personality and may, indeed, be part of the problems the psychiatrist confronts. So the psychiatrist needs to know what books his patient reads, what religion he practices, and what social class he belongs to.

Finally, in this general sounding of what is involved in psychiatry, we have to consider what precisely is to be revealed by a diagnosis. Expressions, we have said, convey mental contents that are then identified and seen more clearly when we put them against their cultural and intellectual background. But we need more than such data as "he was angry on Tuesday afternoon," "he likes motor cars," "he remembers being happy as a child," and so on. They must be fitted together into some order or pattern, and in one sense this is done by the psychiatrist when he entertains hypotheses and constructs theories about the connections between these different mental contents the way other scholars, scientists, and medical practitioners theorize about their data. As such theories are not meant to be pure constructions but to reflect what actually goes on, the researcher must, when constructing them, have a model of the kind of thing he supposes to occur in his patient's mind. He must have an idea what sort of theory would be appropriate, though the specific theory needs to arise from and be tested against specific facts.

In the case of the human studies, our pictures or models of the subject matter, which precede and guide research, have one distinctive feature. They are familiar. Long before we became psychologists or psychiatrists, we became acquainted through our own awareness and experience with what human life is like. We know that we do not experience the states of mind articulated in individual expressions in isolation, but as part of patterns that make our lives coherent and meaningful.

We might briefly remind ourselves that meaning arises from individual experiences becoming linked together as parts of larger wholes. Some are connected thematically because they relate to the same object or to the same kind of activity. Others are part of a continuous and cumulative sequence. Others again directly impinge upon each other. A typical connection within mental life is that between recognizing a situation, responding to it emotionally, and being motivated to action. All this and much more is familiar. It is part of what we know human nature to be like. However, it is not something laboriously learned and tested on case after case, but something we assume to be present in the human beings we encounter and helping us to make sense of the specific things they do or signal.

The points I have made here about expressions, the world of mind, and the way meaning arises in human life and transforms it into a pattern have been examined more fully in other parts of the book (the last point, for example, in the chapter on history). Here I have rearranged them and pointed my exposition toward specific aspects that the context of psychiatry makes particularly relevant. My selection was also governed by the need to introduce the Jaspers quotations I want to examine. It is striking that, taken from a textbook on psychopathology, they bear such striking resemblance to ideas formulated by Dilthey in quite different contexts.

JASPERS' APPROACH

Let me start with a passage that introduces expressions and incidentally contains in its list something like Dilthey's classification:[4]

Psychic life ... becomes an object to us through that which make it perceptible in the world, the accompanying somatic phenomena, meaningful gestures, behaviour and actions. It is further manifested through communication in the form of speech.

Earlier on, he had made an additional point that goes somewhat beyond Dilthey:[5]

We perceive in form and movement a direct manifestation of psychic events or psychic moods ... we are making use of a symbolism which is universal, we are seeing quite directly ... everyone's person and movements of adaptation as ... carriers of mood and significance.

Part of this is plain enough and tallies with Dilthey's views. Such expressions as smiling or shrinking back are usually spontaneous and universally recognized without difficulty. The point of divergence from Dilthey lies in the stress on "directness" of understanding. Whereas Dilthey assumed that a simple, instantaneous argument from analogy lay at the basis of such recognition ("that's how I feel when *I* smile"), Jaspers thought that we had a natural capacity for recognizing expressive movements. M. Scheler took the same view and argued it more extensively. Whether the one or the other view is right does not really affect the main lines of either Dilthey's or Jaspers' arguments.

Jaspers' additional claim that mental states tend to find expression seems right, noncontroversial, and important. It is doubtful, though, that this applies to "*every* inner activity."[6]

Every inner activity is accompanied by a movement which is an understandable symbol for it.

He goes on to suggest that "Natural direct expression gets moulded by a more conscious expression" (p. 271). I take this to mean that we first smile naturally and can then learn to smile deliberately to convey pleasure, or whatever.

Jaspers explains expressions more fully in the following passage:[7]

Expressive phenomena are always *objective,* insofar as they can be perceived by the senses. ... On the other hand, they are always *subjective* since actual perception of them does not make them expressive. This comes only when there has been understanding of their meaning and importance.

I do not think the terminology is particularly happy, but the meaning is clear enough: there is something we can observe, but it only becomes a sign when it is recognized as expressing a subjective content. The suggestion at the end, that it only becomes expressive when we understand its "meaning and importance," seems plainly wrong though. When someone speaks to me in French, I recognize it as an expression without understanding its meaning, let alone its importance. I suspect that in this, as in other cases, Jaspers expresses himself carelessly. However, this is not our concern here. It is enough to illustrate the general thrust of his argument and to show that he tries—in passages scattered throughout this book—to lay the kind of foundations for psychiatry we are talking about.

Here, next, is Jaspers formulation of the point that we have direct insight into the dynamic relations within our mental lives:[8]

. . . in psychology our bent for knowledge is satisfied with the comprehension of quite a different sort of connection. Psychic events "emerge" out of each other in a way which we understand. Attacked people become angry. . . . It [the connection between mental states] strikes us as something self-evident which cannot be broken down any further. The psychology of meaningful phenomena is built up entirely on this sort of convincing experience of impersonal, independent and understandable connections. . . . It carries its own power of conviction and it is the precondition of the psychology of meaningful phenomena that we accept this kind of evidence just as the acceptance of the reality of perception and of causality is the precondition of the natural sciences.

This represents Dilthey's point that, unlike connections in the physical world, links between mental events are themselves experienced. We can watch the movement of iron filings exposed to a magnet, but what moves them is a matter of theoretical construction. What it is like to respond angrily to an attack we know directly from our own experience; even imagining the situation would give us the required insight. So when I see a man responding to an attack, I can know why he reacts as he does, what feelings prompt his actions. It appears "self-evident," because when we are told that a man hit out because he was angry, we do not look for a further explanation. It would be absurd to ask, "but why should he hit out when he is angry?" The situation cannot be usefully broken down further, because examining, let us say, the successive movements of the arm, or the operation of the nerves and muscles, would add nothing to our insight into the angry response—on the contrary, we would lose sight of it. Jaspers describes the connection as impersonal because it is not someone's individual quirk to become angry when attacked—it is how anyone would react—and as "understandable" because the connection is transparent to us. The reason, finally, why Jaspers calls it "independent" is, I think, that our understanding of how something makes us angry does not depend on particular psychological theories.

Jaspers expands on the notion of understanding and consolidates some of the points just discussed in the following passage:[9]

> In depicting connections that can be understood genetically we always find: (i) we have presupposed a *mental content* which is not a psychological matter and which can be understood without the help of psychology; (ii) we have perceived an *expression* which brings an inward meaning to light; and (iii) we have represented a direct *experience* which phenomenologically is irreducible. ... We can have no psychological understanding without empathy into the *content* (symbols, forms, images, ideas) and without seeing the *expression* and sharing the experienced phenomena.

Point (ii) merely reiterates that understanding requires that we should recognize an observable phenomenon as an expression. Point (iii) repeats that the phenomenon cannot be analyzed without loss into its components, physiological equivalents, or the like. Neither a description of the tensing of a particular muscle nor one of the flow of adrenalin into the blood provides a recognizable account of the anger. The point about empathy made at the end of the quotation is also one made by Dilthey, but I have not emphasized it previously because its importance can easily be exaggerated into seeing his whole theory as being based on this psychological state. To understand someone who says that he is angry (or, for that matter, that he sees red), one must somehow be able to conjure up in one's own mind the state described, feel what the other person feels, or, in Jaspers words, "share the experienced phenomena" as you see the expression.

I have left until last an explanation of the point that Jaspers lists first, because it raises a point not present in the earlier quotations; it is a somewhat oblique reference to the world of mind. "Anger," to stick to Jaspers' own earlier illustrtion, is a concept defined in dictionaries and more generally through its use in conversation, books, and so on. We do not have to analyze a person, or consult psychological texts, to know what it means. Earlier he had amplified his view on "mind" in passages such as the following:[10]

> The highest mental creation can still be questioned as to its psychic origins; what involuntary elements are being expressed; what is its effect on the psychic life and what significance has it as a footing the psyche, etc.? The realm of the understandable is, of course, not exhausted by this psychic aspect of the understandable and we should remember that from other points of view the mind is regarded as a world of meaning, divorced from the psyche.

and:[11]

The basic phenomenon of mind is that it arises on psychological ground but is not something psychic in itself; it is an objective meaning, a world which others share. The individual acquires a mind solely through sharing in the general mind which is historically transmitted and at one given moment is defined for him in a contemporary form. ... The general or objective mind is currently present in social habits, ideas and communal norms, in language and in the achievements of science, poetry and art. It is also present in all our institutions.

As in Dilthey, mind is the product of the mental activities of individuals; it is invariably given through physical signs, yet it confronts individuals as an independent sphere, containing the language, culture, and beliefs that persist and develop in time, independent of the existence of particular individuals but affecting and shaping them.

I am a little uneasy about the assertion that the individual acquires a mind *solely* through sharing in the general mind. However, its importance is hardly questionable. What we find—what the psychiatrist finds—as the content of a person's mind are ideas couched in a particular language, fears reflecting shared prejudices, aspirations formulated in his culture, goals defined for him in his society. Without knowing the sphere of mind in which the patient's mind is steeped, the psychiatrist could not even being to treat him, let alone diagnose his problems. He might otherwise mistake for eccentric fantasy what is a common belief of a community, as strange desire what is merely a conventional attitude. Deviations from the norms of his own community may be signals of mental disturbance. A Hindu who has eaten beef might feel guilty even though he may have no objection to eating other meats. This only tells us about his orthodoxy, but a Christian who feels that way gives signs of some abnormality.

In other cases it may be the incompatibility of goals approved of within the same culture that is a causative factor of disturbances. A person encouraged in childhood to be a good Christian by his mother and to be "macho" by his father might be a case in point.

All this is obvious enough and needed saying only because the concept here used, namely that of objective mind, has been looked at with suspicion within the Anglo-Saxon world. But there is no need to treat it as a piece of Germanic metaphysics, carrying dubious and mystifying implications. It is merely a convenient term for something we need to refer to. If we object to the term, we just have to invent another, which equally needs to be protected from misunderstanding. The term "culture," as used by American social anthropologists, has a very similar meaning. In its case, one has to warn users that it does not have a value connotation, as it has when we call some people cultured and others not. K. R. Popper, with an air of original discovery, introduced, and argued for, the same idea under the title "third world," which has since come to be commonly used for something quite different.

Though I have in this book kept Dilthey quotations to a minimum because I did not want to duplicate those I have used in my other writings on Dilthey, I will conclude this section with two quotations that illustrate how close Dilthey's formulations are to the kind of things Jaspers felt he had to say about expressions, mind, and so on to lay the foundations of psychiatry.

What is given always consists of expressions. Occurring in the world of the senses they are manifestations of mental content which they enable us to know. By expressions I mean not only signs and symbols but also manifestations of mental content which make it comprehensible without having the purpose. ... Concepts, judgements and larger thought structures form the first of these classes. ... Understanding, focusing entirely on the content which remains identical in every context ... is here more complete ... it follows from its nature that it does not require us to go back to its psychological context.

and

The greater outer reality of mind always surrounds us. It is a manifestation of the mind in the world of the senses. ... *Every single expression represents a common feature* in the realm of objective mind. Every word, every sentence, every gesture or polite formula, every work of art and every political deed is intelligible because the people who expressed themselves through them and those who understand them have something in common. [*C.W.,* Vol. VII[12]]

It should be plain enough that I did not attempt to do justice to Jaspers either as a philosopher or a psychiatrist, as I have placed neither of his preoccupations into their proper context. I did not even take all aspects of his philosophic approach to psychiatry into consideration. My sole point was to show that the kind of ideas that Dilthey had developed as part of his philosphy of the human sciences are echoed most closely by a philosopher explicitly involved in providing a theoretical framework for psychiatry. Before illustrating this by a number of quotations, I tried to map out the kinds of issues that are relevant in this enterprise. Applying these theories to a discipline that is tested daily by success or failure highlights these theories from a particular point of view.

6

Epistemology
and the Philosophy of Life

Ever since Descartes placed such dramatic emphasis on the subject, epistemology has been a major—and, indeed, often the dominant—theme of philosophy. There are notable exceptions. Heidegger, for example, considered epistemology to be secondary to, and dependent on, ontology, which was his prime concern. Not so Dilthey. Though constantly lured toward historical description and analysis, enchanted by aesthetic problems and immersed in problems of moral or educational philosophy, he steadily envisaged, from early diary entries to the jottings of his last years, the crucial job of laying epistemological foundations for our knowledge and—most urgently—our knowledge of the human world.

His basic approach was influenced by Kant's line of attack, but this is true of almost any philosopher of the nineteenth and twentieth centuries, of idealists, positivists, pragmatists, linguistic analysts, and phenomenologists. In Dilthey's case, the influence was strong and explicitly acknowledged. However, this neo-Kantianism was yoked to a philosophy of life that Dilthey developed and was committed to. From its point of view Dilthey criticized Kant and endeavored to modify and supplement his epistemology.

Some of this work—like that of philosophers more orthodoxly neo-Kantian who were mainly concerned with applying Kant's approach to a philosophy of science—was both original and fruitful. However, some of the deep-seated presuppositions of Kant's philosophy were not compatible with the basic premises on which Dilthey's philosophy of life rests. This produced a tension in Dilthey's thinking that proved more intractable than other conflicts in his thinking and provides the main reason why the epistemological part of the "Introduction" was not completed—indeed, could never have been completed.

THE PHILOSOPHY OF LIFE

Dilthey applied the term "philosophy of life" to a philosophic approach and outlook not confined to professional philosophers. In a lecture, "Present-day Culture and Philosophy" (reproduced in *C.W.*, Vol. VIII, pp. 199–205, tr. 109–21) he discussed—under this label—a group of thinkers, including not only Schopenhauer and Nietzsche, who, though appealing to a wider public, were philosophers, but also writers and artists such as Richard Wagner, Tolstoy, Ruskin, and Maeterlink. Though he criticized these thinkers for their too personal and subjective point of view, he ultimately classed himself with them. G. Misch used the term when he compared and contrasted Dilthey's philosophy with phenomenology and existentialism. Since then, other thinkers such as Bergson, Klages, and Ortega y Gasset have been classed under this label. The distinguished Dilthey scholar, O. F. Bollnow, also assigns G. Simmel to this group in his book *The Philosophy of Life*.

One feature, expressed by the emphasis on "life" and shared by the thinkers listed, is the rejection of a purely academic, theoretical approach to philosophy. Philosophy is not only about life—it is practically relevant to it. Perhaps it is worth mentioning that all these thinkers must have been familiar from childhood with a famous line from Goethe's "Faust," "Grey is all theory, but green life's golden tree" (where green is obviously not just a color but the sign of burgeoning vitality). It is one of Goethe's ironies that the lines are spoken by Mephistopheles.

Essentially, this view of philosophy is a reaffirmation of philosophy's traditional task to which it needs to be recalled from time to time. It is only some modern forms of philosophy that have taken refuge behind the idea that it is merely a particular specialism, sorting out linguistic confusions or puzzles. Traditionally, many functions have been attributed to philosophy, but all are in the service of life. Philosophy crystallizes both awareness of ourselves as individuals and consciousness of the problems of our civilization. It tries to provide a grounding for our moral values and places ideals before us. It serves the quest for knowledge by clarifying its presuppositions. It tries to justify our political aspirations and to pinpoint the goals of education. Plato and Aristotle, Epicurus and Mark Aurelius, Spinoza and Kant pursued all these goals. The "philosophy of life," Marxism, and Existentialism were all movements that apart from their specific aims, had this for their goal. Besides relevance for life, the name "philosophy of life" is also intended to suggest two further, closely linked programmatic points: One is that philosophy finds the sole source of its conclusions in life. The other closely related point concerns the definition of its subject matter.

The first point is essentially epistemological and methodological. The philosophy of life is committed to the belief that all knowledge comes from experience and that the source of this knowledge can be specified as life because that is seen as the sum of our experiences through time. Abstract speculation and the building of dogmatic systems is excluded by this point of view. In this it is at one with British Empiricism and Positivism from Locke to J. S. Mill. However, Dilthey rejects this form of empiricism because of its conception of experience as defined in terms of simple data given to the senses. He maintained that such a conception of experience distorts actual experience by means of a dogmatic, metaphysical presupposition. Experience is not just taking in colored dots or simple sounds; it is seeing my friend cutting the grass, hearing birds singing in the trees, observing a family setting out for a picnic, and the like. It is the intricate tapestry of life into which our past experience and our social and cultural knowledge is interwoven. We shall return to this when we discuss life as the subject matter. Meanwhile here are Dilthey's own words.:

The fundamental idea of my philosophy is that no one, so far, has based his philosophizing on the full, unmutilated whole of experience, and so, on the whole fullness of reality. Speculation is certainly abstract. . . . But empiricism is no less so. It bases itself on mutilated experience, distorted from the outset by an atomistic theoretical view of mental life . . . no complete human being can be confined within this experience. [*C.W.*, Vol. VIII, p. 175]

The empiricism criticized here is, of course, what is often called "British Empiricism," but the distinction Dilthey makes between his philosophy based on experience and empiricism is not easily rendered in English.

Life as the subject matter of philosophy, the third aspect of what is meant by a philosophy of life, is closely connected with the other two aspects, life to be served by philosophy and life being the sole source of our knowledge. This philosophy is relevant to life because it is about life, and it cannot but be about life because its sole source is life.

It is important first of all to be clear about the precise meaning Dilthey gave to the term "life." "In the human studies," he wrote, "I use the expression life only for the human world" (*C.W.*, Vol. VI, p. 314). That he should not be talking about elephants and earthworms in the human studies is not particularly surprising. It means, however, also that the biological aspects of man that he shares with other animals are pushed into the background. He did not deny for a moment the importance of man being an animal or the fact that human life, throughout, is rooted in and affected by biological factors. But his focus of attention is on life as modified and, indeed, transformed by mind. In fact, he uses the terms "life" and "world of mind" as virtually exchangeable. An outstanding example of this is the double title given to the essays collected in *C.W.*, Volumes V and VI, "The World of Mind. An Introduction to the Philosophy of Life." Life is to him what he sometimes describes as "social/historical reality." It is the pageant of social, political, and cultural activities, be it of individuals or groups set up for those purposes. It covers personal relationships, legal proceedings, and economic activities, and this is, clearly, what the human studies are about. All this is so obvious that it needs no further discussion.

There is, however, a point of the utmost epistemological importance; it could have been made under the previous heading, of life as a source of information, but may be more conveniently dealt with in a consideration of what life meant for Dilthey. He distinguished three aspects or functions of mind, which he saw as equally involved in the mind's work of shaping life. They are—in a way that is familiar and traditional—thinking, willing, and feeling. They can all be traced in the manifestations of life. Law or politics are not just creations of thought—they reflect and represent acts of will. The world of art as much as the economic sphere is codetermined by what pleases and displeases—in other words, by feelings.

We have already encountered his insistence that the three are not isolated spheres. Thought, which in this classification covers factual cognition, gives rise to feelings, and these feelings lead to resolutions, acts of will. I become aware of the noise and fumes of my neighborhood; I suffer from it and make every effort to move away. Communities function in the same way. A source of water pollution is diagnosed; this causes concern, which leads to plans for eliminating this health hazard. The order in which one function affects the other is, obviously, flexible. We may feel the discomfort and look for its cause. We form a purpose, and that makes us look at the facts. Almost any social phenomenon or cultural institution can be analyzed in these terms. An art gallery, for example, needs access to such knowledge as the best temperature for pictures, the right light for their appreciation, and so forth. It needs people with a lively appreciation of art and a policy for seeking out and purchasing pictures. Similarly, a political party needs a policy-making body assisted both by experts on public preferences and feelings and researchers into economic and social problems and possible remedies for them. There is no need to multiply examples.

More challenging is Dilthey's claim that the world is disclosed to us not only through our cognitive apparatus but through our feeling and willing. This is implied when, instead of saying that "thought grasps life," he insists that "life grasps life." He argued at length that our assurance of an external world did not rest just on the testimony of our senses or on theoretical arguments, against which the traditional skeptical arguments carry a good deal of weight. (We could be dreaming, we could be systematically deceived, etc.) It is the resistance our will encounters that convinces us that the world is not just our idea. Indeed, we see and interpret a good deal of our environment in terms of the way things serve or frustrate our purposes. This wall is an obstruction to my view; this hammer is a serviceable tool, just the thing to drive in a nail!

Feelings, too, are not "just subjective." They disclose things as being attractive, desirable, depressing, loathsome, repulsive, and so on. This is why Dilthey criticizes past epistemology in the famous words, "no true blood flows in the veins of the knowing subject constructed by Locke, Hume and Kant; it is only the diluted juice of reason, a mere process of thought" (*C.W.*, Vol. I¹). It is, in other words, a mistake to see knowledge as the preserve of a pure detached consciousness. Dilthey probably put this most sharply in the following quotation.

What occurs in this contact [with the world] is life, not a theoretical process; it is what we call an experience, that is, pressure and counter-pressure, expanding towards things which in turn respond, a vital power within and around us which is experienced in pleasure and pain, in fear and hope, in grief over burdens which cannot be shifted, in delight over what we receive as gifts from outside. So the I is not a spectator who sits in front of the world's stage, but is involved in actions and counteractions in which the same actualities are overwhelmingly experienced whether kings figure in them or fools and clowns. This is why no philosopher could ever persuade those involved that everything was appearance or show and not reality. [*C.W.*, Vol. XIX, p. 153, my translation]

In this line of approach, Dilthey undoubtedly blazed a path. It can be found in Heidegger and in the existentialists who followed his lead. I have already mentioned in passing that Dilthey's wide conception of experience is also to be found in pragmatism.

DILTHEY'S EPISTEMOLOGY

Dilthey's commitment to a philosophy of life, to the belief that life was the source, goal, and purpose of philosophy, was persistent and pervasive. Throughout his work are numerous, often quoted references to the effect that in philosophy "life grasps life" (*C.W.*, Vol. VII, p. 121), that life must be understood "out of itself" (*C.W.*, Vol. V, p. 4), that it must be "interpreted in its own terms" (ibid., p. 370), that thought cannot go behind life (ibid., p. 5), etc.

In the projected continuation of his "Introduction," that second volume that was never produced but the drafts of which we now have in *C.W.*, Volume XIX, Dilthey intended to translate his general point of view into a systematic epistemological exposition. It is really only this volume that reveals how seriously Dilthey was concerned with general epistemological issues. His plan for this volume is set out in the drafts of a letter (dated 1882), published in *C.W.*, Vol. XIX, p. 389, under the title "Explanation to the 'Introduction.'"²

I start from a plain basic idea: All science, all philosophy, is empirical science. All experience derives its coherence, and the validity conditioned by it from the coherence of human consciousness. The dispute between Idealism and Realism can be settled by psychological analysis; it can prove: the reality given in my experience is not a phenomenon of my ideas [*in meinem Vorstellen*]; rather is it given to me as something distinguished from myself because I am not only idea but also will and feeling. Reality is what the will, in resistance, in the pressure of the groping hand, etc. becomes aware of, and is as aware of it as it is aware of itself. Self and reality are, therefore, given in the totality of mental life, one in relation to the other and equally immediate and true.

Some of the themes combined in this passage we have already encountered. I have, first, referred earlier to Dilthey's refusal to make a sharp distinction between philosophy and the empirical studies. In the above passage he clearly goes further by squarely identifying philosophy as an empirical discipline. I think that this is a simplified, or careless, formulation of his view. To his credit he was more ambiguous and to my mind less consistent on this matter. The second point we have noted as an influential part of Dilthey's approach is his insistence that reality is disclosed to us not only through our senses and intellect but also through our feelings and will. He wrote at some length on the role of the will in assuring us of the reality of the outside world (in *The Origins of our Belief in the Reality of the External World*, 1890, Vol. V), but I have not, and do not intend to, pursue this subject further.

The third point noted before is Dilthey's insistence on the importance of psychology to the point of replacing epistemology by it, or at least merging the two. Again—to my relief—he is not wholly consistent on this point. The hermeneutical approach supplements the psychological one, and he is also, at times, aware of the limitations of psychology as a basis for epistemology. To these issues I shall revert.

The most striking idea that provides the hub of Dilthey's epistemology is only hinted at in the above programmatic statement. The reason why psychology must supersede or absorb epistemology is that all reality is given to us as contents of the mind. This is brought out very clearly in the two main theses [*Sätze*] that form the cornerstone of his proposed continuation of the "Introduction."

As the "Breslau draft" for the second volume of the Introduction was not available for reference or quotation (except by a few scholars with access to the archives) before 1983 and will not be available in English for some time, I am quoting more fully from this volume than from other texts and reproduce the two theses here.

The axiom of phenomenality [*C.W.*, Vol. XIX, p. 58[3]]

The beginning of all totally serious and consistent philosophy is represented by the insight: all these objects [he had referred in the preceding paragraph to farmers, ploughs, steam engines, etc.] even including the persons with whom I stand in relationships are only given to me as facts of my consciousness. Facts of consciousness are the sole material from which objects are constructed. A fact of consciousness is the resistance which they exert, the space which they occupy, their painfully felt impact as much as their beneficial touch.

The axiom of the totality of mental life [ibid., p. 75]

The second main thesis [*Haupsatz*] of philosophy follows from the thesis analyzed in the previous chapter: the coherence in which the facts of consciousness, hence also perceptions, memories, objects and ideas of them, finally concepts, are linked is a psychological coherence i.e. it is contained in the totality of mental life; corresponding to this the explanation of the way in which perceptions and the other intellectual processes are connected has its basis in the analysis of the totality of mental life.

It is clear that Dilthey's philosophy of life rejects any simple naturalism or realism in favour of a tradition that stretches, in Dilthey's own words, "from Protagoras to Fichte" (ibid., p. 39) and was continued by E. Husserl. It treats reality as given to mind and bearing the traces of its structure. Rodi, in the article referred to in Note 1 to Chapter 6, comments on the two theses (and some earlier drafts, reproduced in *C.W.*, Vol. XIX, p. 38 et seq.) by insisting

one does not do justice to this section … if one tries to locate it as epistemology and/or psychology in the sense commonly used in the last third of the nineteenth century. The kind of experience which is self-reflection aims to be neither speculative nor empirical, and understands itself quite early as a "philosophy of life", can best be described, in terms of today's concepts, as a phenomenologically orientated, epistemological anthropology.

I quote Rodi because he usefully qualifies the idea of Dilthey's simply being committed to psychology, but also because I want to polemize later against the position thus attributed to Dilthey. In that connection I shall expand on the indebtedness of Dilthey's position as just described to Kant and the conflicts between Kantian themes in Dilthey's philosophy and his "philosophy of life" and "epistemological anthropology." First, I want, however, to relate Dilthey's "philosophy of life" to his commitment to hermeneutics.

THE HERMENEUTICS OF LIFE

The sustained effort to analyze and interpret the interconnected totality of our experience, which is life, is the ultimate aim of hermeneutics. This way the clash between the philosophy of life and traditional epistemology can be phrased in terms of the conflict between the methodology of hermeneutics and the way epistemology normally conceives its tasks.

Here one of the crucial issues is that of starting points. Epistemologies, and, for that matter, metaphysical systems underpinning epistemologies, traditionally looked for firm foundations on which knowledge can be built. The two great metaphysical systems of antiquity—the atomic theory of Leukippos and Democritos, and Plato's theory of forms—were both designed to provide a solid foothold for knowledge in an unchanging and comprehensible ultimate reality. Empiricists through the ages have looked for assured foundations in the evidence of the senses, and Descartes had sought an Archimedian point of reliable certainty by attacking all we took to be true by means of systematic doubt so as to find something that was not vulnerable to it. Spinoza's philosophy, like that of other rationalists, rested on the presupposition that a rationally ordered reality corresponded to our rational thought, which, after all, was part of it. To the Kantian attempt to reach solid epistemological foundations I shall return presently.

By contrast, hermeneutics, as we have already seen, rejects any fixed starting point and is, instead, committed to the hermeneutic circle. This applies to the hermeneutics of life as much as to any more specific hermeneutic enterprise. Life has to be understood from within, because there is no other standpoint we can reasonably adopt once we have rejected the absolutist claims of metaphysics. To be faithful to experience (and not to the kind of empiricism committed to the metaphysical belief in simple sensations as a reliable starting point), we have to start from wherever we are when we begin to reflect on life. We are not at any beginning: we are not babies, our minds are not blank tablets waiting to be written on. We have learned a language and are steeped in a culture and tradition, we have adjusted to society and learned from experience. This is life, and these are the terms in which we see it. It is this whole context that needs disentagling from within.

From this point of view, all the starting points of past philosophy appear to be illusory. They have all been rehearsed in the history of philosophy and cancel each other out. Atomism and, for that matter, any materialism cannot fully account for the mind that created or grasps the theory. The Platonic forms cannot easily be given a content when they are completely divorced from any sense content. Kant put this criticism in one of philosophy's great metaphors. The dove cleaving the air and feeling its resistance thinks how much better it could fly if there were no air (*Critique of Pure Reason*). Descartes, using the armory of traditional skepticism, doubts the reliability of the senses and notes the fallibility of reason. But he cannot overcome these doubts by argument; he simply has to dismiss them. Or else his arguments, for example for the existence of God, could themselves be confusions of reasoning or deceptions by the agency of the evil demon he had invented for his skeptical case. Even his certainty of his self-consciousness cannot serve as an adequate starting point. We may be convinced that there is something existing, but his arguments are insufficient to give it any content.

The hermeneutic approach is based on acceptance of these uncertainties, this absence of certain foundations. It is not, however, skepticism, in the sense of doubting the possibility of all knowledge. It only assumes that all the sources of knowledge are corrigible, all starting points provisional. There are no alternatives to relying, for some purposes and to some extent, both on our senses and on our reasoning as long as we consider both corrigible through each other, and more generally through being related to different wider contexts. We could not, for example, understand others and the cultural world around us if we did not have some immediate, introspective awareness of ourselves. Yet this awareness of ourselves can be corrected, enhanced, and deepened by the understanding of others of the world of mind. So we come to know ourselves through the "circuitous road of understanding."

Throughout this book, we have encountered different examples of the hermeneutic assumption that different chunks of knowledge are caught in circles of mutual dependence. Hermeneutics itself in its interpretations profits from psychological knowledge of man, but psychology to gain these insights needs hermeneutical interpretations of human creations, the objectifications of human life. History needs to be made intelligible through the aid of the systematic human disciplines, yet these disciplines depend for their sources on history. Above all, there is the circle in which philosophy and the empirical human studies need to support each other. (I take this to be a more precise statement of Dilthey's position as articulated in his writings than the simplification—quoted in his plan for the continuation of the "Introduction"—that philosophy *was* one of the empirical disciplines.) Finally, underlying these other circles, is the circle in which life and thought are caught up. Life as we catch it is always already "intellectualized" and made comprehensible through judgment (we shall return to this point and illustrate it with quotations), yet thought itself is, according to the philosophy of life, rooted in and colored by the vital processes of which it is a part and a function.

This brief account must serve as a description of how the problems of knowledge presented themselves to Dilthey from the point of view of a philosophy of life. But, as I have mentioned at the very beginning of this book, Dilthey was not consistent in this. He felt some sympathy for positivism and, even more extensively, some commitment to Kant's epistemology. This is a conflict he never managed to overcome. There is little dispute on this. Most commentators are vividly aware of this tension. However, there are three different positions that have been taken up in response to it. One is to accept as inevitable and fruitful this unresolved tension, and I have quoted Bollnow, whom I take to adopt this position. Others deplored Dilthey's failure to commit himself more consistently and wholeheartedly to the hermeneutics of life he had done so much to pioneer. Heidegger and Gadamer and, I think, Rodi belong to this camp. Third, one can also stress the Kantian threads in Dilthey's thinking and wish that he had developed them more fully and consistently. Because of my own regard for Kant's epistemology, I favor the third position, and if I stand condemned of having, in the past, distorted Dilthey's philosophy, it was by overstressing and making as coherent as possible his Kantian heritage. I shall, therefore, turn to what Dilthey took from Kant and the specific ways it conflicts with his philosophy of life.

THE KANTIAN APPROACH

Throughout his working life, Dilthey returned again and again to a project that he called a "Critique of Historical Reason." It makes a repeated appearance in the early letters and diaries collected in Der junge Dilthey, in which he speaks also of "a new Critique of Pure Reason on the basis of our historical-philosophic outlook."[4] (J120). It is mentioned in the dedication to York of Volume One of the Introduction (C.W., Vol. I, p. ix) and repeated in the concluding chapter of that volume (ibid., p. 116).[5] Finally, manuscripts from the last years of his life (probably between 1907 and 1910 and published in C.W., Vol. VII, pp. 191–291) are entitled "Drafts towards a Critique of Historical Reason."

It has been argued, for instance, by Rodi and, as quoted by him, by Groethuysen in his introduction to C.W., Vol. VII, that the title must be understood fairly broadly as being almost synonymous with Dilthey's lifelong effort to lay the foundations of the human studies. Rodi adds that the "Critique of Historical Reason" never figured as the title of a course of lectures, let alone of a complete and finished work of Dilthey's.

I cannot help believing that the repeated and emphatic use of this title by a major philosopher closely acquainted with Kant's work must be taken to mean more. One purpose, and that critical of Kant, which Dilthey must have had in mind, is hardly controversial. He clearly believed that the three critiques of Kant required to be supplented by a fourth, because they did not do justice to the distinct problems of historical knowledge and, indeed, more generally, the understanding of human beings. Little more needs to be said about this. Not only is it noncontroversial as an interpretation of what Dilthey meant by aiming at an additional critique but also reflects, for all those who think that Dilthey is a philosopher to be taken seriously, a task to the accomplishment of which he made a substantial contribution.

But is this enough? Surely Dilthey's choice of title would still have been frivolous if it did not also represent a commitment to at least something of Kant's approach and methods. This is no mere hypothesis but can be amply documented by quotations from Dilthey. Professor Bollnow makes this point in his Dilthey,[6] from which I take the following two Dilthey quotations. (After forty years, Bollnow, as he admits in a more recent article,[7] does not underwrite everything in this book. It remains, however, a stimulating work full of eminently well chosen quotations.)

"It seems to me that the fundamental problem of philosphy has been identified by Kant for all times," wrote Dilthey (*C.W.*, Vol. V, p. 12), and also "We must continue the work of this transcendental philosophy" (*C.W.*, Vol. VIII, p. 14). In *The Poetic and Philosophic Movement in Germany 1770–1800*, he also insists on the importance of "following Kant's critical path, to lay the foundations, in cooperation with researchers from other fields, of an empirical science of the human mind."[8]

However difficult and subject to different interpretations Kant's transcendental philosophy may be, the basic outlines of his approach are not in question, and Dilthey was thoroughly familiar with them. When Kant talked about reason, he talked about a faculty or capacity of man. The *Critique of Pure Reason* was about man's capacity for knowledge, mainly empirical knowledge and knowledge of mathematics. The *Critique of Practical Reason* was about man's capacity for moral judgments. A "Critique of Historical Reason" would accordingly be about man's capacity for forming historical judgments and more generally, as I have already suggested, for understanding human beings and their creations.

In each of his Critiques Kant started from the assumption that the capacities under consideration were, in fact, capable of achieving their aim. In other words, we did have knowledge, made valid moral judgments, and so forth. For philosophy to doubt these achievements could only bring philosophy into disrepute. Instead, it was the philosopher's job to examine critically how these achievments were possible by asking what were the presuppositions, the necessary conditions for these accomplishments. We are not, of course, talking of factual possibility in the sense of "he could have seen it, he was there and is alert," but in the sense of the possibility of something being *justified* as genuine experience or knowledge. If these accomplishments were real and could not be achieved without certain preconditions being fulfilled, then the existence of these preconditions would have been demonstrated. This is the form of Kant's famous transcendental deductions. Only if A (the unity of the cognitive subject is a good example) then B (meaning experience and knowledge). B (i.e. we do have knowledge and experience), therefore A (unity of the cognitive subject).

This deduction is transcendental because it refers to conditions of experience that lie, or at least may lie, outside the sphere of experience. Kant did not care a fig—it must be emphasized—whether the unity of consciousness could be empirically established. The philosopher's job was to establish it by his transcendental deduction and thus provide a firm framework of presuppositions of experience being possible. If philosophy relied on experience for its conclusions, it would simply move in a circle that, for Kant, was not acceptable, was in fact vicious because we would be trying to establish how experience was possible by using that experience.

I shall try to show that Dilthey to some extent explicitly argued against some of these Kantian approaches, but also, at the cost of consistency, followed the Kantian road. By and large I shall take Kant's side by trying to highlight the difficulties Dilthey's abandonment of Kantian positions created for him.

The *Critique of Pure Reason*, like other epistemological enterprises, aimed to justify elements of certainty in our knowledge. Anticipations, predictions, and generalizations based solely on experience, could only—Kant believed—be probable. But he thought that it would shortchange our convictions that events had causes, that objects persisted in time or would be visible from angles other than the one from which we happen to see them, and so on, if we treated them as merely habits of thought or probable extrapolations from experience. So he considered the empiricist account of knowledge inadequate, but he could not accept the—to his mind insufficiently founded—rationalist assumption that a rationally ordered universe corresponded to our rational thought. He sought the solution in what he called his Copernican Revolution. The mind was active in cognition. It organized the raw material given through the senses by imposing its own structures. The features of the world we recognize as certain are so because they are the ways in which the human mind necessarily absorbs experience.

The illustration often used to illuminate Kant's point is that of a man wearing nonremovable green-tinted spectacles (though Kant's point is, emphatically, not about color vision). That man would know a priori that whatever he saw would be tinted green.

This is not the place to attempt a fuller exposition of Kant's epistemology. There are thousands of books that have attempted to do so, and I, too, tried my hand at a more extended account.[9] Here it is enough to indicate the thrust of Kant's revolutionary approach, to which Dilthey's two theses bear strong affinity. Like Kant, he believed that because the world was there for us as given to our minds, it bore the structures of that mind's activities. Kant called the basic forms that the mind in cognition imposes on the data given it "categories." It is further evidence of Dilthey's explicit recognition of Kant's influence that he, too, spoke of categories,[10] though he added his "Categories of Life" to those listed by Kant.

It is not too difficult to work out the scenario of a "Critique of Historical Reason" in Kant's spirit. Building bricks for such an enterprise and hints for putting them together are there in Dilthey's writing, but clearly the project had not been executed. As the works in which these inconclusive attempts occur are fragments and drafts from the last years of Dilthey's life, it is possible that, had Dilthey lived a little longer, they might have been put together with a firmer hand. I tended to take this view in my earlier writings. It seems likelier, however, that the reason why these Kantian lines of thought remained fragments or were phrased rather vaguely was that powerful currents in Dilthey's thinking, which for the sake of brevity we might call his "philosophy of life," were in conflict with them.

A sketch that singles out the Kantian strains in Dilthey's thinking naturally starts by recognizing as a fact to be accounted for our capacity for understanding meaning conveyed through expressions. The philosophic inquiry then takes the form of seeking the presuppositions involved, the conditions—to be orthodoxly Kantian, the necessary conditions—that make understanding as a process achieving knowledge possible.

Two principles used by Dilthey can fill the place of basic presuppositions of this kind. One is represented by the much-quoted statement, "understanding is the rediscovery of the I in the Thou" (C.W., Vol. VII, p. 189). Clearly, this cannot mean that when we understand people, we discover that they are exactly like us. This would be absurd. Not only are the large differences between people a palpable fact, but understanding would be superfluous if that were not the case. It means, as I have argued earlier, that understanding presupposes that we all share some basic human features.

The second main principle can be described as the "Vico-principle" because it received its classical formulation by G. Vico, who referred to "the civil world," "which, since men had made it, men could come to know."[11] What he meant, as is clear from the context of his writings, and what Dilthey presupposed, though he did not quote Vico, was that whatever the human mind had created, the human mind could understand.

By a happy coincidence, these two principles correspond to and are illuminated by two major themes of Dilthey's work on which I have focused attention. What we can presuppose as common human nature is a matter for painstaking examination and analysis, which is the task of what has come to be known as "philosophic anthropology." The other principle obviously provides the basis for hermeneutics, as it stipulates that anything created by the human mind is, in principle, accessible to successful interpretation.

It scarcely needs emphasizing that the special presuppositions of knowledge of the human world take their place in the more general framework, which provides the presuppositions for any kind of knowledge. After all, the human world is embodied physically and encapsulated in the physical world. Expressions, for example, need to be observed before they can be understood. So Dilthey took Kant's view of space as the form of outer experience (though not, as we shall presently see, his view of time as the form of inner experience) on board, accepted basic logical operations as presupposed in all thought (I shall quote him to this effect presently), and agreed to what he called the "formal" categories. The unity of consciousness must, of course, be presupposed both for observational knowledge and knowledge through understanding.

Dilthey's "categories of life" supplement his two main presuppositions and can be construed on Kantian lines. Kant's categories can be described in three supplementary ways, which in fact depend on each other. They are, first, forms of judgment. In other words, to say that the category of causality applies to judgments about events means simply that they take the form of "x causes y." Because, second, the phenomenal world—the only world of which we have knowledge—is itself structured by our judgments, causality can be described as a feature of that world. Third, categories as forms of judgment can also be described as ways in which the subject functions in his acts of cognition.

All this applies—though he does not set this out formally—to Dilthey's categories. Stipulating, for example, the category of purpose (or "ends and means") implies, first, that judgments about the human world take such forms as "x aims at y," "w tries to achieve z," and so forth. It means, second, that the human world *is* shot through with purposes, and that, third, the human mind is preconditioned to judge things in this manner.

Some of Dilthey's deviations from and criticisms of Kant's epistemology are "negotiable" even to Kantians as long as they are not committed to the belief that Kant's exposition is flawless and complete and could not be improved in any way. Other points in which Dilthey departs from Kant's approach—his psychological approach to the structures of the mind is one—raise crucial issues of consistency if Dilthey is to be understood as continuing "this work of this transcendental philosophy." Here lie the deep-seated contradictions to which we have already referred.

Let us start with some of Dilthey's modifications of Kant's philosophy that are—to my mind—reconcilable with the essentials of the "Copernican revolution." First, the categorial framework of cognition cannot, Dilthey believed, be pinned down to Kant's list of twelve categories supposed to be complete and unchanged. So he writes, for example, "Kant's a priori is rigid and dead; but the real conditions of consciousness, as I understand them, are living historical process, are development, they have their history. ..." (*C.W.*, Vol. XIX, p. 51; also in an earlier draft reproduced in ibid., p. 44). Even convinced Kantians consider this part of Kant's philosophy a piece of outmoded and pedantic "architectonic" and are prepared to opt for a more flexible, open-ended body of presuppositions among which new ones may emerge. What matters is that they function as a priori presuppositions, not that they are eternally rooted in human cognition.

This leads directly to a second, more general, point linked to an aspect of the meaning of "Historical Reason," which I have not discussed so far. Kant and his contemporaries did not think of human nature, reason, and the like in historical terms. It was mostly in the nineteenth century that everything came to be considered as being involved in, and explainable in terms of, historical flux. So looking at reason as historical also means for Dilthey that our capacity for knowledge, the transcendentally subjective conditions of cognition, may change and develop, be, in fact, subject to historical processes. It would be hard to resist this suggestion because the history of science, for example, strongly suggests that our presuppositional framework has in the course of time changed even in fairly fundamental ways. However, this is not fatal to the Kantian position either as long as we hold on to two points: (1) There is no problem about holding on to a priori features of our knowledge, even if they have an empirically traceable origin in time. For example, it is not just an empirical fact that Brown comes before Smith in our directory. We know that this would be so before we look, because we know that the arrangement is alphabetical. The fact that someone introduced such an arrangement at a particular moment in history is neither here nor there. (2) If it were suggested that all our categories, presuppositions, and so forth were changing in history, we might, indeed, be in danger of a relativism that Kant would certainly have roundly rejected and Dilthey also wanted to resist, though we shall have to see with what degree of consistency. It is arguable that people in some ages did not operate with the concept of "development," but can we really envisage them pursuing any kind of knowledge without using that of "causality" in some sense? Even in the case of Dithey's "categories of life" it is hard to believe that people understood each other at any point in history without presupposing, for example, purposiveness in their fellow men. On the question of whether mental structures or operations transcended temporal change, Dilthey was not and, given the parameters of his thinking, could not be wholly consistent.

I turn to aspects of Dilthey's theory of knowledge where we can no longer speak of correcting, or supplementing, Kant's work or even of achieving a new synthesis that absorbed what was important in Kant and merged it with the philosophy of life and its hermeneutic approach. There are flat contradictions that Dilthey was reluctant to face squarely. We have reached the point adumbrated earlier where we have to decide whether Kant's "transcendental approach" should be abandoned as ill-conceived, or whether his case is so compelling that it calls for a retreat from some of the positions of the philosophy of life. I am, of course, not saying that Dilthey was not fully aware of his divergencies from Kant. It is quite plain that he attacked Kant explicitly and articulately. What I am saying, however, is that some of what he wanted to retain from Kant depends on presuppositions that he had thus repudiated.

The conflict can be pinpointed in terms of two related issues: the status of inner experience and the question of embodying the cognitive subject. For Kant inner states (we are talking about such things as anger, joy, and so on) are as phenomenal as outer experience, such as seeing a chair. Time, as the form of inner experience, has the same status as space, that of outer experience. Dilthey with his two theses agreed with Kant's view of outer experience. Chairs and, for that matter, other people are given to me as phenomena, as contents of my consciousness subject to the mind's structuring activity. But when we are conscious of our inner states, we touch the bedrock of reality. The experience of time, the very fabric of our lives, is not phenomenal. Anger is not, like the chair, the appearance or phenomenon of something that existed independently outside my mind. What I experience is real anger, not the appearance of something inevitably hidden.

Dilthey is emphatic on this. Kant, he writes, "misjudged the significance of inner experience ... he studied the metaphysical spirit in compounds

[*Preparaten*] not in life" (*C.W.*, Vol. XIX, p. 437). I pick two further quotations from the many references to this issue: "The fundamental mistake of this view lies in extending the concept of appearance to inner experience" (ibid., p. 216), and a few pages later, "With this characteristic of our consciousness we leave mere correspondence and representation and enter a real world which is given to us as it is" (ibid., p. 220).

This divergence of views has important bearings on the second issue I have mentioned, for on the question of whether we can have substantial ultimate knowledge of ourselves depends the possibility of giving flesh and substance to the cognitive subject. Dilthey's view is highly plausible, particularly if we dismiss as irrelevant theories of unconscious mental life such as that of Freud, which operate with the contrast between apparent and real states of mind. (It is irrelevant because subconscious states are eventually made accessible to introspection. Whether insight is immediate or the result of reflection does not affect the question if it reveals ultimate reality.) Nevertheless, it rests, in my opinion, on a misunderstanding of Kant's theory. The phenomenal chair—whether we are talking about what we immediately see, or the atomic structures that science teaches us to look for behind it—is not the appearance of a real chair. Whatever ultimately underlies what we see cannot be described as a chair, it is an X that presents itself to us as a visible chair (or atomic structure). There is *only* one kind of chair, namely the phenomenal one. The chair, or anything else, must be phenomenon, because we cannot but grasp it (thereby structuring it) by means of the perspectives imposed by our cognitive apparatus. This applies to our inner states as much as to outer ones, for the former as much as the latter are experienced in temporal sequence, are grasped in terms of concepts, and so on.

Kant has a second argument against giving privileged cognitive status to mental life. Here I can only mention it very briefly. Inner and outer experience are, in fact, interdependent. For example, our sense of the passage of time depends on cross-reference to spatial relations (such as the movement of the hands on a clock face, the revolutions of the sun, etc.).

There is a third point, which is almost too obvious to make but meets at least some of Dilthey's objections: Kant recognizes, indeed emphasizes, that inner experiences, for instance, to use one illustration much on Dilthey's mind, the experience of temporal flux, are empirically real (though transcendentally phenomenal) and can be distinguished from illusions and fantasies, just as a "real" chair can be distinguished from an illusory chair.

The issue stated so far may almost appear to be a quarrel over words. Both Kant and Dilthey agree that our experience of time, anger, etc. are real as against being fantasies, suppositions, or the like, and that they cannot be contrasted to a real time or real anger outside our experiences. Dilthey also agrees, as I shall presently show by quotations, that even our inner experiences are intellectually structured. But what is substantially at issue is the relation of epistemology to psychology and the possibility of an anthropological theory of knowledge.

THE WHOLE MAN AS THE COGNITIVE SUBJECT

Dilthey's rejection of a bloodless cognitive subject is part of a philosophic reaction against Kantian epistemology that gathered force in the nineteenth century and continues in this. As it has almost become a modern orthodoxy, it may be well to look at it critically in terms of the reason that prompted Kant to his position.

It cannot have escaped anyone—not Kant, not any speculative philosopher, however austere—that cognition takes place in human beings, creatures with a biological makeup, with needs for food, shelter, and the like, which they work to obtain, beings with emotions and social requirements that place them into social and political organizations. These factors undoubtedly influence intellectual life and the pursuit of knowledge. They channel our interests, encourage or inhibit investigations, color and distort our views, create and perpetuate prejudices, and so forth. No one is ignorant of this, no one would dispute it. Dilthey's merit, as that of the thinkers I am about to mention in passing, is to have explored and explained these factors in depth. There is no reason why we should not welcome psychologies of philosophies, sociology of knowledge, and critiques of ideologies.

But does this ultimately affect the autonomy of reason, and if so, how far? There are a thousand reasons, rooted in the factors just mentioned, why we might fall into error or self-deception, produce fantasies, ideologies, or propaganda instead of knowledge, but the question is: can we also, under favorable conditions, achieve objective knowledge, arrived by rational procedures? Can we ever say: here is the evidence for what I think, and my biological needs, class membership, social conditioning, and the like are irrelevant? If the answer is yes, then the psychology, sociology, or biology of thought cannot, whatever their usefulness, replace epistemology.

The best-known attack on the autonomy of the intellectual life comes from Marx and his followers. In his "Towards a Critique of Political Economy,"[12] Marx wrote, "It is not the consciousness of men which determines their existence but, on the contrary, their social existence which determines their consciousness" [my translation] and in *The German Ideology*,[13] he wrote,

One starts from real, active human beings and describes the development of ideological reflexes and echoes of the processes of life in terms of their real processes of life. ... Human beings thus alter their actuality and their thought and the products of their thought. Consciousness does not determine life, but life consciousness [my translation].

The Danish theologian and philosopher S. Kierkegaard is no less incisive in rejecting, from his own point of view, an abstract thinking subject.

. . . I assume that anyone I may have the honour to talk with is also a human being. If he presumes to be speculative philosophy in the abstract, pure speculative thought, I must renounce the effort to speak with him; for in that case he instantly vanishes from my sight, and from the feeble sight of every mortal.[14]

and

In general how does the empirical ego stand related to the pure ego, the I-am-I? Anyone who is ambitious to become a philosopher would naturally like to have a little information on this point, and above all, cannot wish to becme ridiculous by being transformed, eins, zwei, drei kokolorum, into speculative philosophy in the abstract. If the logical thinker is at the same time human enough not to forget that he is an existing individual ... all the fantasticalness and charlatanry will gradually disappear.[15]

If Marx particularly stressed man's social relations—which, as everyone knows, were, for him, closely related with the production of goods necessary for survival—and Kierkegaard emphasized—mainly in reaction against Hegel—the existing individual, whose constitutive characteristic was making personal choices, Nietzsche underlined the biological roots of man's thinking.[16]

Doesn't nature hide from man most things even about his body, to banish him to and envelop him in a deceptive consciousness removed from the convolutions of his bowels, the quick flow of the blood, the intricate tremor of his fibres ... and woe to the fatal curiosity which manages to peep through the gap, out and down from the chamber of consciousness and now gets an inkling that man rests, in the indifference of his ignorance, on what is merciless, greedy, unsatiable and murderous—hanging, as it were, in dreams on the back of a tiger.

and in the Antichrist (14) he adds ". . . consciousness, 'mind' counts with us as the symptom of relative imperfection of the organism"[17]

The continuation of these trends in the twentieth century is due at least partly to the influence of these thinkers, as well as of Dilthey, and to movements more or less directly inspired by them. One thinks above all of Marxism, both in its orthodox form and in such revisionist forms as that of the Frankfurt school on the one hand, and existentialism on the other. I have already referred to Heidegger's "anthropological" approach to epistemological problems, but one can also point to thinkers far removed from either the Marxist or the existentialist positions, such as Wittgenstein who stressed that our ways of talking (and therefore thinking) were embedded in ways of life. P. Winch, following in his footsteps, got himself into the position of the housewife displayed in advertisements who cannot tell margarine from butter. In his case it was philosophy he could not tell from sociology.[18]

In this context I want to give brief attention to the view of J. Habermas, because his work has attracted considerable attention. His background is that of the Frankfurt school, a group of thinkers who combined their allegiance to dialectical materialism with a sympathetic interest in Dilthey. They exhibited considerable interest in epistemology, discussed reason at some length, and described their own theory as "critical." They also tended to theorize—and this is why I mention them here—on the social, psychological, and political conditions of thought.

Habermas writes[19]:

For knowledge is neither a mere instrument of an organism's adaptation to a changing environment nor the act of a pure rational being removed from the context of life in contemplation.

In an Appendix to this work he adds:[20]

My first thesis is this: the achievement of the transcendental subject have their basis in the natural history of the human species.

Finally, in this list of quotations, I add a passage from p. 61:[21]

The science of man, however, extends in methodical form the reflective knowledge that is already transmitted prescientifically within the same objective structure of the dialectic of the moral life in which this science finds itself situated. In this structure, the knowing subject can only cast off the traditional form in which it appears to the degree that it comprehends the self-formative process of the species as a movement of class antagonism mediated at every stage by processes of production, recognises itself as the result of the history of class consciousness in its manifestations, and, thereby, as self-consciousness, frees itself from objective illusion.

Though we need not go into the subtle details of Habermas' position, it might be useful to single out the points relevant here, as Habermas' thought and style is a little convoluted. The first quotation is clear enough in its meaning but poses a question rather than giving an answer. It simply denies that either the Nietzschean position of reason as the tool of an animal species or the Kantian view of a pure rational being as the cognitive subject is adequate. The second quotation suggests that cognition is based on our biological development. The third quotation starts by stating that the human sciences are systematizations of common-sense appreciation of the moral relationships in which we are involved in life. From this the conclusion is drawn that we can only free ourselves from traditional beliefs and illusions by appreciating how man develops through class struggle over the means of production (the last phrase being my shorthand for the Marxist interpretation of history).

Though it may seem unfair to give three short quotations and complain that they do not provide a complete and convincing answer, I suggest that they reflect a dilemma in Habermas' thinking from which he could not escape, just as Dilthey could not escape from a very similar predicament. Habermas should receive credit for his acute awareness of the problem, but his attempt at escape resembles the feat claimed by the famous boaster Baron von Münchhausen, of pulling himself out of a bog by his own hair. If our reason is sufficiently autonomous to reach objective conclusions, as long as we take care to avoid the long familiar dangers of prejudice, sloppy thought, and the like, then all this business about our biological evolution or the history of class struggle is beside the point. If, on the other hand, these factors are seriously formative, why should we believe that they can be vanquished by awareness of their power and by reflection, and, indeed, that the author of such theories had, in fact, freed himself of such influences when developing his theories? This is the traditional predicament of all relativist theories.

There is no need to enter here into the differences between the positions I have outlined. They supplement rather than contradict each other, and Dilthey's view takes its place among them without coinciding with any particular one. While appreciating the biological basis of life, he never emphasized it very much in his work, nor did he emphasize the importance of the individual and his choices as much as did Kierkegaard. While acutely aware of the relevance of social and economic conditions, he was not converted to dialectical materialism. What they all shared, though, was an emphasis on the rootedness of rational activity in life, which meant, of course—if it was not to be a resounding platitude—that the content of our intellectual pursuits was colored and codetermined by factors that were neither evidence nor arguments.

THE AUTONOMY OF REASON AND THE
TRANSCENDENTAL SUBJECT

I turn back to Kant's position, which these various authors explicitly or implicitly attacked and which, in turn, represents an incisive criticism of their position. In the *Groundwork of the Metaphysics of Morals*, Kant wrote:[22]

. . . we cannot possibly conceive of a reason as being consciously directed from outside in regard to its judgement; for in that case the subject would attribute the determination of his power of judgement, not to his reason, but to an impulsion. Reason must look upon itself as the author of its own principles independently of alien influences.

In the context from which the quotation is taken, Kant is mainly concerned with the autonomy of practical reason (i.e. the purely rational source of basic moral principles and the denial that morality could be a matter of feelings or outside pressures), but it applies equally, and is intended to apply equally, to theoretical reason in its pursuit of knowledge. However, I have not found as concise a statement of the point in the *Critique of Pure Reason.*

The quotation is clear enough, and its pivotal point is that reason is nothing if not autonomous. Of course reason can, does, and should serve a variety of purposes. Man employs it as means for securing his survival and pursuing his desires, for arranging his comforts and establishing social harmony. But reason as our capacity for cogent thought and the critical evaluation of factual evidence cannot subject itself in its operations to outside influences. Unless it operates according to rules of its own, it can never claim to attain truth and objective knowledge. If I were to say, "I believe that men make better philosophers than women, because I am a man (and not because I have analyzed this pile of statistical evidence)," or "I cannot accept this economic argument because it is produced by a political opponent (and not because there are logical flaws in the argument)," I would have abandoned any claim to knowledge or rational argument. It would be visibly an expression of prejudice, and if anything I said on such grounds were true, it would be merely a coincidence.

This is, clearly, what Kant means by rejecting the possibility of "reason being consciously directed from outside." If someone replies to an assertion of mine, "you say this because you are a Jew, middle-class, etc.," I must reply, if I believe I speak from knowledge, "What I am and my psychological motives are neither here nor there. What matters are the reasons for my assertion." If I argue correctly to reach *true* conclusions, no psychological or sociological explanation is required for *that.*

However those who question the autonomy of reason would argue—and argue with some justification—that, of course, no one would consciously claim, or even admit being influenced by, outside factors in beliefs he claims to be true. On the contrary, the insidious and pervasive power of such forces as instincts, class interests, race prejudice, and the perhaps more harmless pressure of tradition, habit, and life style, are precisely due to the fact that we are not conscious of them. Hence such processes as unmasking, debunking, and critique of ideologies become necessary.

Here we must make a decisive distinction, which, I think, is sometimes obscured in discussion. Is the claim that desire, self-interest, our hopes, fears, and concerns often interfere with and distort the operation of reason, so that it falls into error, self-deception, and the like? Or is reason inescapably affected by life, of which it is part?

The first alternative presents no insuperable intellectual challenge. We have always known that when people make mistakes, delude themselves, or engage in illusions, we may ask for psychological, sociological, or historical reasons why this should happen. We may also be suspicious of the views of people whose interests are strongly supported and served by their views. If a rich man extols the benefits of private wealth to the nation, we are apt to say, "he would say that." His case may turn out to be rationally founded, but a little suspicion is understandable and justifies a little probing.

If the theories of Nietzsche, Marx, and the rest amounted to no more than a systematic and searching counterpart to the common-sense belief that the causes of errors and illusions can be traced and guarded against, they can be considered as protecting rather than undermining the autonomy of reason.

To avoid misunderstanding, I want to mention a point that, though challenging the authority of reason, is quite distinct from the one we are considering here. Nietzsche, Kierkegaard, and Dilthey also maintained that human beings hold, quite legitimately, beliefs that do not have their source in reason at all and are not subject to rational criteria, so that it is a mistake to treat them as if they were. I have no quarrel with this view. Neither belief in the power of various factors that drive us into error nor acceptance of spheres outside the sway of reason (such as love or religion) are a challenge to the possibility of objective knowledge. (Though it contradicts, of course, the belief of some people that objective knowledge on religious matters is possible.)

It is different with the more drastic interpretations of the challenge to the purity of rational processes. We can distinguish a weaker and a stronger version of this challenge. The weaker claim is that some of our beliefs cannot be corrected by the presentation of argument or evidence, even if the person holding them is aware of the extraneous reasons for holding them. I take it that Marxists, for example, tend to maintain that thinkers and artists cannot help holding certain views because they are part of, have been raised in, and live within a certain type of society. The claim of a thinker that his belief in capitalism (let us say) was not due to his middle-class background, to which he had given due thought, would be dismissed.

The stronger claim, which would justify the weaker claim but goes beyond it, is that all our thinking, all our knowledge claims (except presumably trivial and specific ones such as, "I know there is an ashtray in front of me") are inevitably permeated, shaped, and slanted by outside factors such as sexual drives, spiritual aspirations, class conflict, tradition, and so on.

This position, both in its weaker and its stronger form, cuts at the root of all rational debate and all claims to objective knowledge. Either—according to the stronger version—we are invariably condemned, knowingly or unknowingly, to subjective distortions of our thinking, or—according to the weaker version—we can never know when this might be the case. Some thinkers—I have Marxists and neo-Marxists, particularly, in mind—attempt a compromise. While arguing that all theories are subject to class bias, the distortions imposed by a particular economic system, and the like, they argue or assume that they themselves escaped this bias in their theorizing. They also tend to believe that their analyses—unlike the attempts at criticism by other schools or the self-criticism of the thinkers in question—can remove the bias thus nailed. This strikes me as muddled or presumptuous.

Inevitably, these remarks are sketchy, and my criticisms are not particularly original. All forms of subjectivism and skepticism have traditionally been subjected to the criticism that whatever claim is made cannot reasonably be accepted as more than subjective. I needed to make these points because it may help to explain why Dilthey, who shared this anthropological account of the theory of knowledge to some extent, also felt profoundly uneasy about it. As it was, above all, the Kantian in him that made him uneasy, I want to expand upon the Kantian case against the embodied cognitive subject.

The idea that thought and cognition can proceed within us unaffected by our biological, psychological, or sociological factors to which we are subject as persons, and that therefore there is within us a pure cognitive subject (or perhaps I should say "that I am, in a sense, a pure cognitive subject") is not only strongly supported by philosophic arguments such as those of Kant but also reflects the common-sense view of the matter. Yet it is also curious because the relation between me as a thinking subject and me as an empirically given person subject to a multitude of external influences is difficult and opaque. One can sympathize with the recoil from this position by Marx and Nietzsche, by Dilthey and Habermas. They, too, exhibit in their unease sturdy common sense.

For Kant, the cognitive subject cannot be empirically known, because it is not part of the empirical world. It is that through the activity of which the empirical world is known, so that all we can know about it is what we can deduce—from the fact that we have knowledge—about the nature of these activities, which alone makes that knowledge possible. The empirical self can, of course, be investigated psychologically, and the findings can become part of an anthropology, on which, as a matter of fact, Kant himself had lectured.[23]

Kant was perfectly clear on the need to face this issue, and I quote the most crucial passage on this from from *The Critique of Pure Reason*.[24]

How the "I" that thinks can be distinguished from the "I" that intuits itself ... and yet, as being the same subject, can be identical with the latter; and how therefore, I can say: "I, as intelligence and *thinking* subject, know myself as an object that is *thought*, in so far as I am given to myself beyond that which is given in intuition, and yet know myself like other phenomena, only as I appear to myself, not as I am to the understanding—these are questions that raise no greater nor less difficulty than how I can be an object to myself at all, and more particularly an object of intuition and of inner perception.

He concludes the passage by reasserting that I can only be an inner appearance to myself because all my experiences are given under the transcendentally subjective conditions of seeing them in time and organized by categories. A little later he adds, "The subject of the categories cannot, by thinking the categories, acquire a concept of itself as an object of the categories. For in order to think them, its pure self-consciousness, which is what is to be explained, must itself be presupposed."[25] There is no need to go into further details of Kant's position; all that concerns us are the reasons for his position, which he maintained while clearly aware of its implications and difficulties.

Dilthey was profoundly uneasy about the Kantian position, although he also sympathized with it. He could not accept that the subject matter of epistemology lay outside the realm of psychology and anthropology, lay outside, in fact, the realm of experience. In many passages he rejects or ignores Kant's arguments for inner experience being phenomenal, thus placing the cognitive subject beyond the reach of introspection: "Thought is within life, cannot, therefore look behind it ... thought cannot get behind life because it is its expression" (C.W., Vol. XIX, p. 347). Precisely the same point occurs in Volume V, p. 5: ". . . behind life thought cannot go. To see life as appearance is a contradiction in terms for realities lie in the course of life, in the growth from the past and the extension into the future. ..."

However, Dilthey was too subtle and honest a thinker, and had too acute a knowledge of Kant's arguments, to be wholly satisfied with, and wholly consistent in, his "philosophy of life." We noted earlier that he had been condemned for his compromises with positivism and Kantianism by more radical advocates of a philosophy of life and of hermeneutics. The reason for this tendency was his persistent belief that it was both desirable and possible to provide epistemological foundations that provided criteria for the objective truth of what we considered knowledge, be it in mathematics, science, history, or the social sciences. So there are sprinkled throughout his writings expressions much closer to the Kantian position than the argument I have just quoted would lead us to believe. One must admit, however, that they are sometimes curiously qualified to make them fit his philosophy of life.

So, after agreeing, for example, with Kant that the concept of necessity is an a priori condition of our consciousness, he adds, "necessity is, however, after all a certain kind of feeling of conviction" (C.W., Vol. XIX, p. 43). This seems to me sheer confusion. He is—in my opinion—right in agreeing with Kant's view on the role of necessity for consciousness. What Kant meant—to put it as concisely as I can—is that we could not be conscious of a world without accepting that our observations fitted into an objectively necessary order, such as that of causality. Though I may notice the heat first and the stove afterwards, I know that stoves cause heat, but heat never causes stoves. Though we know about stoves and such from experience, we attribute a necessary causal order a priori. The full argument for this position, given in "The Analogies of Experience,"[26] is one of the glories of philosophic argumentation. Dilthey was only one of many thinkers impressed and converted by it. But what on earth could it mean to add that this necessity is "a feeling of conviction." Of course necessity produces a feeling of conviction, but the feeling by itself is not a criterion of knowledge. Flat-earthers may have a deeper conviction of certainty than adherents of the relativity theory.

A similar stance, namely a muted allegiance to Kant, blunted by psychological qualifications, speaks from the following quotation:

Thus there is solved the final controversial question if there is an absolute beginning of knowledge and if its justification as thought does not presuppose thought and cognition, which it was to justify. The elementary logical operations, as the forms in which we make our consciousness of facts distinct and clear, are the presupposition and condition of all experience. But by means of them we learn that they are themselves ways of experiencing. ... [C.W. Vol. XIX, p. 324]

There seems to me to be a curious confusion. Like Kant, Dilthey recognizes that the world of experience is not simply given but that our knowledge involves presuppositions, such as the application of logical operations. Dilthey is, of course, right in also saying that such operations—say syllogistically deducing something—can be described as forms of experiencing. But surely what is presupposed is not simply their occurrence, but their validity. It was *this* that Kant looked for *outside* experience.

At times Dilthey gives clear evidence of appreciating this point, as can be seen from the following quotation, which, dated 1900, was composed after the quotations just given.

Of the methods which he [Kant] applied to pinpoint the conditions of valid cognition in consciousness was ... the ... conclusive one [*Beweiskräftige*], which presupposed that what itself makes experience possible must not be conceived as product of experience. [C.W., Vol. IV, p. 44]

In the light of these feebly qualified admissions and the more vigorous support for the Kantian point of view of the last quotation, we can stress a Diltheyan point of view that pulls in the opposite direction to his emphasis of thought being part and expression of life. His stress that life can only be given through thought, can only be caught as already intellectualized, is perfectly clear. Thus he says, for example:

So one can see that being cannot be separated from thought and is only an expression for that characteristic of the content of thought by means of which it contains reality partly or wholly within itself; ultimately reality implies both truth and actuality. [C.W., Vol. XIX, p. 231]

The above quotation figures in the context of a sustained discussion to which I cannot do full justice here. Instead, I want to link it to another quotation, which, dated 1911, might be counted as Dilthey's "last word" on the subject. "Life is not given to us unmediated, but clarified through the objectification of thought" (quoted by G. Misch in his Introduction to C.W., Vol. V, p. LX).

We encountered this point already as an important, but apparently epistemologically harmless, methodological principle. To understand others, to understand the human world, indeed to understand ourselves, we study the creations of the human mind, the artifacts, the institutions, the poetry and fiction that men have created. Now that we look at this point again, it does not look quite as harmless. That pulsing life within us is, after all, not immediately and transparently given. It must be grasped by thought, and that thought is aided by having products of thought as fixed subject matter.

As this point is so vital for understanding Dilthey's difficulties, I add another very incisively formulated quotation from *Leben und Erkennen* [Life and Cognition] of 1892.

Everything, simply everything, which enters my consciousness, contains what is given, ordered or distinguished or linked or related, in any case, grasped in intellectual processes; as a consequence even in inner experience nothing given as such can be directly observed or perceived. [C.W., Vol. XIX, p. 335]

If this means anything, it surely means that experience is always structured by thought and that thought cannot go behind thought, rather than behind life. Before we can settle any other matter, we have to satisfy ourselves about the grounds on which any claim to know anything rests. If this order or priority is to be preserved, we are forced, after all, to start from the pure cognitive subject—that is, a consciousness that, although it accepts that outside factors ensure its existence and determine the content of its awareness, cannot, without abandoning any claim to knowledge, accept that its operations by which it absorbs and structures that content can itself be conditioned by its existential foundation or its content.

This sets strict limits to any ecclecticism. It is an illusion to which only the woolly-minded can wholly surrender that you can be a Kantian Marxist, a biological Kantian, or an epistemologist looking for the presuppositions of knowledge in social conditions. You cannot, for that matter, combine without inconsistency Kant's Critical Philosophy with the philosophy of life.

I find it difficult to understand what need there is for blood in the veins of the cognitive subject, what good a cure for its anemia would do. Even given that this is a metaphor, I cannot see either how a view of cognitive processes arising from and being entangled in processes of life can justify the validity of knowledge. Although the pure, anemic cognitive subject is a curious ghost, it is not a dispensible one; without it, there could be closing time for valid knowledge and rational discourse.

By contrast, there is no reason to recoil from the hermeneutic rejection of absolute starting points. I do not think that it matters whether a starting point or presupposition is the only possible one and is, like diamonds, forever. What has to be recognized, though, is that any process of thought, any cognitive enterprise or investigation involves a staring point, some premises or presuppositions. When we think or investigate, the presuppositions on which we proceed govern our activities, even if later we abandon them for others, or even submit them to investigation. But we cannot both accept something as a presupposition or starting point and, at the same time question it.

So Dilthey's theory of knowledge, as so much else in his work, does not lead us unambiguously in one direction. I would have preferred him to be more incisively Kantian; I would like to see a working-out of a "Critique of Historical Reason" in neo-Kantian terms. Others would prefer a more consistent elaboration of his philosophy of life. Whichever case may be the stronger, Dilthey challenges us to think critically about the whole basis of our knowledge and more specifically the foundations on which an understanding of the human world can rest.

7

Postscript

Major thinkers need to be reassessed periodically. Inevitably, we ask what they can mean to us "today"; inevitably we see them within the perspectives of our own time and preoccupations. In Dilthey's case this obvious point gains extra significance because of the way in which his writings have become accessible. Compare his case with that of Kant, whom I have invoked by way of contrast before. Kant continues to stimulate and inspire; new interpretations of his writings are produced and will continue to be produced; difficulties and obscurities remain to be probed. Nevertheless, when Kant died over 180 years ago, his funeral was a national event because Germany was mourning the author of the three Critiques and, of course, much else. How different is the case with Dilthey. It would be only a small exaggeration to suggest that at his death his family mourned at the grave of the unknown philosopher. But, as we have seen, only a small portion of his writings was readily available. Only gradually, as volume followed volume in the edition of his collected works, did his stature as a philosopher become visible. The process of making his works accessible is still proceeding, and we are only now getting to the point of seeing his philosophic opus as a whole. Looking at Dilthey today allows a more comprehensive assessment than had been possible until recently.

The idea of Dilthey as a Romantic irrationalist for whom understanding was a matter of empathy has long been buried. The idea of Dilthey as mainly a historian of ideas did not survive the publication of Volumes V and VII of the *Collected Works*. Now, with the yields from the archives, we are getting a fuller picture, even though it may yet have to be completed and modified when we have access to his lectures on Logic and more of his letters.

A number of aspects of Dilthey's work that were unknown or far from obvious even a few years ago have thus become visible. Volume XIX provides important evidence of his philosophic thinking between the publication of Volume I of "The Introduction" and the fragments of a "Critique of Historical Reason" of his last years, so that we can document a much greater continuity in his thinking than some commentators suspected. Themes prominent in his earlier years were only put on the back-burner for a time, never abandoned. Preoccupations of his later years can be traced to beginnings in his youth or in middle age. Any theory about sharp turns from history to epistemology, or from a psychological to a hermeneutic approach—due allegedly to the encounter with Husserl or the controversies evoked by his work on psychology—have become implausible. Instead, we see him clinging to vast plans into which he tried to fit the work arising from special preoccupations of a particular period.

Even more important is the revelation of how seriously and persistently Dilthey was preoccupied with epistemology. At the same time, we have gained fresh insights into the nature of the epistemology by which Dilthey meant to lay the foundations of the human studies. This enterprise was far from trouble-free. We can now see one of the reasons why Dilthey never completed—could never complete—his planned "Introduction" in the unreconciled conflict between different strands of his thinking.

However, the reassessment of Dilthey in the light of freshly available evidence was not the sole or even the main point I had in mind when I put "today" into the title of this book. That title is meant to make both a negative and a positive point. Negatively, it indicates that some topics that a monograph might normally include have been omitted; positively, it emphasizes a focus on the relevance of Dilthey's thought to contemporary issues.

Omitted was any attempt at placing Dilthey into his historical setting, relevant for a full understanding of Dilthey though it might be. Dilthey was undoubtedly affected by, and alertly concerned with, the various currents of his time: industrialization, the rise of the middle classes, the decline of religion, the development of popular political parties, the emergence of socialism. He was preoccupied, as a liberal, with German aspirations toward constitutional government and the unification of Germany. In his letters, articles, and other writings there are explicit references to such matters, and his view of them may well have colored his outlook on more general issues. In this book I have touched on none of this.

The slant of the book also made me exclude any sustained examination of the philosophers who had influenced Dilthey. A book on Dilthey planned on the lines of his own work on Schleiermacher would have contained substantial chapters on Leibniz and Spinoza, on the British empiricists, on

Hegel and the philosphers of the Romantic movement, with Schleiermacher taking pride of place. For my purposes it seemed sufficient to mention them only in passing, with only a limited exception in the case of Kant, because I thought that Dilthey's epistemological position could be highlighted in terms both of his indebtedness to Kant and of his divergence from him.

Excluded also—to complete the list of my omissions—were some aspects of Dilthey's philosophy. I have been very brief on his conception of philosophy and silent on his typology of world views. I have said nothing about Dilthey's aesthetics and educational theories and very little about his ethics. These matters are significant for understanding Dilthey's philosophy as a whole, but they have little direct bearing on contemporary philosophy in the English-speaking world and were—to my mind—not needed to clarify those aspects of Dilthey's philosophy selected for consideration because of their immediate significance to contemporary debates.

This book is based on the belief that Dilthey's most lasting, original, and incisive contribution to present and future thinking is his philosophy of the human studies, in which he tried to lay the epistemological and methodological foundations of all knowledge about the human world. The view that Dilthey was, above all else, a philosopher of the human studies is, of course, widely shared, and so is the view that his contribution is important. The belief that this was so prompted me to begin my work on Dilthey many years ago. What I have tried to do in this book is to translate this general belief into concrete cross-references to modern developments in different spheres. What originally attracted me to Dilthey was his conviction—which I certainly share—that the empirical studies of man, history, psychology, sociology, and all the rest, can profit from stringent philosophic consideration of their presuppositions and methods.

Dilthey's general achievements as a philosopher and his influence within philosophy must, I think, take second place to his importance for the human studies. Not that his purely philosophic influence is negligible. Not only did he have disciples who remained close to his inspiration, but distinguished thinkers with distinctive philosophies of their own, such as Heidegger and Husserl, acknowledge his influence, and Habermas made use of his ideas. There are striking parallels between his ideas and some of those of pragmatism on the one hand and those of Wittgenstein and his disciples on the other. The origins and nature of these affinities may merit further investigation. Apart from anything else, the study, side by side, of such overlapping philosophies may fruitfully supplement each of them. These are matters I have left aside, but it may be worth stressing that the slant of Dilthey's philosophy toward the philosophy of the human studies itself makes a general point about philosophy. It is dangerous for philosophy to look only inward toward its own problems. Philosophers fail to perform the traditional functions of their discipline if they are content merely to take in each other's washing. Because of the urgency of the problems, the conflict of methodologies, and the confusion of paradigms, the studies concerned with man provide philosophy with a special challenge to raise its eyes above its own navel.

To make good this point, I want to look briefly at some of the reasons why the disciplines I have selected for consideration merit philosophic attention.

History is as old a preoccupation of mankind as any branch of human inquiry, and curiosity about our past has not abated today. Scholarly and popularizing books on history continue to appear, and historical romances are even more popular; there is also a plethora of films and television programs that provide documentary accounts or fictionalizations of historical events, among which recent wars are a particularly popular subject.

All this, combined with the fact that books by historians reflecting on their own craft and philosophic debates on the nature of history have become plentiful,[1] would justify attention to a major philosopher of history. There is, however, a curious paradox about this popularity. While history flourishes to meet an escapist demand for picturesque, romantic, and escapist costume drama, or a nostalgia for the past ("when Britain was great," "when men were men," and the like), its function as a tool for understanding the problems of our time has been overshadowed if not eclipsed by more recent disciplines, such as economics or sociology. Even the historians themselves and the philosophers writing on history tend to sound a little defensive because history, as it only tells stories, seems so much less "scientific" than even subjects like sociology.

In the face of this situation it becomes doubly important to confront the very different conception of the importance of history presented by Dilthey as the spokesman of the historicist school. We can thus be helped to remember that problems need to be understood in terms of the individual, unique sequence of events that brought them about. The continuing bloody conflicts in Ireland, the Lebanon, Palestine, in Sri Lanka and Afghanistan, the tensions in Poland and South Africa, the growth of violent crime in the inner cities of industrialized nations, all have their individual roots in the past. They are also colored by the way the actors in these different dramas themselves interpret their past. Of course, sociology and economics, and indeed psychology, have their contributions to make to the understanding of all our predicaments, but these disciplines can only too easily take flight into platitudinous generalities if they are not clearly linked to a study of what happened, as it unfolded in a particular place at a particular time. A manager facing a strike, a minister confronted with an international crisis needs more than a handbook on management or a text on diplomacy—he needs to know the story, and it can be a long story, of how the trouble arose.

History, more generally, informs us about human nature; indeed, because we are at the very core, historical creatures illuminate our very being.

Furthermore, though it does not foretell the future (because history does not repeat itself, and it is no use doing today what would have worked yesterday), it can prepare us for what is to come by giving us a sense of how things happen in time. Not only comedians, but salesmen, politicians, and seducers have to learn the art of "timing," of choosing the right moment, of being patient or of pouncing quickly.

Dilthey's thinking was permeated by a sense of history understood in this way. As a consequence, he continued to explore every possible aspect of history—the entities that form the subject matter of history, the development of its methodology from the ancient Greek historians to the historians of his own time, the interplay of intellectual and physical factors in the unfolding of events, and the need for interdisciplinary approaches—if the fullest possible historical understanding is to be achieved. Because of the contemporary relevance of all this, Dilthey's views can help us to answer questions posed by the neglected importance of history: Are we encouraging sufficiently the study of history in schools and colleges? Is it taught in the right spirit? Should we teach children about the way history is explored rather than giving them dates and facts to learn? Should there be courses in history for students of management?

However important, the historical approach needs to be balanced and supplemented by systematic human studies, of which psychology and sociology are prime examples. Dilthey's approach to psychology was challenging and controversial in his day and remains so now. Though he did not reject or denigrate experimental and biological psychology or any other aspect of "scientifically" oriented approaches to mental life, he argued strongly that they should be balanced by, and indeed preceded by, the descriptive psychology he advocated. Such a psychology deals with the whole person and with what is distinctly human, such as the capacity for abstract thinking or the creative imagination. Such a "humanistic" psychology is also particularly suited to serve as an adjunct to other disciplines and to enter interdisciplinary projects.

Now that scientific psychology has made such vast progress, emphasis on a counterbalancing psychology in Dilthey's spirit is doubly needed. It remains particularly important as the basis of such branches of psychology as "social psychology," "the psychology of personality," and "abnormal psychology." By way of illustrating these themes—to which I could, of course, not do justice—I expanded in the text on the methodological framework that Dilthey's philosophy provides for psychiatry.

Sociology is equally, if not more, in need of an epistemological and methodological underpinning. As yet it has no unified paradigm or agreed methodology. Outright behaviorism, whose ghost lingers in such terms as "the behavioral sciences," has been proved to be neither theoretically justifiable nor practically sustainable. Some researchers have merely attenuated its principles or ignored them without providing a new methodological framework for these departures. Sometimes such common sense proved a sound guide, but the reaction from a "scientific" paradigm has also led to too easy an acceptance as evidence of the merely subjective and anecdotal. However, "humanistic" sociologies with a distinctive methodology of their own have also emerged. They carry such labels as *Verstehens*-sociology, ethnomethodology, phenomenological sociology, and the like. Some of these have been more or less directly influenced by Dilthey's approach, but all fit into the broadly based philosophic framework for the human studies that he provided.

Let us then rapidly review the outstanding features of that framework, which, with minor variations, applies to all the human studies. Its three closely related ingredients are his theory of understanding, supplemented by accounts of experience, meaning, and expressions, his hermeneutics and his philosophic anthropolgoy.

At the heart and core of Dilthey's epistemology and methodology is the concept of understanding as a distinct cognitive process by which the meaning of expressions is grasped. The analysis of the nature of this process, the conditions for its success, and its operation on different levels of complexity is, by a wide agreement of Dilthey scholars, the most distinctive and original part of his philosophy. To start with, the recognition of understanding as a distinct cognitive process not reducible to other cognitive processes challenges a great deal of traditional philosophy that recognizes only observation and thought as legitimate roads to knowledge. It made it necessary to redraw the epistemological map and to scrutinize critically the presuppositions involved in this kind of knowledge.

Dilthey's theory of expressions, an essential ingredient of Dilthey's theory of understanding, extended systematic attention to a large range of forms of communication besides conventional languages. Not that he ignored language, which has for some time been a prominent subject matter of philosophers, from the linguistic analysts and pragmatists of the English-speaking world to the existentialists, structuralists, and poststructuralists spreading their influence from Germany and France. Indeed, that interest is not confined to philosophers; not only such specialized disciplines as linguistics or semantics, but psychology and sociology have also turned their attention to linguistic communication. Even new disciplines such as communication theory and information science have sprung up. All this is very understandable in a world in which the vast amount of communication that is going on is matched by the number of misunderstandings that occur.

However, side by side with attention to language there has been a spectacular growth in the study of nonlinguistic communication. Freud and his disciples systematically exploited the fact—known to common sense and reflected in fiction—that human acts, gestures, ways of walking and standing, facial expressions, and clothes reveal and communicate what their authors think or feel. Such forms of expression have come under increasing scrutiny under such titles as "body language," "expressive behavior," and the like. In all this Dilthey was a pioneer. Though he never engaged in a detailed study of it, his continued importance in this area of study lies in his creation of a systematic framework that embraces all types of expressions, both linguistic and nonlinguistic.

As understanding is always concerned with what is meaningful, a theory of meaning must take its place beside a theory of understanding. Here I need only recall one significant feature of Dilthey's treatment of meaning. He extended—not without ambiguity, yet fruitfully—the use of meaning beyond the linguistic sphere, and, indeed, beyond the sphere of expression or signification in any sense, to cover experiences, actions, and all kinds of relationships within life. This opened up helpful vistas—for example, it allowed for the distinction between behavior and meaningful action.

A short step takes us from understanding to hermeneutics as the art and methodology of interpretation when understanding is not easy and immediate interpretation is required. Until fairly recently, only high-grade specialists had heard of, let alone knew the meaning of, hermeneutics. Now it has become almost fashionable, and numerous books and articles carrying the term in their titles have appeared. Heidegger and his followers treat it as an essential method of philosophy itself, and many scholars have embraced it as a necessary ingredient in the study of the human world, once the methodology of the physical sciences has proved itself inadequate for the study of man.

Much of this is due to Dilthey's influence, either directly through the spread of his own writings, or probably more extensively indirectly through the work of thinkers such as Heidegger and Habermas, who took their original inspiration in this matter from Dilthey.

It also meets a practical need. Today, even more than in Dilthey's time, we need a scholarly discipline, well equipped to help us interpret the flood of messages to which we are exposed, because misunderstandings, failures in communication, and undetected misrepresentation are prominent features of our social and political problems. Often it is not the facts that are troublesome but the uncertainty as to what the facts we are told about really are. Similarly, the difficulty frequently lies not in what people do but in what we *think* they have promised or threatened to do.

On the theoretical side, much work is yet to be done to establish the canons of a methodology of interpretation and to define the relationship of such a methodology to the methods of science. It would be a gross misrepresentation to think that in most spheres there is a clear and simple alternative between science and hermeneutics. We are beginning to appreciate the hermeneutic factors of scientific enquiry, as well as the scientific underpinning from which hermeneutics can profit. In the social sciences we are moving cautiously toward syntheses between scientific and hermeneutic approaches, but this cannot be accomplished mechanically or with one stroke.

Philosophic anthropology, which in Dilthey's view provides essential presuppositions of understanding and hermeneutics, is, as yet, not a familiar subject matter in the English-speaking world. The term, at least, has not come into wide use. However, the issues that make up its subject matter are familiar in the United States and in England, and there is a long history of thought about them. I specifically discussed two reasons for the new urgency with which we must reexamine our fundamental concepts of man.

One is the twin challenge presented by the growing complexity of modern societies and the increasing technological powers in human hands that have made our world so dangerous. We have been shocked and frightened by the violence, callousness, and cruelty that can be released in citizens, even of highly cultured nations, by leaders such as Hitler or Stalin, or by industrial disputes, racial conflicts, or even occasions such as football matches. It is quite literally a matter of life and death to get things right in human relationships; so we must try to get a clear view of human nature and its potentialities for the most practical of reasons.

The second reason is the rapid development and expansion of various disciplines concerned with man, ranging over physiology, various branches of psychology, sociology, and so on. Their findings, and, indeed, their presuppositions, need absorbing and coordinating. We need some kind of guide or map to take us through the maze of discoveries and theories that cast such varied and confusing light on human nature.

There is a third reason: the eclipse, or at least dimming, of traditional conceptions of man. Describing man—in the tradition going back to ancient Greece—as the rational animal was always an ideal, a model to live up to rather than a description. But the stupidity, bigotry, fanaticism, superstition, prejudice, incompetence, and destructive passion they have witnessed have made many people doubt whether even ascribing an aspiration to, or potentiality for, rationality to man is more than idle self-congratulation. The long-held religious conception of man as a spiritual being, carrying the image of god in his soul, has fared no better and looks more than a little tarnished in the midst of a widespread decline in faith. With these ideas tottering, the idea of progress—be it the individual's progress toward growing wisdom and maturity, or that of humanity toward a happier and more harmonious future—has lost its apparent plausibility. So we have to look afresh at what man is, what he can be, and what he should be, because we need the answers not only to guide our research, or to avoid the disasters of war, industrial conflict, delinquency, and the like but to direct our educational programs, our social arrangements, cultural institutions, and political planning.

Dilthey's writings contain notable contributions to a conception of man's fundamental nature. There is man's historicity—the way he is affected by and responds to the passage of time—which I raised when discussing Dilthey's approach to history. The unity of the mind and its structure was emphasized in his psychology. His epistemology involved consideration of the way meaning arises in human life, the roles and relation to each other of thinking, feeling, and willing, and the categories of life as ways in which the mind grasps the human world around it. He makes other points about human nature, but I did not make an attempt to deal with them if they were not significant for understanding his approach as a whole. The details matter less than the inspiration he gave toward resuming the quest for a unified concept of man that reflects our experience and knowledge of human beings and can guide us in the solution of human problems.

Finally, I want to reassert how interesting and fruitful the very tensions and unresolved conflicts in Dilthey's thinking have proved to be. Not that these tensions are left there by design. Despite his open-mindedness and recoil from any dogmatic foreclosures, Dilthey longed to achieve a coherent and comprehensive philosophy. There is ample evidence for this in his continuously renewed attempts to organize and place into an embracing context his various individual studies. It is equally, or even more, clear that such unity eluded him, and we have listed various reasons for it.

However, a passion for clarity and consistency may also lead to a tendency to simplify and even to falsify. Life is complex and confusing, and things not always clear-cut, so seeing both sides of an issue is not invariably a fault. Refusing to come down on one side of the fence can be a perfectly reasonable choice. Our subject matter—in this case, life—may resist adequate explanation from a single point of view. Something like this is, I gather, the case in microphysics, because explanations in terms of waves and those in terms of particles cannot be reconciled with, or reduced to, each other. It is one of Dilthey's virtues to have been constantly alert to these dangers.

One apparently unreconcilable tension in the human studies that is prominent in Dilthey's work is that between historical and systematic approaches. From the historical point of view everything is subject to change in the temporal flux and must be explained in terms of its origins and development. Yet if there were nothing but that flux, there would be nothing to get a firm grip on. Knowledge itself becomes impossible, because we have lost not only any fixed subject matter but a fixed point of view from which to grasp it, and so we are cast adrift on a tide of relativity. I change all the time, but there is someone throughout who changes. Human beings are dramatically different in different ages and places and yet have a common human nature. Somehow we have to hold on to both points. We are left with the difficulty of where to draw the line. Confronted with a particular human manifestation, we are faced with the intractable problem of whether, and to what extent, we see a basic manifestation of human nature or its temporal guise.

On the methodological level Dilthey teaches us to look for knowledge by flexibly combining historical and systematic approaches. On a deeper level the possibility of objective truth is worth consideration. We need to avoid both dogmatic complacency and skepticism. Experience shows that well-established and firmly held convictions have turned out to be corrigible. Today's presupposition, today's range of available information, appear more adequate than yesterday's, but then surely tomorrow today's truths will be outdated.

Yet skepticism is as fatal in the quest for knowledge as complacency. Truth cannot be just yesterday's or today's convention. It is not just what people at a particular time happen to believe. The long training and hard work, the frustrations and triumphs of scientists and scholars of all kinds presuppose a goal toward which they are struggling, and that, surely, is approximation to a truth, which exists, however elusive it may be.

This ambiguous position is as unsatisfactory as it is necessary. Modern philosophy of science, familiar with this predicament, can look to Dilthey, who stoutly sustained this uncomfortable stance.

The epistemological problem I discussed in the last chapter concerns the same tension on a more general and abstract, more purely philosophical, level. It, too, touches on issues under debate today. No reasonably sane person doubts that he is a physical being living in and dependent on a physical world around him. He takes it for granted that he can only think and pursue knowledge if he is fed, is kept in the kind of atmosphere in which he can breathe, and is maintained in the right kind of temperature. He knows that the malfunctioning of his liver, let alone his brain, but also fear, mass hysteria, jealousy, and the like may interfere with his thought processes. We are not only historically but biologically, psychologically, and socially conditioned. This makes our conclusions fallible, our arguments unreliable, our opinions biased.

Surely all this is true beyond question—but how can this be so if what we hold true is that nothing can be true beyond question. To escape from this circle we need to assume, as I have argued in defence of Kant, the autonomy of reason—that is, the possibility that our cognitive faculty can function independently, in its form and content, from the external conditions we have listed, and some of which are the very conditions of its existence. Here, too, Dilthey—though vulnerable to the criticism of doing insufficient justice to the need for an autonomous reason if there was to be any objective truth—highlighted a paradox that continues to occupy contemporary philosophy.[2]

I believe today, as I did when I first started work on him many years ago, that Dilthey is an important and original thinker whose ideas merit attention because of their bearing on philosophic and methodological issues that continue to perplex us. Not that he was invariably right. On the contrary, he was, to my mind, exasperating and wrong-headed on some issues. However, this is of secondary importance compared to his power to stimulate and challenge, which is the very life blood of philosophy. This is the point I wanted to bring out by relating his thoughts to developments in different intellectual spheres that he had influenced.

Notes

Preface

1. Ulrich Herrmann, *Bibliographie. Wilhelm Dilthey* (Berlin: Beltz, 1969).

2. H. U. Lessing, "Bibliographie der Dilthey Literatur," in *Dilthey Jahrbuch für Philosophie und Geschichte der Geisteswissenschaften,* edited by F. Rodi, for years 1969–1973, Vol. 1/83; for years 1974–1978, Vol. 2/84; for years 1979–1983, Vol. 3/85 (Göttingen: Vandenhoeck & Ruprecht).

3. H. P. Rickman (ed.), *Pattern and Meaning in History* (New York: Harper & Row, 1962) is a collection of my translations from Vol. VII, with an introduction and commentary of some 70 pages. Idem (ed.), *Dilthey Selected Writings* (Cambridge, England: Cambridge University Press, 1976) provides a wide range of translations, with a 30-page general introduction and some brief introductions to individual works translated. Idem, *Wilhelm Dilthey, Pioneer of the Human Studies* (Berkeley: University of California Press, 1979) is a general introduction to the life and work of Dilthey. Idem, *Understanding and the Human Studies* (London: Heinemann, 1969) is not explicitly an exposition of Dilthey but a general discussion of ideas largely based on Dilthey's point of view. See the bibliography for my list of articles on Dilthey.

4. W. Dilthey, *Collected Works* (Göttingen: Vandenhoeck & Ruprecht, 1914–) (henceforth *C.W.*). Volumes XV–XVII deal with the intellectual history of the nineteenth century. They are a collection of newspaper and journal articles, book reviews, and the like. Volume XVIII contains early work on the philosophy of the human studies.

5. H. A. Hodges, *Wilhelm Dilthey: An Introduction* (London: Routledge & Kegan Paul, 1944) contains 50 pages of translations comprising 29 separate passages from Dilthey's works. S. A. & W. T. Emery, *The Essence of Philosophy* (Chapel Hill:

University of North Carolina Press, 1954) is a translation of *Das Wesen der Philosophie*, Vol. V, pp. 339–416. William Luback & Martin Weinbaum, *Philosophy of Existence: Introduction to Weltanschauungslehre* (New York: Bookman Associates, 1957) is a translation of Dilthey's *Die Typen der Weltanschauung*, Vol. VIII, pp. 75–118. J. J. Kuehl, "The Understanding of Other Persons and Their Life Expressions," Vol. VII, pp. 205–20, in *Theories of History: Readings in Classical and Contemporary Sources*, ed. Patrick Gardiner (New York, Free Press, 1959), pp. 213–25.

6. However, there is still inadequate use made of Dilthey's work by Anglo-Saxon philosophy. In *Philosophy and Literature*, ed. A. Ph. Griffith (Cambridge: Cambridge University Press, 1984), for example, there are two lectures—Professor Frank Coffi's "When do empirical methods by-pass 'the problems which trouble us'?" and Martin Warner's "Philosophic autobiography: St. Augustine and John Stuart Mill"—that deal with topics prominent in the writings of W. Dilthey and those influenced by him who have revived and adapted the hermeneutic tradition. Though both Cioffi and Warner quote or briefly refer to Dilthey, neither of them elaborates on the connections. In the case of Cioffi's paper particularly, it might have been interesting to note that the thrust of his argument—and that of Wittgenstein as presented in the paper—coincides with the chief reason for presenting hermeneutics as an alternative method to empirical science.

7. O. F. Bollnow, "Dilthey und die Phenomenologie," in *Dilthey und die Philosophie der Gegenwart* (Freiburg/Munich: Karl Albert, 1986); my translation.

8. J. E. Smith, *Themes in American Philosophy* (New York: Harper, 1970). Idem, *Purpose and Thought: The Meaning of Pragmatism* (New Haven: Yale University Press, 1978).

9. The letter is quoted by Hermann Nohl, *Die Grossen Deutschen*, Vol. IV (Berlin: Propyläen-Verlag, 1957), p. 199.

10. C. S. Peirce, *Collected Papers of Charles Saunders Peirce*, Vol. 12–13 (Cambridge, Mass.: Harvard University Press, 1931–58); quoted from Israel Scheffler, *Four Pragmatists* (London, New York: Routledge & Kegan Paul, 1974), p. 14.

Chapter 1

1. Husserl's letter to Misch, 27 June 1929. Quoted in a postscript in Georg Misch, *Lebensphilosophie und Phenomenology* (Darmstatt: Wissenschaftliche Buchgesellschaft, 1967).

2. Martin Heidegger, *Sein und Zeit* (Halle: Max Niemeyer, 1941), p. 366.

3. José Ortega y Gasset, *Concord and Liberty* (New York: Norton, 1963), p. 129, quoted from Kurt Muller Vollmer. Ortega y Gasset initiated a comprehensive translation of Dilthey's works into Spanish.

4. Erich Feueter, writing in the *Schweitzerische Hochschulzeitung*, 36 (1963): 233.

5. German scholars, among whom F. Rodi of Bochum University plays a leading role, have been at work on the unpublished manuscripts at the central archives of the Academie der Wissenschaften of the DDR in Berlin. Already in preparation is *C.W.*, Volume XX, based on lectures on the systematic epistemological founding of the

Human Studies (logic, system of philosophy, etc.). Volume XXI is to contain lectures and supplementary texts on psychology and anthropology, Volume XXII on educational theory. Volume XXIII will be on practical philosophy (ethics), and Volume XXIV will present a history of modern philosophy with its connection to general culture and the individual sciences. Volume XXV will take up the theme of logic of the Human Studies with Dilthey's responses to Rickert and Husserl. Volume XXVI will provide additional material on the philosophy of world views. Volume XXVII (also already in preparation) will incorporate, with editorial changes, the independently published *Das Erlebnis und die Dichtung* [Experience and Poetry] into the *Collected Works*. It will also include additional material on poetic theory. Volume XXVIII is to continue the Studies towards the history of the German spirit, and Volume XXIX assembles essays on the Berlin Academy of Sciences. Volumes XXX–XXXII are to present a selection from the large collection of Dilthey's letters.

6. R.-A. Makkreel and F. Rodi (eds.), *Wilhelm Dilthey: Selected Works* (Princeton, N.J.: Princeton University Press, 1985). The first volume to appear was Vol. V, *Poetry and Experience.*

7. Peter Krausser, *Kritik der endlichen Vernunft, Dilthey's Revolution der allgemeinen Wissenschafts und Handlungslehre* (Frankfurt: Suhrkamp, 1968).

8. The Schleiermacher biography has now been incorporated in the *Collected Works*: the completed part makes up Volume XIII (1 & 2), the material for the continuation of the work Volume XIV (1 & 2).

9. This material is to be found mostly in *C.W.*, Volumes III and XII, in *Von Deutscher Dichtung und Musik* (Stuttgart: B. G. Teubner, 1957) and in *Das Erlebnis und die Dichtung* (Stuttgart: B. G. Teubner, 1957).

10. Max Dessoir, *Buch der Erinnerungen* [Book of Memories] (Stuttgart: Enke-Verlag, 1946).

11. There is widespread agreement that test results are conditioned both by heredity and by environment (nature and nurture), but investigators disagree (often along political lines) on the relative importance of the two factors. Particularly keen controversy has raged over the question of racial differences in intelligence. There are two obvious difficulties in the way of a straightforward settlement of this question: one is that those who provide a child's hereditary endowment usually also provide its early environment; the other is the problem of devising "culture-free" tests.

12. Margaret Mead, *Male and Female* (Westport, Conn.: Greenwood Press, 1977).

13. Thucydides, *History of the Peloponnesian War*, Book VII, Chapters 43–44—quoted from A. J. Toynbee, *Greek Historical Thought* (New York: Mentor Books, 1952), pp. 101–2.

14. See Heidegger's later writings and H. G. Gadamer, *Truth and Method* (London: Sheed and Ward, 1975).

15. The letters on this affair are in a collection of his letters kept by Mrs. Lisl Wittel in Munster. She kindly allowed me access and, indeed, drew my attention to letters of special interest.

16. Kurt Müller-Vollmer, *Towards a Phenomenological Theory of Literature: A Study of Wilhelm Dilthey's Poetic* (The Hague: Mouton & Co., 1963).

17. Clara Misch (ed.), *Der junge Dilthey: Ein Lebensbild in Briefen und Tagebüchern, 1852–70* (Stuttgart: B. G. Teubner, 1960; first published in 1933).

18. Ibid.

19. See Bernd Peschken, *Versuch einer germanistischen Ideologie-kritik* (Stuttgart: Metzler, 1972).

20. Letter to his sister written in 1867; quoted from W. Nohl, "Wilhelm Dilthey" in *Die Grossen Deutschen*, Vol. IV (Berlin: Theodor Heuss and Benno Reifenberg, 1957).

21. Misch, *Der junge Dilthey*.

22. *Briefwechsel zwischen Wilhelm Dilthey und dem Grafen Paul York von Wartenburg, 1877–97*, ed. S. von der Schulenburg (Halle: Max Niemeyer, 1923).

23. Dessoir, *Buch der Erinnerungen*.

24. In "Wilhelm Dilthey," in *Die Grossen Deutschen: Deutsche Biographie*, Vol. 4, edited by Hermann Heimpel, Theodor Heuss, and Benno Reifenberg (Berlin: Propyläen-Verlag, 1957), pp. 193–204.

25 Jim Hakinson, *Bluff Your Way in Philosophy* (London: Bluffers Guide, 1985).

26 *Das Erlebnis und die Dichtung* (Stuttgart: B. G. Teubner, 1957; first published in 1906).

27. See Note 5.

Chapter 2

1. Clara Misch (ed.), *Der junge Dilthey: Ein Lebensbild in Briefen und Tagebüchern, 1852–70* (Stuttgart: B. G. Teubner, 1960), p. 152.

2. Ibid., pp. 79, 80, 92, 120, 124.

3. F. D. E. Schleiermacher, 1768–1834.

4. The reader will notice that there is no chronological, and not much of a thematic, order in the collected works. They started with the most readily available texts and gradually moved on to articles in journals, manuscripts, and lecture notes.

5. Dilthey's own disciple, Herman Nohl, worked in this field, and O. F. Bollnow was—and still is—active in it. They have influenced a younger generation of educational philosophers. Ernst Lichtenstein ("Schleiermachers Pädagogik," *Neue Zeitschrift für systematische Theologie und Religionsphilosophie* 10, 1968, pp. 343–359) writes: "It was ... the circle of Dilthey's disciples who after the first world war followed Schleiermacher by making educational theory to understand itself, culturally, philosophically and methodologically as a human discipline" [freely translated by me]; quoted from O. F. Bollnow, "Einige Bemerkungen zu Schleiermachers Pädagogik" in *Zeitschrift für Pädagogik*, 32, No. 5 (Basel: Beetz, 1986), p. 723.

6. "The system of nature: with this name we designate the theories which describe themselves as 'natural law,' 'natural theology,' 'natural religion' etc. whose common characteristic is that they deduce social phenomena from causal connections within man ..." (*C.W.*, Vol. I, p. 379).

7. J. S. Mill (1806–1873), A. Comte (1798–1875), H. T. Buckle (1821–1862).

8. D. E. Lee and R. N. Beck, "The Meaning of Historicism," *American Historical Review*, Vol. LIX (October 1953–July 1954).

9 F. Meinecke, "Values and Causalities in History," essay first published in 1928, translated by J. H. Franklin in *The Varieties of History from Voltaire to the Present*, edited by Fritz Stern (London: Thames & Hudson, 1957), p. 269.

10. F. M. Powicke, *Modern Historians and the Study of History* (London: Odham Press, 1955), p. 16.

11. B. Niebuhr, *History of Rome,* new edition by M. Isler, Berlin, 1873, translated by Fritz Stern, in *The Varieties of History from Voltaire to the Present,* edited by Fritz Stern (London: Thames & Hudson, 1957).

12. H. Taine, source unknown.

13. N. D. Fustel de Coulanges, *The Ancient City,* edited by Willard Small (New York: Doubleday, 1950), p. 123.

14. J. Huizinga, in an essay that first appeared in 1934, translated by Rosalie Colie in *The Varieties of History from Voltaire to the Present,* edited by Fritz Stern (London: Thames & Hudson, 1957), p. 292.

15. Ibid., p. 301.

16. L. B. Namier, *Avenues of History* (London: Hamish Hamilton, 1951), p. 1.

17. The acknowledgment previously noted (see Note 2, Chapter 1) refers in fact to Dilthey's analysis of temporality.

18. Immanuel Kant, *Critique of Pure Reason,* A 314.

19. A collection of representative essays in the debate about collectivism and "methodological individualism" are to be found in John O'Neill (ed.), *Modes of Individualism and Collectivism* (London: Heinemann, 1973).

20. H. P. Rickman, *Pattern and Meaning in History* (New York: Harper & Row, 1962), p. 146.

21. Namier, *Avenues of History.*

22. F. Braudel, "La geographie force aux sciences humaines." *Annales Economies, Societés, Civilisations,* Vol. 6, No. 4 (1951): 491.

23. Ibid., p. 726.

24. *Dilthey Jahrbuch,* Vol. 2 (1984), pp. 65–91.

25. Immanuel Kant, *Critique of Pure Reason,* B 172–73.

26. One must remember that Kant, having dealt with our capacity for knowledge in his first Critique and with the basis of morality in the second (i.e., with theoretical and practical reason, respectively), wanted to complete his work by a *Critique of Judgment.* The two parts of that work deal specifically with aesthetic and teleological judgment, but it may be doing one of the world's great thinkers less than justice to think of the title as merely a collective name for these two preoccupations. It is arguable that he intended—even if, in his advanced age, he did not fully accomplish—what the title promises, namely, a critique of judgment.

Chapter 3

1. The relevance of Dilthey's methodology for modern scholarship opens up vast areas of discussion. What is said in this section—and to some extent also, the references to history, psychology and anthropology elsewhere—could be linked extensively to modern developments. To give just one additional example from the methodology of history: When I read J. H. Hexter's *On Historians: Reappraisals of Some of the Makers of Modern History* (Harvard: Harvard University Press, 1979), I was struck by a number of crucial points that could have come straight from Dilthey. In psychology one would want to look above all to personality theories to which Eduard Spranger, one of Dilthey's close disciples, made significant contributions— see E. Spranger, *Lebensformen, geisteswissenschaftliche Psychologie und Ethik der Persönlichkeit* (Halle: Niemeyer, 1914), and idem, *Zur Theorie des Verstehens und zur geisteswissenschaftlichen Psychologie* (Munich: Beck, 1918). Most important and

extensive, however, are the connections between the Diltheyan theories discussed in this chapter and the development of sociology. There is, to start with, Max Weber's use of *Verstehen* and the influence it exercised on subsequent sociology. There is an affinity with G. E. Mead's Symbolic Interactionism, and Dilthey's approach is also reflected in Ethnomethodology. In fact, all that goes under the title of "humanistic sociology" could be profitably reexamined in terms of Dilthey's methodology. (I am, of course, not saying that all this is due to Dilthey's influence—merely that all this can be usefully related to Dilthey's philosophic framework for the human studies.) A thorough discussion of all this would have transcended the scope of this book, and brief references can amount to little more than name-dropping. I considered the alternative of providing extensive bibliographies of the topics I have just mentioned. As I have given courses on the philosophy of sociology, this would have been easy enough, and, of course, the texts I have used, in turn, contain bibliographies that can be judiciously copied. I have decided against it as I could not see much point to it. Readers particularly interested in the hearing of Dilthey's theories on sociology will know about these books and bibliographies in any case. So I have, instead, concentrated on as simple and straightforward an account of Dilthey's own theories as I could manage, and I leave the reader to make some of the connections that cannot be adequately made in a single volume.

2. I have discussed Dilthey's use of "understanding" and the widespread misconceptions about it in H. P. Rickman, *Understanding and the Human Studies* (London: Heinemann, 1969), pp. 24–26.

3. By way of illustration, I reprint two quotations used in the above text. G. A. Lundberg wrote in "Foundations of Sociology," "The error lies in overlooking that insight and understanding are the ends at which all methods aim, rather than methods in themselves" (in *A Study in Human Understanding*, New York: Macmillan, 1939), and Richard von Mieses said in *Positivism* (New York: Dover, 1968), "Understanding then is nothing but the subsumption of an event in a primitive 'theory.' ..."

4. The husband who complains that his wife understands him, rather than that she does not understand him, uses the term essentially in Dilthey's sense.

5. Lundberg was not the only one to attribute to Dilthey the belief that understanding was a method. W. S. Outhwaite put the idea into a title in order to shoot it down: "The Method called 'Verstehen,'" in *Understanding Social Life* (New York: Holmes and Meyer, 1976). Even as sound and perceptive a critic as Michael Ermarth talks about understanding as a method—in *Wilhelm Dilthey: The Critique of Historical Reason* (Chicago: University of Chicago Press, 1978).

6. Commentators thought that this represented a particularly obscure and difficult usage. For example, H. S. Hughes called it in *Consciousness and Society* (New York: Knopf, 1958, p. 24), "the most difficult intellectual problem that I have confronted in the present study—the murkiest of the dark corners in the labyrinth of German social science methods."

7. Discussions on how far meaning should, or should not, be defined in terms of the author's intended meaning continue to this day. Scholars such as E. D. Hirsch, Jr., in *Validity in Interpretation* (New Haven, Conn.: Yale University Press, 1967), define meaning in terms of the author's intentions. Modern deconstructionists such as Derrida go to the other extreme and consider the meaning of the text the creative achievement of the reader or critic.

8. It has been argued that the move from psychology to hermeneutics was

influenced by Husserl; that Dilthey's late manuscripts—for example, his discussions of the categories of life reproduced in *C.W.*, Vol. VII—represent a development triggered off by reading Husserl and exchanging views with him. But Bollnow has argued convincingly that there is much evidence, including specifically the recently published material of *C.W.*, Vol. XIX, for the fact that the themes of Dilthey's old age were rooted in his earlier thinking, from which they naturally grew—O. F. Bollnow, "Dilthey und die Phenomenologie," in *Dilthey und die Philosophie der Gegenwart* (Munich: Karl Albert, 1986). See also F. Rodi and H. U. Lessing (eds.), *Materialien zur Philosophie Wilhelm Diltheys* (Frankfurt: Suhrkamp, 1984), pp. 103–84 and 236–74.

9. Immanuel Kant, "Groundwork for the Metaphysic of Morals" (tr. H. J. Paton), in *The Moral Law* (London: Hutchinson, 1972).

10. Pareto, quoted from Werner Stark, *The Fundamental Forms of Social Thought* (London: Routledge & Kegan Paul, 1962), pp. 126–27.

11. Lundberg, in ibid., pp. 153–54.

12. One of the outstanding exponents of hermeneutics as the methodology of the human studies is Emilio Betti, *Allgemeine Auslegungslehre als Methodik der Geisteswissenschaften* (Tübingen: Mohr, 1967) and idem, *Die Heremeneutik als allgemeine Methode der Geisteswissenschaften* (Tübingen: Mohr, 1962). Other recent books on hermeneutics are: K.-O. Apel, Jürgen Habermas, H. G. Gadamer, Claus von Bormann, Rüdiger Bubner, and H. Y. Giegel, *Hermeneutik und Ideologie Kritik* (Frankfurt: Suhrkamp, 1971); R. E. Palmer, *Hermeneutics: Interpretation Theory in Schleiermacher, Dilthey, Heidegger and Gadamer* (Evanston, Ill.: Northwestern University Press, 1969); and Janet Wolff, *Hermeneutic Philosophy and the Sociology of Art* (London: Routledge & Kegan Paul, 1975). A survey of different approaches to hermeneutics, illustrated with translations of substantial texts, is provided by Joseph Bleicher, *Contemporary Hermeneutics, Hermeneutics as Method, Philosophy and Critique* (London: Routledge & Kegan Paul, 1980).

13. This point is made clearly and succinctly by E. D. Hirsch, Jr., in "Three Dimensions of Hermeneutics," in *New Literary History*, Vol. III, No. 2 (Charlottesville, N.C: University of Virginia, 1972), p. 251: "Adherents of Heidegger's metaphysics take the view that all attempts accurately to reconstruct past meanings are doomed to failure since not just our texts but also our understanding are historical. It is the nature of man to have no permanently defined nature distinct from his historically constituted existence. Whatever we know is decisively accommodated to our own historical world and cannot be known to us apart from that determining context. An interpreter must therefore learn to live with his historical self."

14. Paul Ricoeur, *The Conflict of Interpretations, Essays in Hermeneutics* (Evanston, Ill.: Northwestern University Press, 1974); idem, "The Model of the Text: Meaningful Action Considered as a Text," in *Social Research: An International Quarterly of the Social Sciences*, 38 (Autumn 1971).

15. Jürgen Habermas, *Knowledge and Human Interest* (London: Heinemann, 1968); and idem, *Der Universalitätsanspruch der Hermeneutik* in K.-O. Apel, 1971, see Note 11.

16. Heinrich Rickert, *The Limits of Concept Formation in Natural Science*, ed. and tr. Guy Oakes (Cambridge: Cambridge University Press, 1986). The terms "ideographic" and "nomothetic" had been coined by his teacher, Wilhelm Windelband.

17. On the Hawthorne Experiment see F. J. Roethlisberger and W. J. Dickson, *Management and the Worker* (New York: Science Eds., 1964).

18. An outstanding example of this approach is an analysis of Goethe's imagination (based on autobiographical remarks) in Dilthey's very long essay on Goethe. It first appeared in 1877 and was incorporated in *Das Erlebnis und die Dichtung* (Göttingen: V & R, 1957).

19. *Discourse on Method,* Part 2.

20. The outstanding exponent of demythologizing is Rudolf Bultmann in such works as *Jesus Christ and Mythology* (New York: Scribners, 1958), and idem, "New Testament and Mythology," in *Kerygma and Myth,* ed. H. W. Bartsch (New York: Harper & Brothers, 1957).

21. See Note 7.

22. See Note 7.

23. The literature on questionnaires and interviews is rich in illustrations of how questions can be misunderstood and lead to misleading answers; one illustration, which sounds like a joke, is provided in Alan Garfinkel, *Forms of Explanation: Rethinking the Questions in Social Theory* (New Haven, Conn.: Yale University Press, 1981): We are told there about a clergyman who asks a criminal why he robs banks. "Because that's where the money is," the robber replies.

24. "Concluding Unscientific Postscript," in Robert Bretall, *A Kierkegaard Anthology* (Princeton: Princeton University Press, 1973), pp. 202–3.

25. Habermas, *Knowledge and Human Interest.*

Chapter 4

1. *Briefwechsel*: Dilthey/York.

2. In *C.W.*, Vol. VII, *Der Aufbau der geschichtlichen Welt in den Geisteswissen-schaften* (my translation in *Selections*, pp. 199–207). For a discussion of the relevance of Dilthey's writing for sociology see especially Helmut Johach, *Handelnder Mensch und objectiver Geist* (Meisenheim: Hain, 1974).

3. *C.W.*, Vol. VIII, *Weltanschauungslehre: Abhandlungen zur Philosophie der Philosophie* (transation in *Dilthey: Selected Writings*, pp. 133–154).

4. G. E. Moore, *Principia Ethica* (Cambridge: Cambridge University Press, 1903).

5. See especially Plato, *The Republic,* and Aristotle, *The Nicomachean Ethic.*

6. See Spinoza, *Ethic.*

7. J. S. Mill, *Utilitarianism,* Chapter IV.

8. Max Scheler (1874–1928): among his extensive writing on various topics is *Die Stellung des Menschen im Kosmos* (Darmstadt: Reichl, 1928). Also relevant in the context of his philosophic anthropology is the work mentioned in Note 15. Finally, there is his last and unfinished work, *Philosophische Anthropologie* (ibid.), *Gesammette Schriften* (Munich: Franke), pp. 71–79. H. Plessner (1892–): see particularly *Die Stufen des Organischen und der Mensch. Einleitung in die philosophische Anthropologie,* (Berlin; de Gruyter, 1928).

9. Helmut Plessner in his Preface to *Die Stufen des Organischen und der Mensch*: "It is Dilthey among the great thinkers of the most recent past whose philosophy and historiography—with its method and content—seems an essential source of the new approach [*Problemstellung*] of Philosophic Anthropology" [my translation]. I

should add, perhaps, that Dilthey's influence was by no means confined to philosophic anthropology. Karl Acham, in "Dilthey's Beitrag zur Theory der Kultur- und Socialwissenschaften" (*Dilthey Jahrbuch* 3, 1985) notes the fact that F. Boas, the founder of cultural anthropology, had read Dilthey, and that A. L. Kröber supported his concept of culture by explicit reference to Dilthey.

10. *Nachlass,* C 34, II, p. 156, quoted from H. Johach book cited in Note 16.

11. Ludwig Landgrebe, *Philosophie der Gegenwart* (Bonn: Atheneum, 1952), p. 21 (my translation). H. O. Pappe's article on philosophical anthropology in the *Encyclopedia of Philosophy* (New York: Macmillan, 1967) describes the work of Hobbes, Locke, and Shaftesbury as the root of philosophical anthropology and suggests that they formulated its program. The article treats philosophical anthropology largely as a school of philosophy with widely shared views (though different slants toward biology, psychology, or theology, respectively, can be discerned).

12. See, for example, Maurice Roche, *Phenomenology, Language and the Social Sciences* (London: Routledge & Kegan Paul, 1973).

13. Ralph Dahrendorf, "Homo Sociologicus" and "Sociology and Human Nature," *Essays in the Theory of Society* (London: Routledge & Kegan Paul, 1968), pp. 19–107; "homo sociologicus" is defined on p. 25, psychological and economic man on pp. 20–21.

14. *Concluding Unscientific Postscript,* quoted from Bretall, *Kierkegaard Anthology* (Princeton, N.J.: Princeton University Press), p. 205.

15. Martin Heidegger, *Sein und Zeit* (Halle: Niemeyer, 1941).

16. Ernst Cassierer, *An Essay on Man* (New York: Doubleday, 1953), chapter 1.

17. In Max Scheler, *Philosophische Weltanschauung* (Munich: Lehnen, 1954).

18. See Note 7, Chapter 3.

19. The following is a selection of texts in the field of philosophic anthropology: Arnold Gehlen, *Der Mensch, seine Natur und Stellung in der Welt* (Berlin: Junker & Dünnhaupt, 1940); Hans Lipps, *Die Menschliche Natur* (Frankfurt: Klostermann, 1941); O. F. Bollnow, *Mensch im Raum* (Stuttgart: Kohlhammer, 1963); idem, *Das Wesen der Stimmungen* (Frankfurt: Klostermann, 1941); Paul Häberlin, *Der Mensch: Eine philosophische Anthropologie,* (Zurich: Scheiger & Spiegel, 1941); F. J. J. Buytendijk, *Mensch und Tier* (Hamburg: Rowohlt, 1958).

20. A substantial body of literature is relevant here. Let me just mention Mary Hesse, "Theory and Value in the Social Sciences," in Christopher Hookway and Philip Pettit (eds.), *Action and Interpretation* (Cambridge: Cambridge University Press, 1978) and P. K. Feyerabend, "Explanation, Reduction and Empiricism" in his *Realism, Stationalism, Scientific Method* (Cambridge, Cambridge University Press, 1981).

21. All the quotations from this section come from Dilthey's *Ideen über eine beschreibende und zergliedernde Psychologie* (1894), *C.W.*, Vol. V, pp. 139–226. (Selected translations, *Wilhelm Dilthey Selected Writings*, pp. 88–97).

22. Translated in *Selections,*, p. 89.

23. Ibid., p. 91.

24. Ibid., p. 93.

25. Loc. cit.

26. Loc. cit.

27. Ibid., p. 89–90.

28. *Experience and Poetry* (Cambridge: Cambridge University Press, 1976).

29. Theodor Adorno, Else Frenkel-Brunswick, Daniel J. Levinson, and R. W. Sanford, *The Authoritarian Personality* (New York: Harper & Row, 1950).

30. Basing themselves theoretically on *The Authoritarian Personality* and on Erich Fromm, *The Fear of Freedom* (London: Routledge & Kegan Paul, 1942), a team of psychologists and psychiatrists applied to a sample of distinguished Nazi suspects a battery of personality tests, interviews, free-association tests, and questionnaires, with the aim of assessing the presence of a series of personality traits supposed to constitute the authoritarian personality.

31. Richard Christie and Marie Jahoda, *Studies in the Scope and Method of the Authoritarian Personality* (Glencoe, Ill.: The Free Press, 1954).

32. Translated in *Selections,* p. 92.

33. Ibid., p. 94.

34. Ibid., p. 95.

35. I am, of course, referring to the Vulcan in the voyages of the spaceship *Enterprise,* as depicted in "Star Trek."

Chapter 5

1. Karl Jaspers, *General Psychopathology* (Chicago: Regnery, 1963).

2. Karl Jaspers, *Philosophie der Weltanschauungen* (Berlin: J. Springer, 1919).

3. See, for example, T. S. Kuhn, *The Structure of Scientific Revolutions* (Chicago: University of Chicago Press, 1962).

4. Jaspers, *General Psychopathology,* p. 355.

5. Ibid., p. 255.

6. Ibid., p. 200.

7. Ibid., p. 253.

8. Ibid., p. 302–3.

9. Ibid., p. 310.

10. Ibid., p. 251.

11. Ibid., p. 287.

12. Quoted from *Selections,* pp. 218–19.

Chapter 6

1. *C.W.,* Vol. I, Preface to "An Introduction to the Human Studies," p. xviii, tr. p. 162.

2. In a letter referring to his *Dilthey's Kritik der historischen Vernunft— Programm oder System* (in *Dilthey Jahrbuch* 3, 1985, pp. 140–165), Professor F. Rodi directed my attention to this passage as the basis for his theory that Dilthey did entertain a draft or program for the systematization of his philosophy. Though stating that it remained a program, he suggests that "one can develop a systematic connection of epistemology, Logic and methodology from the two main theses of Philosophy (the thesis of Phenomenality and the thesis of the Totality of Mental Life)." The two theses are quoted in the text.

3. The translations are mine; *Zusammenhang* is translated as "coherence," but no translation of this term is entirely satisfactory.

4. Clara Misch (ed.), *Der junge Dilthey: Ein Lebensbild in Briefen und Tagebüchern 1852–1870* (Stuttgart: B. G. Teubner, 1960; first published in 1933).

5. I was reminded of these two references by Rodi's article referred to above.

6. Bollnow, *Dilthey* (Stuttgart, Kohlhammer, 1936), p. 18 et seq.

7. In "Paul Ricoeur und die Probleme der Hermeneutik" in *Zeitschrift für Philosophische Forschung*, Vol. 30, No. 2 (April–June 1976): 397.

8. *Die Dichterische und Philosophische Bewegung in Deutschland 1770–1800*, Inaugural lecture in Basel, 1867, in *C.W.*, Vol. V.

9. H. P. Rickman, *The Adventure of Reason* (Westport, Conn.: Greenwood, 1983), pp. 99–128.

10. "This," he wrote, "is Kant's great discovery: to recognise in the forms of judgement, underlying metaphysical presuppositions—the categories," *C.W.*, Vol. X, p. 112.

11. Gambatista Vico (1668–1744), *The New Science*, III, *Principles, 331*, translated by T. G. Bergin & M. H. Fisch (New York: Doubleday, 1961), p. 53.

12. Karl Marx, "Towards a Critique of Political Economy," Preface to *NEW*, Vol. 13, p. 8.

13. Karl Marx, in *The German Ideology, I* Feuerbach, 5.

14. Bretall, *Concluding Unscientific Postscript*, p. 196.

15. Ibid., p. 200.

16. Friedrich Nietzsche, "About Truth and Lie in a Non-moral Sense," 8 (1873); this is taken from *Nietzsches Werke* (Leipzig: Kröner, 1922), Vol. 2; *Ueber Wahrheit und Lüge im aussermoralischen Sinne*, 1873, p. 5 [my translation].

17. Ibid., Vol. 8, p. 220.

18. Peter Winch, *The Idea of a Social Science and its Relation to Philosophy* (New York: Humanities Press, 1962).

19. J. Habermas, *Erkenntnis und Interesse* [Knowledge and Human Interest,] (Frankfurt: Surkamp, 1968), p. 197. I quote from the translation of the work by J. J. Shapiro, which appeared under the title *Knowledge and Human Interest* (Boston: Beacon, 1971). The Appendix of the American edition reproduces an article also called "Erkenntnis und Interesse," *Merkur*, 1965, where my quotation appears on p. 312.

20. Ibid., p. 312.

21. Ibid., p. 61.

22. Immanuel Kant, *Grundlegung der Metaphysik der Sitten*, p. 101. I have used H. J. Paton's translation from *The Moral Law* (London: Hutchinson, 1948).

23. *Anthropologie in pragmatischer Hinsicht* [Anthropology from a pragmatic point of view], (Königsberg, 1798), translated, with an introduction and notes, by Mary J. Gregor (the Hague: Martinus Nijhoff, 1974).

24. *Die Kritik der reinen Vernunft*, B155. I quote from the translation by Norman Kemp Smith (London: Macmillan, 1929), p. 167. I have omitted some of the translator's bracketed insertions as superfluous in the present context.

25. Ibid., B 422.

26. Ibid., B 218–65.

Chapter 7

1. Examples of contemporary historians who have written on their craft are: Geoffrey Barraclough, *History in a Changing World* (Oxford, Blackwell, 1956); Marc Bloch, *The Historian's Craft*, tr. Peter Putnam (Manchester: Manchester

University Press, 1953); Herbert Butterfield, *Man on His Past* (Cambridge: Cambridge University Press, 1955); E. H. Carr, *What Is History?* (Middlesex: Penguin, 1964). Among books on history by philosophers are: Isaiah Berlin, *Historical Inevitability* (Oxford: Oxford University Press, 1954); R. G. Collingwood, *The Idea of History* (Oxford: Clarendon Press, 1970); W. H. Dray, *Philosophic Analysis in History* (New York, Harper & Row, 1966); W. B. Gallie, *Philosophy and the Historical Understanding* (New York, Schocken Books, 1964); Maurice Mandelbaum, *The Anatomy of Historical Knowledge* (Baltimore: John Hopkins University Press, 1979).

2. Within days of writing this I read Brian Sayer's "Wittgenstein, Relativism and the Strong Thesis in Sociology" in *Philosophy of the Social Sciences,* Vol. 17, No. 2 (June 1987), pp. 133–45. I found it not only interesting, but compatible with the position I have tried to present. I also found myself more closely in accord with Wittgenstein's views (as presented by Sayers) than my limited knowledge of the "late" Wittgenstein had led me to expect.

Bibliography

DILTHEY'S WRITINGS

Collected Works

I have given all titles in English translation. A list of the works included in each volume can be found in Rickman, *W. Dilthey: Selected Writings* (Cambridge: Cambridge University Press, 1976).

Collected Works. Göttingen: Vandenhoeck & Ruprecht. 1914–

Volume I. *Introduction to the Human Studies,* edited by Bernard Groethuysen; 7th ed., 1973. (First published in 1922.)

Volume II. *World View and Analysis of Men since the Renaissance and Reformation,* edited by Georg Misch; 10th ed., 1977. (First published in 1914.)

Volume III. *Contributions to the History of the German Spirit,* edited by Paul Ritter; 5th ed., 1976. (First published in 1921.)

Volume IV. *The History of the Young Hegel and Other Treatises towards the History of German Idealism,* edited by Herman Nohl; 5th ed., 1975. (First published in 1921.)

Volume V. *The World of Mind. Introduction to the Philosophy of Life. First Part: Treatises towards the Foundations of the Human Studies,* edited by G. Misch; 5th ed., 1968. (First published in 1924.)

Volume VI. *The World of Mind. Introduction to the Philosophy of Mind. Second Part: Treatises on Poetics, Ethics and Theory of Education,* edited by G. Misch; 5th ed., 1968. (First published in 1924.)

Volume VII. *The Construction of the Historical World in the Human Studies,* edited by B. Groethuysen; 6th ed., 1973. (First published in 1927.)

Volume VIII. *The Theory of World-views: Treatises towards the Philosophy of Philosophy,* edited by B. Groethuysen; 4th ed., 1968. (First published in 1931.)

Volume IX. *Theory of Education: History and Outlines of the System,* edited by O. F. Bollnow; 4th ed., 1974. (First published in 1934.)

Volume X. *System of Ethics,* edited by H. Nohl; 3rd ed., 1970. (First published in 1958).

Volume XI. *The Origin of Historical Consciousness. Youthful Essays and Reminiscences,* edited by Erich Weniger; 4th ed., 1971. (First published in 1936.)

Volume XII. *Contributions to Prussian History: Schleiermacher's Political Outlook and Activity. The Reorganisation of the Prussian State. The Legal Code* [Das allgemeine Landrecht], edited by Martin Redeker; 4th ed., 1973. (First published in 1936.)

Volume XIII. *The Life of Schleiermacher,* Volume One, edited by M. Redeker; 1970. (First published in 1870.)

Volume XIV. *The Life of Schleiermacher,* Volume Two: *Schleiermacher's System as Philosophy and Theology,* edited by M. Redeker; 1978. (First published in 1966.)

Volume XV. *Contributions to the Intellectual History of the 19th Century,* edited by Ulrich Herrmann; 1970.

Volume XVI. *Contributions to the Intellectual History of the 19th Century,* edited by Ulrich Herrmann; 1972.

Volume XVII. *Contributions to the Intellectual History of the 19th Century,* edited by Ulrich Herrmann; 1974.

Volume XVIII. *The Sciences of Man, Society and History,* edited by Helmut Johach and Rithjof Rodi; 1977.

Volume XIX. *The Foundations of the Sciences of Man, Society and History,* edited by H. Johach and R. Rodi; 1982.

Other writings of W. Dilthey

Das Erlebnis und die Dichtung [Experience and Poetry]: Lessing, Goethe, Novalis, Hölderlin. Göttingen: Vandenhoeck & Ruprecht, 1957.
The Great Poetry of Imagination and Other Studies in Comparative Literature, edited by H. Nohl. Göttingen: Vandenhoeck & Ruprecht, 1954.

German Poetry and Music, edited by H. Nohl and G. Misch. Göttingen: Vandenhoeck & Ruprecht, 1977.

English translations of Dilthey's work

Emery, S. A., and Emery, W. T. (tr). *The Essence of Philosophy* (from *C.W.,* Vol. V, 339–416).

Makkreel, R. A., and Rodi, F. (eds.). *Poetry and Experience* (translation of Vol. VI, pp. 103–287). Princeton, N.J.: Princeton University Press, 1985.

———. "The Imagination of the Poet," "The Three Epochs of Modern Aesthetics and Its Present Task," and "Experience and Poetry," in *Poetry and Experience,* edited by R. A. Makkreel and F. Rodi (pp. 124–185, 242–317). Princeton, N.J.: Princeton University Press, 1985.

Rickman, H. P. (tr.). *Patterns and Meaning in History. Dilthey's Thought on History and Society* (selections from *C.W.,* Vol. VII). New York: Harper & Row, 1962.

———. "W. Dilthey: Selected Writings" (selections from *C.W.,* Vols. V, VII, VIII and XIII, *The Great Poetry of Imagination* and *Experience and Poetry*). Cambridge: Cambridge University Press, 1976.

SECONDARY SOURCES

Books

Antoni, Carlo. *From History to Sociology.* Detroit, Mich.: Wayne State University Press, 1959.

Betti, Emilio. *Die Hermeneutik als allgemeine Methode der Geisteswissenschaften.* Tübingen: Mohr, 1962.

———. *Allgemeine Auslegungslehre als Methodik der Geisteswissenschaften.* Tübingen: Mohr, 1967.

Bleicher, Joseph. *Contemporary Hermeneutics.* London: Routledge and Kegan Paul, 1980.

Bollnow, O. F. *Das Verstehen: Drei Aufsätze zur Theorie der Geisteswissenschaften.* Meinz: Kirchheimer, 1949.

———. *Dilthey: Eine Einführung in seine Philosophie.* Stuttgart: Kohlhammer, 1955.

———. *Die Lebensphilosophie.* Berlin: Springer Verlag, 1958.

———. "Paul Ricoeur und die Probleme der Hermeneutik." *Zeitschrift für Philosophische Forschung, 30,* 2 (April–June 1976), Meisenheim: Anton Hain.

———. "Dilthey und die Phenomenologie." In *Dilthey und die Philosophie der Gegenwart.* Munich: Karl Albert, 1986.

———. "Philosophische Anthropologie." In *Universitas* 41. Stuttgart: Wissenschaftliche Verlagsgesellschaft, 1986.

Brock, Werner. *An Introduction to Contemporary German Philosophy.* Cambridge: Cambridge University Press, 1935.

Cassirer, Ernst. *An Essay on Man.* New York: Doubleday, 1953.

————. *Zur Logic der Naturwissenschaften.* Darmstadt: Wissenschaftliche Buchgesellschaft, 1961.

Ermarth, Michael. *Wilhelm Dilthey, The Critique of Historical Reason.* Chicago:
University of Chicago Press, 1978.

Gadamer, H. G. *Truth and Method* (tr. Gawen Burden and John Cumming). New
York: Sheed and Ward, 1975.

Habermas, Jürgen. *Knowledge and Human Interests* (tr. J. J. Shapiro). Boston:
Beacon Press, 1971.

Heidegger, Martin. *Being and Time* (tr. John Macquarrie and E. S. Robinson). New
York: Harper and Row, 1962.

————. *Introduction to Metaphysics* (tr. Ralph Manheim). New Haven, Conn.:
Yale University Press, 1959.

————. "Hölderlin and the Essence of Poetry" (tr. Douglas Scott). In *Existence and
Being.* Chicago: Henry Regnery, 1949.

Hirsch, E. D. *Validity in Interpretation.* New Haven, Conn.: Yale University Press,
1967.

Hughes, H. S. *Consciousness and Society: The Reorientation of European Social
Thought 1890–1930.* New York: Knopf, 1958.

Ineichen, Hans. *Erkenntnistheorie und geschichtlich-gesellschaftliche Welt: Diltheys
Logik der Geisteswissenschaften.* Frankfurt: Klostermann, 1975.

Jaspers, Karl. *General Psychopathology* (tr. Jon Hoenig and M. W. Hamilton).
Chicago: Regnery, 1963.

Johach, Helmut. *Handelnder Mensch und Objectiver Geist: Zur Theory der Geistes-
und Sozialwissenschaften bei Wilhelm Dilthey.* Meisenheim: Hain, 1974.

Kant, Immanuel. "Groundwork of the Metaphysic of Morals" (tr. H. J. Paton). In
The Moral Law. London: Hutchinson, 1972.

————. *Critique of Pure Reason* (tr. Norman Kemp Smith). London: Macmillan,
1976.

Krausser, Peter. *Kritik der endlichen Vernunft: Diltheys Revolution der allgemeinen
Wissenschafts- und Handlungstheorie.* Stuttgart: Kohlhammer, 1969.

Landgrebe, Ludwig. *Philosophie der Gegenwart.* Frankfurt: Ullstein, 1958.

Makkreel, R. A. *Dilthey: Philosophy of the Human Studies.* Princeton, N.J.:
Princeton University Press, 1975.

Meinecke, Friedrich. *Die Entstehung des Historismus.* Munich: Oldenbourg, 1946.

Misch, Georg. *Lebensphilosophie und Phenomenologie: Eine Auseinandersetzung
der Diltheyschen Richtung mit Heidegger und Husserl.* Stuttgart: Teubner,
1967.

————. "Vorbericht des Herausgebers" in Dilthey's *Collected Works*, Vol. V, pp.
7–117.

Müller-Vollmer, Kurt. *Towards a Phenomenological Theory of Literature: A Study
of Wilhelm Dilthey's "Poetic."* The Hague: Mouton, 1963.

Nietzsche, Friedrich. *Nietzsches Werke.* Leipzig: Alfred Kroner, 1922.

Ortega y Gasset, José. "Wilhelm Dilthey and the Idea of Life." In *Concord and
Liberty* (tr. Helene Weyl). New York: Norton, 1946.

Palmer, Richard. *Hermeneutics: Interpretation Theory in Schleiermacher, Dilthey,
Heidegger and Gadamer.* Evanston, Ill.: Northwestern University Press,
1969.

Rickert, Heinrich. *Kulturwissenschaft und Naturwissenschaft.* Freiburg: Mohr, 1899.

————. *Die Grenzen der naturwissenschaftlichen Begriffsbildung*. Tübingen: Mohr, 1902.

Rickman, H. P. *Pattern and Meaning in History*. New York: Harper, 1962.

————. *Understanding and the Human Studies*. London: Heinemann, 1967.

————. *W. Dilthey: A Selection*. Cambridge: Cambridge University Press, 1976.

————. *W. Dilthey: Pioneer of the Human Studies*. Stanford, Calif.: University of California Press, 1979.

————. "Vico's First Principle and the Critique of Historical Reason." In *Vico: Past and Present*. New York: Humanities Press, 1981, pp. 206–15.

————. *The Adventure of Reason*. Westport, Conn.: Greenwood, 1983.

Ricoeur, Paul. "The Model of the Text: Meaningful Action Considered as a Test." *Social Research: An International Quarterly of the Social Sciences, 38* (Autumn 1971): 529–62.

————. *The Conflict of Interpretations: Essays in Hermeneutics*. Evanston, Ill.: Northwestern University Press, 1974.

Rodi, Frithjof. *Morphologie und Hermeneutik: Zur Methode von Diltheys Aesthetik*. Stuttgart: Kohlhammer, 1969.

———— (ed.). *Dilthey Jahrbuch für Philosophie und Geschichte der Geisteswissenschaften*, Vol. I (1983); Vol. II (1984); Vol. III (1985).

Sauerland, Karol. *Diltheys Erlebnisbegriff: Entstehung, Glanzzeit und Verkümmerung eines literaturhistorischen Begriffs*. Berlin: de Gruyter, 1972.

Scheler, Max. *Die Stellung des Menschen im Kosmos*. Darmstadt: Reich, 1928.

————. *Philosophische Weltanschauung*. Munich: Lehnen, 1954.

Smith, J. E. *Themes in American Philosophy*. New York: Harper, 1970.

————. *Purpose and Thought: The Meaning of Pragmatism*. New Haven, Conn.: Yale University Press, 1978.

Spranger, Eduard. *Zur Theorie des Verstehens und zur geisteswissenschaftlichen Psychologie in Festschrift für Johannes Volkelt*. Munich: Beck, 1918, pp. 357–403.

————. *Lebensformen: Geisteswissenschaftliche Psychologie und Ethik der Persönlichkeit*. Halle: Niemeyer, 1937.

Vico, Gambatista. *The New Science* (tr. T. G. Bergin and M. H. Fisch). New York: Doubleday, 1961.

Wolff, Janet. *Hermeneutic Philosophy and the Sociology of Art*. London: Routledge & Kegan Paul, 1975.

Zöckler, Christopher. *Dilthey und die Hermeneutik*. Stuttgart: Metzler, 1975.

Journal Articles

I list all my articles relevant to the subject of this book as I have drawn ideas (though not quotations) from them.

Rickman, H. P. "Philosophic Anthropology and the Problem of Meaning." *Philosophic Quarterly, 10*, 38 (1960): 12–20.

————. "The Reaction against Positivism and Dilthey's Concept of Understanding." *British Journal of Sociology, 11*, 4 (Dec. 1960): 307–18.

————. "W. Dilthey and the Philosophy of Education." *International Review of Education, 8*, 3–4 (1963): 336–43.

———. "Seeing the Whole Picture." *The Dialogist*, *1*, 2 (Summer 1969): 7–17.

———. "Vico and Dilthey's Methodology of the Human Studies." In *Gambatisto Vico*. Baltimore, Md.: Johns Hopkins, 1969, pp. 447–56.

———. "Dilthey and the Writing of Intellectual History." *Journal of World History*, *13*, 3 (1971): 475–83.

———. "Discourse de la Method." *Zeitschrift für Philosophische Forschung*, *28*, 1 (January–March 1974).

———. "Hermeneutics." *Journal of the British Society of Phenomenology*, *7*, 3 (October 1976): 167–76.

———. "Dilthey Today." *Inquiry*, 19 (1977): 493–509.

———. "Historical Judgement and Our Knowledge of Man." *Humanitas*, *15*, 1 (February 1979): 47–58.

———. "Dilthey and Biography." *Biography*, *2*, 3 (Summer 1979): 218–29.

———. "Rhetoric and Hermeneutic." *Philosophy and Rhetoric*, *14*, 2 (Spring 1981): 100–11.

———. "What Need for Blood in the Cognitive Subject?" *Dilthey Jahrbuch*, 2 (Oct. 1984): 159–70.

———. "Dilthey on Nietzsche." *International Studies in Philosophy* (1985): 81–85.

———. "Is Philosophic Anthropology Possible?" *Metaphilosophy*, *16*, 1 (January 1985): 29–46.

———. "The Philosophic Basis of Psychiatry." *Philosophy of Social Science*, *17* (1987): 173–96.

Name Index

Subject Index

action, 32, 51
acquired structure, xii, 68, 103, 108, 112
ages, 22, 23, 25, 32
aesthetics, 20
aesthetic values, 36, 161
animism, 77
anthropological epistemology, 137, 147, 148, 153
anthropology, x, xi, 23, 43, 48, 57, 65, 86, 88–107, 114, 153, 154, 166, 173; cultural, 179; epistemological (or anthropological epistemology), 137, 147, 148, 153; philosophic, 6, 80, 143, 164, 178–79; physical, 82, 89; social, 5, 41, 70, 80, 82, 89
atomism, 105, 138
art, 35, 57, 80, 83, 109, 111, 128, 134
Archimedian point, 66, 138
authoritarian personality, 111, 180
autobiography, 29
autonomy of reason, 147, 150–57, 168
axiom: of phenomenality, 136; of the totality of mental life, 137

behavior, 30, 52, 54, 165

behavioral sciences, 40, 80, 163
behaviorism, 4, 6, 57–58, 70, 92, 96, 100, 163
biography, 6, 15, 17, 18, 25, 29–30, 31, 44, 48, 122
biology, 133, 147, 148, 150, 153
body language, 185
body/mind, *see* mind/body

care, 103
categories, 109–10, 142, 181; of ends and means, 27, 44; formal, 27, 143; of inner and outer, 28; of life (or real categories), 26–27, 85, 95–96, 100, 103, 142, 143–45, 167, 177; of meaning, 26; of part and whole, 26, 27; of power, 27; of temporality, 28, 175; of value, 27
cognitive subject, 99–100, 104, 145–50
complexity, 67–68
consciousness, 23, 137, 143, 144, 145, 148, 156; *see also* historical consciousness
"construction of the historical world," 32

About the Author

H. P. RICKMAN is a Visiting Professor at the City University, London, England. He is the author of many books on philosophy, including *Preface to Philosophy, W. Dilthey: A Selection,* and *The Adventure of Reason* (Greenwood Press, 1983) and has contributed extensively to *Fortnightly,* the *London Quarterly,* the *Hibbert Journal,* and the *Philosophical Quarterly.*